BIBLE CULTURE AND AUTHORITY
IN THE EARLY UNITED STATES

Bible Culture and Authority in the Early United States

Seth Perry

PRINCETON UNIVERSITY PRESS

PRINCETON & OXFORD

Published by Princeton University Press
41 William Street, Princeton, New Jersey 08540
6 Oxford Street, Woodstock, Oxfordshire OX20 1TR

press.princeton.edu

Library of Congress Control Number: 2017963656
ISBN 978-0-691-17913-1

British Library Cataloging-in-Publication Data is available

Editorial: Fred Appel and Thalia Leaf
Production Editorial: Karen Carter
Jacket Design: Amanda Weiss
Jacket Credit: Image courtesy of the Library Company of Philadelphia
Production: Jacqueline Poirier

This book has been composed in Miller

Printed on acid-free paper. ∞

Printed in the United States of America

10 9 8 7 6 5 4 3 2 1

For my parents.

"Pretty soon I'll read it to you."

Moreover, any speaker is himself a respondent to a greater or lesser degree. He is not, after all, the first speaker, the one who disturbs the eternal silence of the universe.

—MIKHAIL BAKHTIN, *SPEECH GENRES*

It might, or might not, have helped Anathema get a clear view of things if she'd been allowed to spot the very obvious reason why she couldn't see Adam's aura.

It was for the same reason that people in Trafalgar Square can't see England.

—NEIL GAIMAN AND TERRY PRATCHETT, *GOOD OMENS*

CONTENTS

ACKNOWLEDGMENTS

THIS PROJECT STARTED as a dissertation and benefited from the careful advising of my committee at the University of Chicago—Catherine Brekus, Clark Gilpin, and Richard Rosengarten. They were humorous, pointed, and congratulatory, all in due course. As my advisor, Catherine was unfailingly supportive through all of the twists and turns my thinking took while I worked on that project. During graduate school, I also benefited from a dissertation fellowship from the Martin Marty Center for the Advanced Study of Religion at Chicago, the input of the members of the American Religious History Workshop, and the informal advice of a number of gifted graduate student colleagues.

My work has evolved in ways I could not have imagined through interactions with a number of academic communities I encountered near the end of graduate school and in the years thereafter. I could not have finished my dissertation without the support of Dan Richter and the McNeil Center for Early American Studies at the University of Pennsylvania. The center provides money and infrastructure to people like me, but everyone there knows that academic community is the most important thing the place provides. It wasn't until I went to the McNeil Center that I really understood what all this is for.

I have been honored to participate in several summer Material Texts Workshops at the Library Company of Philadelphia, during which other participants helped me put some foundations under my "book history" pretensions while teaching me how to read, and how to be read. Jim Green and Michael Winship have been patient and generous sources of advice, and have taught me how to value the precious thing that is academic community. A guiding question that I once heard Michael pose to a conference has become my own: "If I know a thing and I don't share it, do I really know it?"

My first academic community was, as an undergraduate, the Theology Department at Georgetown University. I am grateful to Fran Cho, Julia Lamm, Joseph Murphy, and everyone there for introducing me to everything that religious studies can be. Early in graduate school, Dan Wotherspoon, then of Sunstone, took me seriously as a scholar long before I knew what I was doing, and I've never forgotten that.

James Bielo, Travis Webb, Vincent Wimbush, and all of my colleagues in the Institute for Signifying Scriptures have been invaluable in keeping me honest with respect to my theoretical interests. Special thanks goes to Travis, who offered crucial advice on the introduction to this book.

I have benefited from interactions with students and colleagues at the University of Washington, Indiana University, and Princeton University. Special thanks to the freshmen in my Spring 2016 seminar, What is Authority?—the "spongy onion" has been a crucial part of my thinking.

A month before starting at Princeton, making small talk in line for food at a conference, I confessed to a stranger that I was nervous about joining such a distinguished department as my first tenure-track job. My fellow conference-goer—I still don't know who he was (I am by nature confessional with strangers)—was nonplussed. He assured me that working with world-class colleagues would be like playing tennis with world-class professionals. "Playing with better players makes *you* a better player," he said. He was right. Whatever this book is now, it is far, far better than it could ever have been without the input and the support of my colleagues. I owe special thanks to my sub-field colleagues: Wallace Best, Jessica Delgado, Eddie Glaude, Judith Weisenfeld, and our graduate students in Religion in the Americas. From everyone in the department, though, I have learned something that is represented in this book. Special thanks to John Gager for his mentoring and to our amazing staff for keeping the ship running. Other than being married, I have never wanted to be good at something the way that I want to be good at this job, and my colleagues both amplify that desire and make me think I can fulfil it.

As a researcher, my most important thanks must go to the libraries that make my work possible. A month-long fellowship at the American Antiquarian Society jump-started this project and gave me a sense of just how much was possible. In the project's later stages, the holdings of the Library Company of Philadelphia had an immeasurable influence. The tireless librarians and staff at both AAS and LCP went out of their way to help me. Special thanks to Nicole Joniec and Ann McShane for facilitating images from LCP's collections. Clinton Bagley and Laura Heller at the Mississippi Department of Archives and History answered my every random question. Gabriel Swift at Princeton's Department of Rare Books and Special Collections has become an invaluable resource, and a friend. I have also benefited from the assistance of librarians at Andrews University, the Buffalo and Erie County Public Library, the Church History Library of the Church of Jesus Christ of Latter-day Saints, Cornell University, Haverford College, the Historical Society of Pennsylvania, the New London County (Connecticut) Historical Society, the Mercer Museum Library, the Ontario County (New York) Historical Society, the Oyster Bay (New York) Historical Society, Swarthmore College, the University of Chicago, and the University of Pennsylvania.

Much of chapter 5 appeared as an article in the *Journal of the American Academy of Religion*, and I am indebted to the editorial staff and the anonymous reviewers who helped improve that piece. My sincere thanks to my editor, Fred Appel, to Thalia Leaf and Karen Carter, and all of the staff at Princeton University Press, as well as my copyeditor, Emily Shelton, my indexer, Colleen Dunham, and the anonymous readers who reviewed my manuscript and offered such thorough and encouraging comments. Fred's confidence in this project and his patient advice for a first-time author are deeply appreciated.

Thanks to Sari Altschuler and Sarah Imhoff, my friends who became my models for how to do this.

I hereby acknowledge Brendan Pietsch, world-famous acknowledger.

I have a group of friends from college who know a lot more about bibles in America than they could possibly care to. They haven't just listened, but through the lenses of their own disparate fields they've contributed, over beer, over cards, at all hours. My work and my life are enriched by the time we spend together.

My parents read to me and valued my education, even when it went places they didn't anticipate. My wife, Stephanie, makes everything both possible and worth doing.

A NOTE ON CAPITALIZATION

THIS STUDY is about "The Bible" as well as about "bibles." I take the former to be an idea: a concept in Judeo-Christian traditions regarding the special status of a set of texts imagined to be more or less consistent. Those texts, on the other hand, are encountered as material objects that vary from one another and from the idea to which they refer. The idea I take to be a proper noun; the objects, common. I have tried to be consistent in capitalizing "Bible" only when referring to the idea as a proper noun.

BIBLE CULTURE AND AUTHORITY
IN THE EARLY UNITED STATES

Authority, Identity, and the Bible in the Early Republic

IN THE SUMMER OF 1802, Lucy Hurlbut, of Connecticut, went to hear Lorenzo Dow preach and he pointed at her. At that time Dow was not as famous as he would be, but he was famous enough, especially in Hurlbut's environs, near Dow's own hometown. Lucy had made a special plan to make it to this sermon, having missed another one six weeks before. She went hoping to be touched by God's word as related by one of His more eccentric spokesmen, and she was not disappointed. "When the preacher arrived and began his discourse the word was set home to my sole," she wrote in her journal. "After preaching a while he left the subject and pointing to me the Lord enabled him to speak to my case[:] he told of my former convictions and how the spirit of the Lord had been striving with me[.]" Dow, Hurlbut felt, told her about herself: "I thou[gh]t he described the sit[u]ation of my mind better than I co[u]ld have done."[1]

Dow pointed a lot. He was a talented rhetorician, and that pointing finger, the identifying of individual members of his vast audiences, was an unusually transparent demonstration of the strategy of all rhetoric: it situates, names, *subjects* its audience. Dow identified Lucy Hurlbut as a suffering soul, guilty over past sins, feeling God's judgment, and by doing so he helped create that Lucy Hurlbut. Dow's polemic print publications from this same era of his career read like raw transcriptions of his frenzied oral performances, and they, too, *point*, figuratively and, in a way, literally. Dow frequently punctuated his allusive, impressionistic arguments with a manicule attached to a signature phrase: ☞ "And you cannot deny it."

In these written moments, as in the sermon that so affected Lucy Hurlbut, Dow does not argue or persuade: he positions his reader or listener as someone already implicated in what he is saying and subjected to his authority to say it. In her response to Dow's pointing, Hurlbut likewise positioned Dow as an authority, one who could pronounce God's judgment: "[T]he Lord enabled him to speak to *my* case." Rhetoric, when it works, creates such relationships. Each subject position makes the other possible.

This relationship—that of the suffering sinner and the bearer of the Word—itself depended on a shared set of symbols, types, behaviors, and vocabulary that came from another authority: the English Bible. Dow was not ordained by any ecclesiastical body or trained in theology by any seminary; he represented no school of thought, no powerful social set, no disciplinary body, civil or religious. He had, that is, no particular authority to cast judgment on Lucy Hurlbut, other than that accruing to any white man. Dow's performance of judgment worked, though, because he could make himself recognized as an apostle, as one having such authority from God. That recognition depended on Hurlbut's ability to know an apostle when she saw one—on her facility with the Bible. While contemporaries and subsequent scholars refer routinely to "the authority of the Bible" in the early national period, I will argue here for a fuller understanding of that authority, one that recognizes that it inhered not in a book, but in the relationships that users such as Hurlbut and Dow created with it.[2]

This is a study of the authority of the Bible in the early national period that attends to its actual rather than idealized terms. Historians have long recognized the decades after the American Revolution as a period of upheaval with respect to religion as well as politics. These same historians have often identified the way that the Bible was positioned as an answer to the era's problem of authority. The dominant Protestant rhetoric of the time proclaimed the "Bible alone" to be authoritative bedrock—"an anchor of religious authority in a churning sea of demographic, social, and political turmoil," as Mark Noll has put it.[3] Books do not act as authorities without readers, though. In this period, "the authority of the Bible" was a statement about the Bible's status as a complicated site of contestation with respect to religious authority. As above, the Bible served as a source of symbols and models for the creation of authoritative relationships. Each use of those symbols was a possible disruption of the Bible's authority. In its rhetorical use, the text itself could not remain static or unchanged.

A variety of relationships among would-be religious authorities and their potential followers, created and maintained through reference to the Bible, flourished during the post-revolutionary era. This period matters because the question of how roles were to be made recognizable was particularly acute during this time. The changes wrought by the revolution created new opportunities for new roles, but they also unsettled the terms by which those roles could be made legible, understandable, and recognizable. For Protestants, Catholics, and those they proselytized, the Bible was the shared script for responding to this uncertainty. All authority is fundamentally rhetorical, and rhetoric like that acknowledged by Hurlbut was unusually effective in developing relationships of authority in the decades after the revolution.

This book pursues an understanding of early national American religion grounded in detailed moments of biblically-constituted relational authority in the context of large-scale cultural characteristics that determined what it meant to read or otherwise use bibles during this time. While previous studies of this era have tended to echo its Protestant rhetoric in suggesting that the Christian Bible became the era's preeminent religious authority, this study asks the many questions that underlie such an assertion: What does it mean for a text to act as an authority? What is the relationship between personal and textual authority? What did the concept of religious authority mean to those bound by it in the early nineteenth century? Any answer to these questions must come from investigating the Bible's *authoritative use* by individuals in their relations with others, not from the assumption that the inert book itself possessed authority. Moreover, it must also consider forms of authoritative bible use beyond the learned, considered articulations of argumentative theology. The authoritative use of bibles in the early national period was the means of creating and maintaining authoritative relationships that departed from eighteenth-century conceptions of what it meant to be a religious subject. This study will explore the print-bible culture that made various forms of bible usage possible in early national America. It will treat those forms of bible usage—written, oral, and performative biblical citation, carried out in more and less explicit ways, in more and less formal settings, by more and less privileged Americans—as bids for and responses to authority that had effects on both relationships of authority and on the Bible itself. This approach reorients arguments about early national biblicism and its authoritative stakes toward the practical, lived, material experience of rhetorical worlds and away from static notions of biblical and bible-based authority. This reorientation is the primary goal of this book.

Charles Nisbet, staunch Presbyterian and first head of Dickinson College, was a consummate representative of established Protestant authority entering the last decade of the eighteenth century. Trained in divinity in Edinburgh and Princeton, he spoke nine languages and was responsible for Dickinson's course of lectures in systematic and pastoral theology. In October of 1791, as the Bill of Rights neared ratification, Nisbet was characteristically sarcastic about his expectations for the religious environment promised by what would be the first amendment to the Federal Constitution. In a letter to printer William Young, Nisbet proposed that Young write a pamphlet "showing that although toleration is indeed begun among us, yet it is as yet very imperfect." The problem, Nisbet slyly suggested, was that not only did "the several sects keep their pulpits to their own people only, excluding all others," but they only let one minister speak at a time. Nisbet suggested that this was "expressly contrary to the spirit of the federal constitution, which places all sects, teachers, and doctrines on an equal footing." Congress itself, he thought, should be encouraged to set an example of true toleration for the nation's religious institutions.

> [P]ropose to that august body, to make an addition to their present places of meeting, so as to contain a stage large enough to hold the representatives of all the sects on the continent, including Indians, & that all the teachers of those sects be employed to officiate at once as chaplains to Congress, at the same time, that no sort of preference may be given to one above another, & when a sermon is to be preached before congress, that it be preached by all the chaplains of the different sects at the same time time [*sic*] and in the same place, & that the congress make a law that in all congregations the same form of worship be observed as above described, & that each congregation entertain a preacher of all the different sects on this continent, as it can not be said that our pulpits are free & unrestrained, while any one Sect is kept out of them, either altogether or for a time.[4]

Nisbet's sarcasm came from a place of concern. The cacophony of all sects preaching at once—a cacophony made dangerous as well as absurd to a reader like Young by Nisbet's specific inclusion of "Indians"—was a symbol of the disorder that men like Nisbet feared as the logical outcome of his era's undermining of traditional models of religious authority.

Disestablishment, Noll has argued, was a symptom of and goad to late colonial Americans' reverence for the Bible. In the eighteenth century, he writes, "recourse to Scripture fueled rejection of church-state establishments" at the same time that a "deepened attachment to Scripture heightened the feeling that all of life required divine direction from the Bible." Noll argues that in this vacuum which biblicism itself had created, devotion to the Bible allowed an "'informal Christendom' to continue even when Americans rejected church-state establishments."[5] The atmosphere of biblical reference that Noll gestures to, in which nearly everyone presumed the relevance of the Bible while nearly no one agreed on *how* it was relevant, is the setting of this book.

During the early national period, the latent questions of religious authority were laid unusually bare. With the dissolution of British control over the colonies and the uncomfortable negotiation of relationships among the new states, everything from the political language available to name those relationships to the self-perceptions of their citizens to economic matters such as the notional value of paper currency came unmoored from traditional meanings.[6] This upheaval manifested in religious matters as a popular rhetoric that rejected previously accepted ecclesiastical and clerical means of validating religious authority. For many, clerical education and ecclesiastical office became irrelevant or in fact damaging to one's capacity to lead in religious matters. Congregational,

Presbyterian, and Anglican establishments were challenged by Baptists (present in the colonies since the seventeenth century but newly ascendant in the late eighteenth) and Methodists (arriving from England in the 1760s), by ministers from within their own ranks, and by entirely new denominations and popular movements.[7]

Still, rhetorical deference to the Bible remained.[8] The standard work on religion in the early national period, Nathan Hatch's *The Democratization of American Christianity*, is organized around the tropes of individualism and lay empowerment, specifically with respect to the interpretation of the Bible. "[C]ommon people, Bibles in hand," Hatch wrote, "relished the right to shape their own faith and submit to leaders of their choosing." Hatch overlaid early national religiosity with the republican impulse of the revolution: the Awakening, he wrote, was spurred by an "ideology of communications . . . driven by the exhilarating sense that people could break free of elite domination and speak and write whenever they felt led."[9] Many religious leaders of the era declared that each of their listeners could read and interpret the Bible for him- or herself, discovering through his or her own reading how it answered the various questions to which they sought authoritative answers. In the rhetoric of this period of upheaval, religious authority rested with, as the catchphrase of the period went, "the Bible alone."

Approaching this era with a robust conception of religious authority, what does it mean to take a text as an authority? Stephen Greenblatt has written that the Reformation invested scripture "with the ability to control, guide, discipline, console, exalt, and punish that the church had arrogated to itself for centuries."[10] Such abilities, though, require discursive exchange. Protestants of all stripes profess that the Bible speaks to them through the Holy Spirit, but bibles as objects do not have the agency required of authority—they do not speak. Human authorities, rather, speak through bibles, or with them. The written text may be said to have authority, but only a reader can control, exalt, and punish.[11]

Underlying that key phrase—"the Bible alone"—is the fact that the authority of the Bible is not a timeless, abstract, inviolable truth, but a *process*, one that moves in multiple directions and features multiple interacting components, strategies, and products. Religious studies scholar Vincent Wimbush has argued that approaches to scripture as a concept need to be oriented not toward texts such the Bible and Qur'an as such, but toward the ongoing practices that distinguish those texts as "scriptural": "[T]he primary focus should be placed *not upon texts* per se (that is, upon content-meanings), but upon textures, gestures, and power—namely the signs, material products, ritual practices and performances, expressivities, orientations, ethics, and politics associated with the phenomenon of the invention and uses of 'scriptures.'"[12] Rather than "scriptures," he argues, we should be thinking about "scripturalization." Wimbush intends this deverbal noun to carry the implication of an ongoing, dialogic process, replacing "scripture" and its connotations of fixity. This approach "regards 'text' in more layered and expansive terms and positions the narrowly construed 'text' in the complicated middle," not at the end or the beginning of the enterprise.[13]

As I read them, Wimbush's theoretical interventions are of a piece with Catherine Bell's reorganization of ritual studies around "ritualization." Bell insisted that ritual be thought of as a process of creating "privileged differentiation" of some actions from other actions, "a way of acting that specifically establishes a privileged contrast, differentiating itself as more important or powerful."[14] Likewise, scripturalization is about suggesting or sustaining for some texts a privileged distinction from other texts. Scripturalization in this sense, as Bell held with respect to ritual, runs in all directions. It concerns both those texts thought of as scriptures, such as the Bible, as well as the universe of texts that cite that scriptural text and each other, from commentaries and concordances to bible-based performatives and biblical quotations worked into everyday speech. Biblical citation—through oral quotation, physical performance, written imitation—is a way of distinguishing some speech or activity from the usual, as special. *At the same time*, scriptural citation marks the cited text itself as special, worthy of citation. This co-constitutive operation that sustains privileged contrast—or, in the case of new scriptures, creates it—is scripturalization.[15]

To take full stock of the implications of this approach, it is important to remember Wimbush's charge that the text be located in the middle of scripturalization as a phenomenon, not at the beginning or the end. The status, nature, and content of scriptural texts change constantly through the operations of scripturalization. This changing text is nevertheless real, both notionally and materially; the Bible is both a concept and a set of print objects. The ability to cite such a text as if it were static and to have such citation be recognizable is what makes scripturalization possible, providing the ostensibly shared objects of citation necessary to distinguish some speech from other speech. The terms by which the scriptural text is recognizable are never more than contingent, however. As Bell emphasized with respect to ritualization, context is everything for the functioning of scripturalization.[16] In early national America, for instance, sometimes citing the Bible meant only producing English sentences with a structure and word choice typical of the early modern period. Countless commentators, from the 1830s to the present, have noted that much of the nonbiblical content of the *Book of Mormon* "sounds like" the King James Bible. This is an operation of scripturalization—the text of the new scripture cites and improvises on the old—and yet it would only be such in an anglophone context in which the King James Bible was widely known.

The contingency of the text speaks to the imaginary nature of scripturalization. The privileged distinction of a scripture is contingent; the power relations conjured by reference to a scripture are relationships of fictional asymmetry.

As Wimbush argues, scripturalized power is "the power of, and to, make-believe, that is, to make the social collective believe certain things in certain ways, to make it accept the reality of things that are made up."[17] Other scholars have distinguished such relationships of asymmetry in terms of authority rather than power, distinguished by its constitution through discourse alone rather than violence or the threat of violence.[18] However it is named, the asymmetry of the authoritative relationship is fictional. This is an especially salient point with respect to religious authority. To say that a relationship of authority is religious is to posit that the asymmetry of the relationship is grounded in the relative access to or possession of assets that are unseen, of skills that must remain unproven or, at best, tautologies: demonstrated by the same authoritative discourse that they would support. Authority—fictive asymmetry, produced discursively—is an essential component of religion. Authority engenders belief, contextualizes experience, scripts ritual. It does not, however, transcend any of those things: it is constituted from within them even as it effects them.

The practical consequence of ritualization, Bell wrote, is that it renders ritualized subjects: individuals in relationships of power constituted by ritual activity. Expanding on Bell's terms, this study will speak of late colonial and early national America as a scripturalized culture, and its residents as scripturalized subjects. In my approach to relational subjectivity, I am particularly influenced by genre theory as a subset of rhetorical studies. Weaving together Mikhail Bakhtin's dialogic approach to discourse, Kenneth Burke's dramatistic analysis of rhetorical action, and J.L. Austin's notion of speech acts, genre theorists have argued that particular forms of speech and action are constituted by the aims of speakers, the expectations of audiences, and the universe of shared historical and material factors that make up both. In her field-defining article "Genre as Social Action" (1984), Carolyn Miller argued that genre should be considered not in terms of taxonomies of texts but as a way of naming "typified rhetorical action" taken in response to "recurrent situation[s]." Genres "have conventional forms," she wrote, "because they arise in situations with similar structures and elements and because rhetors respond in similar ways, having learned from precedent what is appropriate and what effects their actions are likely to have on other people."[19] With this theoretical armature in mind, biblical citation can be analyzed as a genre, as a recurrent form of rhetorical action. Viewed this way, the citational possibilities of scripturalization both regulated existing relationships of power and provided for the possibility of new ones. Scripturalized subjects are the products and the wielders of the rhetorical power that comes from having recourse to a scriptural text.[20]

This, then, is what "the Bible alone" meant in early national America: a renewed rhetorical emphasis on the scripturalized terms of religious authority. This emphasis coincided with a culture-wide change in scripturalization's materiality. The contingent text had never been more complicated. In early national America, advances in the technologies of print production and distribution made possible a print-bible culture of unprecedented variety and volume, exacerbating the inherent tensions of scripturalized authority. The early national print market was flooded with bibles created by competing publishers, editors, and commentators, along with a universe of bible-citing material. For the most part, the content of this material was not new. Before 1800 and only slowly evolving thereafter, the domestic print market in America, across all genres, was primarily involved in reprinting British books.[21] What was new was the diversity and volume of available religious print, and the circumstances of its rhetorical use.

This market developed at precisely the post-revolutionary moment when reliance on a bible—an idealized text made usable in printed, material copies—as a source of authority took on new analogues. Printed matter had an increasingly important role in the creation of authority of all kinds in the decades after the revolution. From the Declaration of Independence to the Constitution, and in texts such as the Federalist Papers that worked to establish the legitimacy of the founding documents, the new nation was founded in writing, and renewed focus on the Bible was part of this moment. Scripturalization operates in a universe of cultural, economic, environmental, and interpersonal variables. In the revolutionary era, the rhetorical creation of the United States and its citizens was a new variable added to the longstanding scripturalization of the Bible in North America. "Trust in the Bible was a religious analogue to political trust in the Constitution," Noll has written.[22]

On a conceptual level, such new political analogues for the Bible had long-term effects on the Bible itself. Michael Warner argued in *Letters of the Republic* that the early American "national state grounded its legitimacy not just in the people or the rule of law ... but in the very special cultural formation of print discourse."[23] Because a large part of print discourse in the early republic was biblical or bible-based, the association of print and state legitimacy necessitated the association of state and Bible. This association had consequences not just for the state, but also for the Bible. The use of the Bible to create an American national identity added a new referent for bible-based rhetoric.

As will be discussed at length in chapter 1, scripturalization constitutive of British national identity was a long-standing fact, which made its operations readily available to the making of American national identity. James Byrd's *Sacred Scripture, Sacred War* tracks the martial aspect of this rhetorical work, demonstrating the ways in which ministers used the Bible to sell the Revolutionary War. In *American Zion*, Eran Shalev examines the centrality of the Old Testament to early national rhetorical creations of American identity. Shalev's study is particularly useful in its attention to the broad, general implications of early national biblicism, the difference that the Old Testament made to political discourse in ways that are not reducible to or immediately evident in "straightforward declarative propositions."[24]

Both Shalev and Byrd focus on biblically-inflected public rhetoric, primarily that articulated by elites. This is, to be sure, an important element in the operations of scripturalization in the early national period, but I am more interested in authoritative uses of the Bible better described as interpersonal, implied, and popular. Taking public rhetoric as representative of an actual public is dangerous, as it risks confusing authorial intention with audience response. Here, I have examined a wide variety of sources to try to get at the mutually-constitutive nature of speaker, audience, and Bible in the early national period.

My primary area of focus with respect to the consequences of the early national association of the Bible with political identity has to do with the rhetoric surrounding the founding era's democratic ideals. "Democratization" is a crucial aspect of American national creation in which the Bible's scripturalization is deeply implicated. Expressing confidence in every reader's ability to comprehend and use the Bible was, as Hatch suggested, a rhetorical resource for democratization. Hatch's view of the democratizing tendencies of the early national period depended on "leveling" as democracy's defining feature. As Jeffrey Stout argues, however, leveling is not necessarily what democracy is about: "As a social formation democracy has more to do with structures of earned and accountable authority than it does with leveling."[25] I argue that the scripturalized environment of early America meant that biblical usage—citation of and creation from the Bible—served as the terms for earning and accounting for authority as institutional and traditional means faltered. At the same time, the rapid proliferation of American print-bible culture in this era resulted in an environment in which the biblical means of creating and sustaining relationships of authority were more available to more individuals and communities than ever before. The scripturalization of early national America provided both means for and constraints on relationships of authority. Moreover, the exercise of both those means and constraints in specific circumstances had an ever-developing effect on the scripturalized status of the Bible itself.

This, to be clear, is an argument about the expectations of readers and the volume of print-bible culture in the scriptural formation that was early American democratic nationalism, not an argument about the liberating effects of early national democratic scriptural rhetoric. Access to literacy, print, and the circumstances for claiming biblical authority would remain unevenly distributed across lines of race, gender, class, and geography throughout the early national period, and this study will attend to those differences. I will maintain, though, that as technologies of reading and citation proliferated, democratizing rhetoric did have both authorizing and constraining effects on popular bible usage, even among and across demographic groups.

It must be noted here that one of the most important demographic lines to attend to with respect to early national biblicism is that between Catholics and Protestants. Wrapped up in the nation-making aspects of early national scripturalization is a native anti-Catholicism. The rhetorical focus on textual authority in the era of the American founding was a manifestation of Protestant assumptions that surfaced more and less explicitly. While the prerogatives of institutions, clergy, and tradition loom as large in the history of Protestantism as they do in the history of Catholicism, from the sixteenth century Protestants used rhetorical insistence on textual authority to distinguish themselves from Catholic forms of authority. Inheriting this legacy, a largely Protestant early national print-bible culture (re)asserted the importance of the Bible often against an imagined Catholic other. Anti-Catholicism was not incidental to late colonial and early national scripturalization, but constitutive of it. Scholars concerned with the underlying assumptions of secularism in American history, such as Tracy Fessenden, have emphasized that Noll's "informal Christendom" that followed disestablishment was specifically an informal *Protestantism*.[26] Fessenden and others have brought attention to the unmarked, "soft" Protestantism of early American Christianity, but there was plenty of hard Protestantism, too. Catholics made up a small portion of the population at the beginning of this period, but took up an outsized space in the Protestant imaginary, particularly where authority was concerned.[27] Early American biblicism is inseparable from its anti-Catholic edge.[28]

For the period of this study, the operations of scripturalization played out in primarily intra-Protestant discourse inflected with anti-Catholic assumptions, and the subjects investigated here will reflect this. At the same time, I hope to make clear that Catholics did not cede biblicism—or the operations of scripturalization—to Protestants. Thomas Ward's *Errata of the Protestant Bible*, first published in 1688 and based on Catholic criticisms of Protestant bibles going back to the sixteenth century, was well known in early America and printed in several American editions in the early nineteenth century.[29] Irish Catholic Mathew Carey published what was probably the first English-language family bible printed in the United States, in 1790. It was a Douay-Rheims, subsidized by John Carroll, the nation's first Catholic bishop, who also consulted on the text and helped find subscribers.[30] Carey's considerable efforts to sell the book were focused on its status as an avowedly Catholic bible. His advertisements for the Catholic bible demonstrate, all at once, the Catholic biblicism, Protestant biblicism, and presumption of anti-Catholic bias regnant in the post-revolutionary era. On the one hand, he wrote in advertisements that he expected "every Roman catholic family throughout the union, who can afford the expense" to buy one, not least out of the need to refute the Protestant assumption "that [Catholics] are forbidden the use of the sacred volume."[31] On the other hand, he also addressed advertisements to Protestants, urging them to pick it up as a second bible. Pointedly referring to the

King James as "the common church-of-England translation" (a jibe at a time when all things English were out of favor), Carey argued that it was a matter of common knowledge that "there are various and important errors in it," and therefore suggested that an attentive Protestant needed a second translation with which to compare the Authorized Version, to "enable him to detect most, if not all of [the errors]—and thus to remove from his mind those doubts and difficulties, which are so fatal to true religion." Carey also encouraged Protestants to see the purchase of a Douay-Rheims as an opportunity to demonstrate enlightened American tolerance, by placing their names on the subscriber list next to those of the nation's Catholics.

Carey sold his entire print run of five hundred copies of the Douay-Rheims, but many copies were returned by the buyers for being defective. Carey sent the bibles to Craig and Lea, a firm in Wilmington, Delaware, to be bound, and hundreds of them came back misbound: sections of the books were upside down, missing, and dramatically out of order. "Were the sheets put together by a child, and never examined afterwards, they could not be worse," Carey wrote in anger to his binder. Even after he started complaining, between December of 1790 and March of 1791, batch after batch of unreadable bibles reached Carey. He was particularly annoyed because of the special status of the book compared to others: "Heavens! If it was a collection of primers surely they would deserve more attention." Having never had a problem with Craig and Lea's work before, Carey intimated in his complaints that he believed the mistakes were so gratuitous as to be intentional, though he never openly stated the ostensible motive for a binder to deliberately ruin Catholic bibles. Craig apologized and claimed that the mistakes were the work of one person responsible for sewing the books, but he, likewise, never named a motive. Remembering the incident decades later, Carey was more direct: "I supposed that the affair must have resulted from the malice of Some besotted Sectarian who worked in the office & whose zeal & malice were inflamed by the appearance of a Catholic Bible."[32] Carey did not return to bible publishing until 1800, and when he did he turned to Protestant bibles. While an active and prominent Catholic, Carey published more than sixty editions of the Authorized Version between 1801 and 1825 and became one of the most prolific and successful bible publishers in the country.[33]

Those Catholic bibles, their text deliberately scrambled by Protestants, are evocative if idiosyncratic artifacts of the operations of scripturalization in early national America. In these unreadable books, the mediation, the stakes, and the contingencies of biblical authority are made manifest. This study reorients understandings of early national biblicism toward such contingent, mediated, and contested artifacts of early national bible-based authority. This means looking closely at the material culture of bible production and distribution, the vast body of parabiblical materials that contributed to the ability of an ever-widening set of people to effectively use the Bible, the ways in which they did so, and—crucially—the effect of all of this biblical activity on the Bible itself. Part I will focus on the characteristics of late colonial and early national print-bible culture. Part II will turn toward the consequences of this scripturalized environment for religious authority and the place of the Bible itself.

Chapter 1, "Creating the American Bible Reader, 1777–1816," traces the development of the imagined American bible reader out of seventeenth- and eighteenth-century British print-bible culture. At the turn of the nineteenth century, the burgeoning American bible market, embedded in the broader market of bible-oriented print, imagined a reader who was in many ways the inverse of the dominant religious authority of the eighteenth century: rather than educated, upper-class, and male, this reader was some combination of barely literate, lower-class, and female. This imagined reader's relationship to actual readers was uneven, but her presence in early national print-bible culture was fundamental to the era's creation of new religious subjects, because it created space for readers to imagine the self-sufficient authority of their own bible reading. This imagined reader, manifest in the material bibles of the period, had important consequences for early national bible usage across the American population.

Chapter 2, "Taking a Text: Reading and Referencing the Bible in the Early Nineteenth Century," focuses on reference as an aspect of biblical facility essential to Protestant religious authority in the early national period. Reading has its own authoritative aspects, but it is reference that defines bible usage as an authoritative act because of its public implications: reference is by definition an attempt to make one's reading authoritative for others. Early national bible culture disseminated the skills necessary to authoritatively cite the Bible—"chapter and verse"—among a wide range of readers. At the same time, this dissemination consisted of bringing the textual mediations of intellectual and theological elites to a larger set of readers, encouraging novel forms of religious authority to develop along traditional lines.

Where part I will demonstrate the authoritative importance of explicit reference to the Bible in the early national period, part II elucidates the ways in which communities interacted with the Bible as the defining part of the era's discursive field, imaginatively building on and expanding the Bible through their references to it. These chapters will think through the mechanics of reference and citation to explore the scripturalized terms of religious authority in the period and the consequences of those terms both for religious subjects and for the Bible itself.

Chapter 3, "Joshua, When the Walls Fell: Biblical Roles in Changing Times," examines forms of bible usage that were performative, popular, and implicit. Here, under the rubric of "performed biblicism," I am interested in elucidating the Bible's ability to act as a script for the performance of new and invented roles in an era of shifting identities. Performed biblicism offers a way of making sense of the ways in which the Bible participated in the construction of relationships of religious subjectivity as a dynamic aspect of lived circumstance. In the early nineteenth century, congregations gathered to playact the New Testament church, performing the Pentecost according to the script provided in Acts. Mormon missionaries, dispatched two by two on the apostolic model, stopped at the edges of towns that rejected them and knocked the dust from their feet (Matthew 10:14–15; Acts 13:50–51). Slave owners made themselves over into Abraham. Visionaries such as Isaac Childs and Chloe Willey cast themselves as Isaiahs and Daniels and Miriams. Would-be authorities extracted roles from the Bible that invited audiences, real and imagined, to respond with coordinating roles, conjuring relationships that pushed against the limits of early national structures of power and authority. Moments of biblical self-identification in the early national archive are not monolithic. What distinguishes those discussed here under the rubric of performed biblicism is the expansion of the ostensibly static biblical text into the contingency of embodied life.

Chapter 4, "'Write These Things in a Book': Scripturalization and Visionary Authority," homes in on one particularly dramatic form of performed biblicism that highlights the relationship between performed and written scripturalized authority. Visionary accounts placed the authority of a given speaker front and center. At the same time, while at the level of the text these accounts were monologic—stories told by a uniquely privileged storyteller—they depended on an existing field of discourse shared among speakers and audiences for their comprehensibility. As texts created and authorized by communities of authors, editors, copyists, and readers, visionary accounts are uniquely ideal sites for thinking about the stakes and effects of scripturalization in the late colonial and early national period. This chapter features a detailed study of the history of *The Vision of Isaac Childs*, a virtually unstudied late colonial visionary text that circulated widely in both print and manuscript throughout the nineteenth century.

Chapter 5, "The Many Bibles of Joseph Smith: Scripturalization in Early National America," brings together the various themes of the book to document the creation of a new scripturalized community. This chapter highlights the place of print-bible culture, citationality, performance, and the scripturalization of biblically-resonant visionary texts in earliest Mormonism. Smith's texts invited their readers and auditors to regard them as scriptures and therefore to regard Smith, their immediate source, as a prophet. These texts functioned by citing the Bible, both implicitly and explicitly. The scripturalized community conjured by Smith and those around him is the preeminent example of the type of religious authority made possible by early national bible culture and an important window on the ways in which the authoritative use of bibles changed the Bible itself.

Finally, this book's conclusion will gesture toward the consequences of early national biblicism for subsequent American religious history. The Bible's availability for citation and re-citation fundamentally changed the desire, effectiveness, and circumstances of its citation. While the Bible's cultural presence in the early national period has been treated as flat and simple, the identities quarried from it were of infinite diversity and particularity; its ability to conjure those identities in concert with circumstance and other presences was at the nexus of religious authority in the early national period. The Bible's capacity to sit at that privileged position, however, was dependent on a set of circumstances that changed. The terms, processes, and effects of scripturalization are never static. The conclusion, "Abandoned Quarries," will gesture toward not the "decline" of the Bible's importance in America, but this shift in the nature of the Bible's persistent authoritative use.

Much existing scholarship on the use of the Bible in America has a difficult time separating itself fully from the assumptions of its subjects. Even where hermeneutics is made the central concern—i.e., where scholars focus on interpretation rather than on the innate characteristics of scripture—this is generally carried out with a sense of irony or even condemnation drawn from the tacit assumption of a core or base reality to the text. The operations of scripturalization are nevertheless implied, though, in this work. My intention here is not to draw a sharp line between scripturalization and more traditional arguments about the historical presence of scriptures, but to emphasize that the text's contingency, as a necessary product of its very use and usefulness, *is* the story, not an ironic or unfortunate aspect of the story.

My approach to dialogic, co-constitutive discursive environments has important analogues in existing scholarship. In *Jeremiah's Scribes*, Meredith Marie Neuman uses seventeenth-century sermon notebooks to reconstruct the creation and dissemination of Puritan sermon literature. Neuman uses notes of oral sermon delivery kept by audience members alongside ministers' own sermon notes to highlight the ways in which "sermon culture" was the product of both ministers and their community in a discursive, collaborative process. In this way, she challenges "static notions of authorship, authority, and authenticity," showing how "[a]cts of hearing, notetaking, and applying the sermon implicate the auditor in the work of the pulpit."[34] Neuman's construction of seventeenth-century "sermon culture" as a discursive process rhymes with nineteenth-century "bible culture" as I will explore it here.

Neuman's primary sources consist of a cache of sermon notes which are the enviable product of Puritan religious practices. Because of the density and structural rigor of Puritan sermons, note-taking was both possible and often presumed necessary for audience comprehension. The current study concerns a much broader discursive community surrounding the scripturalization of the Bible in the early United States. The processes of scripturalization took place across theological and denominational distinctions and were active in the co-constitution of clerical and lay roles, rather than observant of supposed distinctions between them. Scripturalization operated in performative moments, in oral speech, and in written texts both public and private, manuscript and print. Out of this vastness, my sources are necessarily selective. There is no single, delimited body of texts that would facilitate the argument I want to make here about the developments of biblical usage in the early national period. As in any such study, questions of representativeness can be fairly asked. I have attempted to highlight moments and readers—known, lesser-known, and unknown—that illustrate widespread tendencies and practices. What my subjects have in common is that their words are preserved in the archive. This alone makes them in some sense atypical. For every usefully marked-up bible I looked at for this study, I looked at twenty whose margins were silent, who may as well have been fresh from the binder's, with no legible evidence of having ever been touched by a reader. I don't think that any of my well-known subjects are less representative of their time for being published, even though the outlets for their bible usage certainly can't be said to be typical. Likewise, the stray marks in old books that came into my view during this research are no less admissible than all of those that didn't. As an historian I am indebted to those readers who made marks that I can read, two centuries later. David Paul Nord, writing about the less-than-perfect nature of colporteur reports as sources for talking about what people read, observes that, whatever their faults, they are recommended by the fact that "they are what we have."[35] The historian's hope is that in the aggregate the voices speak for the silences. But let it be said that there will always be more silences than voices; these are the terms we accept when we look at the past. Like any scholar, all I can say is that I looked, and I saw.

PART I

Print-Bible Culture in the Early United States

THAT PROCESSES OF SCRIPTURALIZATION cohered around the Bible for Europeans at the time of English colonization of the Western Hemisphere is beyond question. The eighteenth-century English Atlantic operated in an environment of scripturalization inherited from, ultimately, second-century BCE Palestine.[1] Scripturalization is a constant, dynamic process, however—its terms, extent, and effects are never static, always co-constituted with circumstance. Scripturalization set the terms for questions of translation, readership, and interpretation in early-modern Europe; the privileged difference of the text made these questions matter. At the same time, the fact that these questions mattered is what constituted the text's privileged difference.

Part I examines the authoritative presence and effects of bibles and parabiblical material in America in the late colonial and early national periods. Emblematic of the scripturalized assumptions this era's bible culture inherited from earlier eras is a "To the Reader" essay that appeared in many of the first American-made English-language bibles. Written by John Witherspoon, president of Princeton and a signer of the Declaration of Independence, the essay framed the commitments of English bible culture for a new American print-bible market. Sensitive to the challenges of higher criticism, still little-known to Americans in 1790, Witherspoon set out to tell the story of the Bible's providential transmission history. Characteristic of the author's Enlightenment humanism, Witherspoon's introduction is preoccupied with the Bible's original Hebrew and Greek texts. Less characteristic of Enlightenment sensibilities is Witherspoon's confidence in the perfect integrity of the transmission history of these sources. "The providence of God," he asserts, is "particularly manifest in [the scriptures'] preservation and purity." God trusted the Hebrew text to "the Jews," Witherspoon wrote, and they fulfilled their responsibility with "scrupulous exactness." The New Testament, meanwhile, is imagined as a solitary whole. Witherspoon's "To the Reader" was commonly accompanied by a chart, also of his composition, giving the "Account of the Dates or Time of Writing the Books of the New Testament." In accordance with most scholarship of Witherspoon's time, it presents all of the texts as having been composed in the first century CE, such that "the Bible" (he makes no mention of the process of canonization) existed in pristine manuscript form in time to be translated into Syrian "as early as the year 100." [2]

Having established the enduring purity of the Hebrew and Greek manuscripts, Witherspoon then relates the history of their translation, evaluating the value of various versions with reference to their derivation from the originals. In the 1790 version of the essay, he marvels that so many translations— "not only the Popish translations, but those of the Protestants, for a considerable time after the Reformation"—have relied on the Vulgate rather than on the Hebrew and Greek originals. Witherspoon tells the story of the Authorized Version's creation, making it the culminating episode in the Bible's providential transmission history. He extols the authority of the King James on the basis of the fact that its translators worked from the originals, and that it "has been generally approved by men of learning and piety of denominations, of which its having never been superseded by any other, for one hundred and eighty years, is sufficient proof." Witherspoon's introduction established the Bible as a unitary text and the King James as its English-language point of access; it simultaneously historicized and idealized the text, establishing the Bible as a book with a transmission history while making a bald statement about the providential quality of that history. [3]

The Bible's presumed reliability, solidity, efficacy—these were the enduring surface-level assumptions of American bible culture at the beginning of the period of this study. As repeated and re-repeated over the ensuing decades, these assumptions would change little for the vast majority of the American population. Witherspoon's "To the Reader" was still in use in American bibles at least into the 1870s. This image of the providentially reliable Bible, however, was a rhetorical figure. Because of the inherent nature of scripturalization, there never was any such singular text, only an ever-churning process of production, circulation, reading, citation, re-citation. Assumptions such as Witherspoon's about the Bible would remain perfectly recognizable over the period of this study, but the actual processes of scripturalization would change a great deal. Chapters 1 and 2 track the evolution of early American bibles and bible readers against the backdrop of the Bible's presumed reliability. [4]

CHAPTER ONE

Creating the American Bible Reader, 1777–1816

[I]t is a mere bobtail thing, and its fort lies in telling "how many chapters, verses, words, syllables, and letters there are in the Bible; which is the shortest, which the longest, and which the middle chapter . . . all such goodly discoveries as are fit to make Old Women & Children wonder." However, as many of our Readers are of that sort, insert it by all means.

—MASON LOCKE WEEMS TO MATHEW CAREY, SEPTEMBER 28, 1801

THE "MERE BOBTAIL THING" to which Mason Weems was referring was this chart:

THE OLD AND NEW TESTAMENT DISSECTED.

Books in the Old Teſtament,	39	Bible, is Pfalm cxvii.	The leaſt verfe is 1ſt of Chronicles,	
Chapters,	929	The middle verfe is the 8th of Pfalm	ch. 1. and 1ſt verfe.	
Verfes,	23,214	cxviii.	The middle book in the New Teſtament	
Words,	592,439	The word *And* occurs in the Old Teſta-	is 2d Theffalonians.	
Letters,	2,728,109	ment 35,543 times.	The middle chapters are Romans xiii.	
Books in the New Teſtament,	27	The fame in the New Teſtament alfo	and xiv.	
Chapters,	260	occurs 10,684 times.	The middle verfe is in Acts xvii. 17th	
Verfes,	7,959	The word *Jehovah* occurs 6,855 times.	verfe.	
Words,	181,253	The middle book of the old Teſtament	The leaſt verfe is in John xi. verfe 35.	
Letters,	838,380	is Proverbs.	The 21ft verfe, ch. vii. of Ezra, has all	
The Apocrypha hath 183 chapters, 6081		The middle chapter is Job xxix.	the letters of the alphabet.	
verfes, and 152,185 words.		The middle verfe is 2d Chronicles, chap.	The chap. xix. of ye 2d of Kings and	
The middle chapter and the leaſt in the		xx. the 17th verfe.	chap. xxxvii. of Iaiah are both alike.	
				JUDEA,

FIGURE 1.1. "The Bible Dissected." The Holy Bible (Philadelphia: Mathew Carey, 1802).
Image courtesy of the Library Company of Philadelphia.

Mathew Carey, the Philadelphia printer for whom Weems peddled books in the Southeast, included "The Old and New Testament Dissected" at the foot of a page near the end of his first King James Bible, which reached consumers in 1802.[1] Weems was a bit of a card—he was being characteristically flip when he urged Carey to use it. He was also serious: he had seen the chart in other contemporary bibles and did not want Carey's to be found wanting in any respect. "To have it said that Carey's bible contains more Curious things than were ever seen in any other bible, wou'd be a great Matter," Weems argued. He based the value of "curious things" on the nature of the readers he imagined for Carey's bibles—"old women and children." Putting aside, for the moment, the question of the appeal of "bobtail things" for any particular class of reader, Weems's blunt description of the intended or imagined readership of Carey's bibles brings into relief a crucial aspect of early national print-bible culture: that it was self-consciously oriented toward a sort of reader who was defined as somehow *lesser than* those variously responsible for that print.[2] At the turn of the nineteenth century, the interests involved in the burgeoning American bible market, embedded in a broader market of bible-oriented religious print, imagined a bible reader who was in many ways the inverse of the dominant religious authority of the eighteenth century: rather than educated, upper-class, and male, some combination of marginally literate, lower-class, and often female. Different aspects of this need or deficiency were emphasized in different contexts, and this imagined reader's relationship to actual readers was uneven, but her presence in early national print-bible culture was fundamental to the era's processes of scripturalization. Print-bible culture's address to this imagined reader created space for actual readers to imagine the self-sufficient authority of their own bible reading.[3] At the same time, because this address to readers was accomplished largely through the textual mediations of intellectual and theological elites, it encouraged novel forms of religious authority to develop along traditional lines.

The inversion of the imagined agent of religious authority (male, patrician, and educated) in the subject constituted by print-bible culture (female, common, and in need of teaching) is a key to understanding the development of bible-based authority in the early national period. The era saw a proliferation of cheap, spare bible-society bibles oriented toward those supposed to be in need. Meanwhile, more substantial "family" bibles also became familiar, uniformly addressing themselves to "common" readers, often containing illustrations oriented toward women. These bibles constituted a print-bible culture that imagined a reader both subject to the bearers of religious authority and potentially empowered by those authorities' address.

In two telling respects, though, the distinction between bible-authority and bible-user was not complete. The early national bible reader was generally imagined to be a Protestant, although a robust Catholic print-bible culture was present from the late eighteenth century. Less ambiguous is the question of race. Despite all manner of missionizing rhetoric, both the face of religious authority and that of the imagined reader of print-bible culture were emphatically white. While a large amount of pedagogical print was directed at Native and African Americans throughout the eighteenth and early nineteenth centuries, bibles were not. This, I will argue, had to do with the nation-building assumptions embedded in this print-bible culture: the American bible reader was not just a Christian (real or potential), but also a citizen. This classification naturally excluded indigenous peoples and the enslaved but included white women, unable to participate fully in political culture yet rhetorically held responsible for the promulgation of American nationhood.[4]

This chapter will trace the development of early national print-bible culture from the built-in pedagogical assumptions of scripturalization itself to its evolution in the specific history of eighteenth-century British bible culture. At their most straightforward, the pedagogical goals embedded in colonial-era print-bible culture concerned readers' understanding of the biblical text. Bibles of this era also reinscribed the Bible's privileged status—they participated actively, that is, in the processes of scripturalization. Beyond that, though, they conjured an image of the British bible-reading subject and of the relationship between the Bible and Britishness. Early national American bibles would inherit these pedagogical goals, with the significant difference that nationalist interests would necessarily be turned toward creating *American* bibles and readers.

In early national America, bibles were constitutive of religious subjectivities not just in the mechanics of the text's rhetorical use, but at the material level of their format and composition. Just as tropes and symbols of the biblical text made identities recognizable and performable, American bibles rhetorically constituted approaches to and regard for the Bible itself. The visceral metaphor of Weems's chart, for example—advertising the Bible *dissected* and inviting the reader to handle it as a palpable, limited object with countable words and a precise midpoint—did not just say something about that bible's imagined readers: it told its actual readers something about the Bible. The co-constitution of the American Bible and its readers will be the key to understanding bible-based authority in the nineteenth century.

Scripture and Pedagogy

Written scripture demands authority. The Word of God, or divine truth, or transcendent wisdom may be imagined as self-authenticating and eternally changeless, but writing it down is an act of mediation that must be justified, explained, and legitimated. In the New Testament, before Luke begins his account of the gospel, he announces his qualification for writing it down: "[P]erfect understanding of all things from the very first" (1:3).

This act of mediation, moreover, is fundamentally pedagogical. Written scriptures teach. (Luke, again, says that he writes "[t]hat thou mightest know the certainty of those things, wherein thou hast been instructed" [1:4]). Various mediating voices are built into any given example of a written scripture—

author, transcriber, translator, indexer, publisher—but each alike assumes the asymmetrical apportioning of relevant knowledge that defines a pedagogical relationship. Each voice found in a scripture is, at base, a voice that teaches.

This fact has been particularly salient in the history of Western Christianity. Early modern Catholicism found authority in its own body of thought and tradition as the institution founded and headed by Christ to carry out his work on earth. Reformers, on the other hand, insisted that authority for doctrine and practice rested only with scripture, that anything that was not so grounded had to be left off, and that it was the responsibility of each Christian to pursue the understanding of such distinctions through the reading of scripture. The doctrine of *sola scriptura* placed an extreme burden on the proper presentation and reception of the Bible at the same time that it undermined the Catholic Church as the institution presumed to be responsible for ensuring scripture's purity and correct interpretation.[5]

While Reformation leaders insisted that the Bible be accessible to all Christians—and promoted vernacularization to this end—their connection of this access with *teaching* is often overlooked in favor of the suggestion that they encouraged lay freedom in the reading of scripture.[6] Early on, Martin Luther himself moderated his rhetoric about the laity's bible reading in the face of what he considered dangerous tendencies toward misinterpretation. He was less sanguine than typically suggested with respect to lay bible reading, and even among the clergy he suggested a tiered system of authority based on humanist pedagogy. "There is a vast difference therefore between a simple preacher of the faith and a person who expounds Scripture," Luther wrote. "A simple preacher (it is true) has so many clear passages and texts available through translation that he can know and teach Christ, lead a holy life, and preach to others. But when it comes to interpreting scripture, and working with it on your own, and disputing with those who cite it incorrectly, he is unequal to the task; that cannot be done without languages."[7]

Preaching, for all the Protestant rhetoric about the minister acting as a mere vessel for the Word, is fundamentally pedagogical. The earliest English bibles, appearing in the fifteenth century, were created specifically to facilitate preaching to a vernacular audience, and it was this attempt to teach, rather than the fact of translation itself, that caught the Catholic Church's ire.[8] Reformers, citing both the Bible's difficulty and the radical beliefs which could be generated by what they saw as incorrect readings, were essentially as uncomfortable with laypeople reading without supervision as the Catholic Church. Vernacular bibles right away became cluttered with guidance for readers—notes and commentary in the margins; personal addresses from commentators and translators and crowned heads; charts and lists at the front, at the back, between the testaments.[9] The first edition of Luther's own 1534 German translation has cross-references and marginal explanations, a preface, and introductions to the testaments. *Scriptura* was never, ever, *sola*.[10]

The Protestant bible reader, then, has always been a reader who must be taught, and not only by the Spirit. The pedagogical impulse at the core of Protestant biblicism, materially embedded in a pedagogically-focused print-bible culture, identifies a reader in need. The characteristics by which this need has been defined, however, have varied according to the contexts of bible production.

The need that defined the imagined reader of the first English bibles was, as Luther indicated in his distinctions among preachers, philogical: scripture required translation. In the mid-sixteenth century, Henry VIII—who broke with Rome but remained religiously conservative—opposed the vernacular bible until persuaded that a sanctioned, regulated English Bible for which he could claim responsibility was less likely to spread heresy (and more likely to enhance his authority as head of the English Church) than the illicit translations already circulating.[11] The title page of the Great Bible of 1539 features a looming, enthroned Henry literally handing out bibles, and a very small God peeping out above him, voicing His support.[12] Though apparently wanting in humanistic education, the recipients of Henry's largesse are depicted as affluent and male. From these readers, vernacular scripture might spread farther, as it first issued from Henry. A royal decree of 1542 held that "[i]t shalbe lawfull to everye noble man and gentleman being a householder to reade or cause to be red by any of his famylie or servants in his house orchard or gardeyne, and to his owne famylie, any texte of the Byble or New Testament, so the same be doone quietlie and without disturbaunce of good order." Absent a nobleman's instruction on his own lands, women were prohibited from reading the Bible to others, and the lower classes were forbidden to read it at all. "[N]o woomen nor artificers prentises journeymen serving men of the degrees of yeomen or undre, husbandemen nor laborers shall reade within this Realme or in any other the Kings Domynions, the Byble or Newe Testament in Englishe, to himself or any other pryvatelie or openlie, upon paine of oone monethes imprysonement for every tyme so offending."[13]

Education and class, with varying degrees of emphasis and differing assumptions, would continue to be the primary ways in which the imagined readers of English bibles were identified. The Geneva Bible was the work of Protestants who had fled England in the 1550s at the threat of persecution under Henry's Catholic daughter, Mary. The Geneva translators justified their work on the basis of their learning, positioning the reader according to education rather than class or status, strictly speaking. In an introductory note, the translators professed concern for "simple readers," and contended that their translation mediated not just the original languages of the Bible but the vast scholarship on interpretation and translation: "[W]e have also endeavored both by the diligent reading of the best commentaries, and also by the conference with the godly and learned brethren, to gather brief annotations upon all the hard places." The Geneva is thus explicitly pedagogical in its content and tone. Each book is headed with a summary of its "argument"; the text is supplemented by tables including chronologies of both the Old and New Testaments and an extensive index of biblical events and proper names arranged alphabetically. The presence of woodblock illustrations is explained by the translators' determination that "certeyne places in the bookes of Moses, of the Kings and Exekiel semed so darke that by no description thei colde be made easie to the simple reader." These readers, they hope, will benefit from "figures and notes for the ful declaration thereof."[14] The Geneva's most famous feature, its marginal commentary, amounts to three hundred thousand words, by Harry Stout's count, "a self-contained theological library" that guided "common readers" through the text.[15]

Religious partisanship was also a defining characteristic of the Geneva's imagined reader; that reader was a Protestant, and a Calvinist one. The definitive English bible translation for Catholics, the Douay-Rheims, appeared in the same era as the Geneva, its Latin imprimatur and exhaustive polemical notes constituting a Catholic reader. Partisanship likewise inflected intra-Protestant controversies over bible production. When the subject of a new state-authorized translation to replace the Geneva was raised in 1604, James I voiced his dislike of the Geneva on the grounds that he found "some notes very partial, untrue, seditious, and favoring too much of dangerous and traitorous conceits." Specifically, he thought the Geneva commentary promoted disobedience to kings, singling out a note at Exodus 1:19 which allowed that the midwives who refused to carry out Pharaoh's order to kill Israel's male babies were acting in a "lawful" manner. In commissioning a new translation, James directed that it bear no marginal commentary at all.[16]

Rhetorically, the 1611 King James Version attended to the needs of "common readers": "[W]ithout translation into the vulgar tongue, the unlearned are but like children at Jacob's well (which was deepe) without a bucket or something to drawe with."[17] In keeping with its official nature, though, the first editions promoted a sense of what David Norton calls "ecclesiastical splendour" through their size, quality of paper, and use of black letter type.[18] The size suggested that these bibles were for the preaching of clergy, not the study of lay people. Its extrabiblical material was primarily of a liturgical nature: a liturgical calendar, an "Almanacke" chart giving lunar information relating to the timing of Easter, and thirty-five pages of meticulously illustrated biblical genealogies. Its margins had no commentary but did bear cross-references, potentially useful to lay readers but at this early date most commonly associated with ministers' needs in preparing sermons.

James reasserted Henry's claim to authority for the English Bible, legibly and self-consciously, and by the late seventeenth century the King James text had supplanted the Geneva's.[19] The Geneva's intentionally accessible, pedagogically oriented style, however, prevailed over the Authorized Version's relative austerity. Into the mid-seventeenth century, the Geneva would be the bible that English-speaking settlers were likely to carry to the New World. Geneva bibles remained common in the colonies among Reformed groups, and were widespread in popular preaching into the eighteenth century.[20] After the Puritan Commonwealth was established in England—James I's sensitivity about disobedience to kings proved justified—the Geneva commentary came back into favor. From 1642 at least nine editions of the King James were published with the Geneva commentary, and publishers developed a new set of annotations in the 1660s and 70s.[21] Like Weems and his chart, seventeenth-century bible publishers recognized the addition of notes to the Authorized Version as "a sensible commercial move," as Norton calls it.[22] At the same time, it is also important to recognize how, at the level of the text, theological and market considerations combined in the hybridization of the Geneva and the Authorized Versions to create a distinctively new imagined English bible reader in the eighteenth century.

Eighteenth-Century English Bibles

Ironically, state attempts to control the content of English bibles contributed to their increasing variety. In 1577, Elizabeth I granted London printer Christopher Barker exclusive right to print "all and singular Bibles and New Testaments whatsoever, in the English tongue or in any other tongue whatsoever, and any translation with or without notes," an authorization known as the "bible patent."[23] Later, exclusive patents were granted to selected printers in Wales and Scotland, and to the Universities of Cambridge and Oxford.[24] For the first half of the eighteenth century, London printer John Baskett and his sons, through a series of purchases and leases from 1710 on, controlled both the royal and the Oxford patent, which meant that they dominated the legal bible market.[25] At the same time, the profitability of bible printing led many others to find ways into the market. Straight piracy, based primarily in Holland, was common from the early seventeenth century: nearly eighty unlicensed editions of English bibles were published in Holland or elsewhere on the continent between 1599 and 1746.[26] Other printers, though, composed bibles that could nevertheless be presented, for legal purposes, as something other than bibles. Beginning in 1659, printers shut out of the official bible business began producing sets of bible illustrations, ostensibly to be bound into bibles published by the patented printers. By 1688 printers were restyling these sets of pictures as illustrated bibles under titles such as "History of the Bible," a title that would remain widespread well into the nineteenth century. These went so far as to incorporate scriptural text to accompany the pictures, and eventually nonpatented printers were printing full illustrated bibles.[27] The practice extended beyond illustrations, to elaborate annotations. Titles proliferated which identified a publication as a bible and yet as something else: *The Compleat History of the Old and New Testament: or, a Family Bible*

(1736); *The Universal Bible: or, Every Christian Family's Best Treasure* (1759); *An Illustration of the Holy Scriptures, by notes and explications on the Old and New testament* (1759).[28] This was also the era of the proliferation of heavily-annotated bibles with a particular commentator's name prominently attached to them, and these, too, were published outside of the provisions of the bible patent: Samuel Clark's *The Holy Bible, containing the Old Testament and the New: with Annotation and Parallel Scriptures . . .* (1690); Philip Doddridge's *Family Expositor* (1739–1756); *Mr. Whiston's Primitive New Testament* (1745); John Brown's *Self-Interpreting Bible* (1778).[29] While the majority of English bibles were still produced by a handful of patented printers under the generic Authorized Version title (*The Holy Bible, Newly Translated out of the Original Tongues . . .*), these too became distinguishable for their aesthetic qualities and expanding content.

The titles of the bibles produced by nonpatented printers and the contents they signaled suggest a shared sensibility. Though partly inspired by concern about copyright restrictions, they evolved in ways that spoke to issues unrelated to anything so banal as copyright law. Three recurring themes stand out: these bibles imagined their readers as constitutive of a "family," accentuated the narrative or "historical" aspect of the Bible, and promised "completeness." These elements conjured an image of both the Bible as an object and the imperial British subject as bible reader that would be crucial antecedents of the imagined American bible reader. The pedagogical interests of English bibles in the colonial era would set the terms of the development of American print-bible culture beginning in the 1780s.[30]

"Complete" "Family" "History"

It is important to place the family bible in the context of "family prayer" as its imagined site of reading and use.[31] "Family" in the titles and general description of English bibles should be thought of as a place and an occasion as well as an audience: just as later "school bibles" were for students in the classroom and "pulpit bibles" were for ministers in church, family bibles were imagined as suiting a father's reading in the home.

In that context, two aspects of "family" are key. One is that this imagined reader is, as most often expressed, "common." The commentators responsible for family bibles' paratextual content invariably prefaced their work with lengthy introductions, and here these authors proclaimed their interest in bringing the Bible to readers with little money or education.[32] The imagined reader of a "cottage bible" was a "cottager"—a Britishism referring to rural laborers—who would read aloud to his family. Samuel Clark addressed his preface to "the plainer sort of Christians" and included explicit "Directions to the less Intelligent, for their more easy understanding these Notes."[33] *The Self-Interpreting Bible*, Brown wrote in his preface, was intended to present commentary "in a manner that might best comport with the ability and leisure of the poorer and labouring part of mankind."[34] Philip Doddridge, in the *Family Expositor*, explained that he paraphrased the New Testament to make it more accessible "to those that wanted the benefit of a learned education"; paraphrase, he said, "is the most agreeable and useful manner of explaining [scripture] to common readers, who hardly know how to manage annotations."[35] In the 1754 preface to his "Expository Notes upon the New Testament" (appearing in American editions beginning in 1791), John Wesley dedicated his work to "serious persons, who have not the advantage of Learning" and was more explicit than most about whom he really meant and whom he did not: his notes are "not principally designed for Men of Learning; who are provided with many other helps: And much less for Men of long and deep Experience in the ways and word of God. . . . I write chiefly for plain, unlettered men, who understand only their Mother-Tongue, and yet reverence and love the Word of God, and have a Desire to save their souls."[36]

In addressing "common readers" explicitly, each of these authorities for the Bible cultivated both a rhetorical respect for that reader and a fundamentally superior pedagogical attitude toward him. George Whitefield's widely-circulated preface to Samuel Clark's bible, first used in a 1760 edition, takes Peter's attitude toward the Ethiopian eunuch (Acts 8:26–40) as paradigmatic for all such presenter-reader relationships. "An instructive passage this!" Whitefield writes. "Not only as it shews us how the greatest Personages ought not to think themselves above perusing God's lively Oracles, but also points out to us that teachable and child-like disposition, with which all ought to come to the reading of them, as well as the care the Holy Spirit of God takes to furnish such as have a mind to do his Will, with proper Instructors, that they may know it. The Meek will he guide in his Way."[37]

The imagined reader of a family bible in a moment of family reading remained emphatically male; as Henry's decree two centuries earlier had imagined, family bible reading meant men reading aloud to their families. This will be one of the differences between the colonial and early national imagined bible reader in America, as the diversification of the market for bibles and the feminization of literacy instruction turned family bibles into feminine commodities after the end of the eighteenth century.

The pedagogical focus on simple readers also informed these bibles' promise of "Completeness." Cottagers tended not to own many books, and these bibles promised that they didn't need to. Just as the Geneva translators had promised that they had sifted scholarly work on the Bible in order to present it to common readers, heavily-annotated eighteenth-century bibles promised that they were all-encompassing: all that a given reader needed in order to understand the Bible was contained within the covers of a given artifact. *Brown's Self-Interpreting Bible* promised both to allow the Bible to explain itself and to present in a single volume "the principal substance" of a range of major commentaries: "Pool, Patrick, Clark, Henry, Burkitt, Gill, Doddridge, Guyse, &c. &c."

Completeness held the sense of universality, as in *The Universal Bible or, Every Christian Family's Best Treasure* (1759). Here, an English bible becomes *the* Bible, which told readers something both about the Bible and about the English. In the title of 1764's *The British Bible: Or, A Compleat System of Rational Religion*, "British" is identified with rationality itself, and both are made to inhere in the English-language bible.[38] In a similar fashion, one of the most popular lines of bibles in the early nineteenth century would be referred to as "polyglots": while the word, prominently featured on title pages, implied broad linguistic scope, the only language actually present was English.[39]

This triple identification of true religion, the Bible, and Britishness was carried also in the eighteenth century's increasing historicization of the Bible. This development is typically associated with German scholarship, and what scholars generally think of as higher criticism would not have a significant impact with respect to English bibles until well into the nineteenth century. Elements of historicism, however, are plainly obvious in early English bibles. These include a cognizance of the origins of the Bible as a text, of its translational and archaeological complications, and an impulse toward contextualizing sacred stories according to events of world history. In 1699, the convocation of Anglican bishops commissioned William Lloyd to supervise an improved edition of the Authorized Version. Lloyd's bible, first appearing in 1701, contained extensive historicizing material: revised marginal dates, a lengthy chronological index plotting biblical events on the timeline of world history, and an essay comparing biblical weights and measures to contemporary ones. Lloyd's timeline was reprinted in countless editions of the Bible well into the nineteenth century under the title "An Index to the Holy Bible" and quickly became such an expected part of English bibles that by 1741 the Society for the Propagation of the Gospel in Foreign Parts (SPG) specified that the bibles used by its missionaries in churches contain it.[40] The Index relies primarily on scriptural references, but it also cites extensively from noncanonical histories, such as Josesphus's *Antiquities* and *Bellum Judaicum*, Eusebius's *Ecclesiastical History*, and Dionysius Exiguus's *Liber de Paschate*. The explicit blending of works of history with scripture to plot biblical events historically is of a piece with the maps and images of the Holy Land that also proliferated in bibles of this era. The historicizing attributes of eighteenth-century English bibles may be read as the products of scholarship, but in the context of print-bible culture their pedagogical effects on the imagined reader were, in part, imperial. Plotting biblical events on the timeline of world history made them antecedents to English history, inviting readers to imagine their national past as part of the sacred past. Running dates in the margins of these bibles likewise allowed a reader to track the relationship between the biblical period and her own.[41]

The title of *The Grand Imperial Bible* (1766) said explicitly what all copies of the Authorized Version implied in the dedication to King James, bound in at the front to honor James I as "the principal Mover and Author of the Work": England had a special relationship with the Bible. Scholars have theorized extensively about Christianity's colonialist logic, and specifically about the Bible's status as a key tool of colonialism. Vincent Wimbush argues that belief in the Bible's importance and the nation's importance were mutually constitutive, that the respective fictions of England's preeminence and the Bible's preeminence depended on one another.[42] English colonization of the New World was couched in missionizing terms that emphasized the unique responsibility of the English to spread the gospel. By the Victorian era, this would manifest in the British and Foreign Bible Society taking responsibility for providing translations of the Bible in the various languages of the British Empire, famously emblematized by "The Secret of England's Greatness," Thomas Jones Barker's circa 1863 painting of Queen Victoria presenting a bible to an African prince fairly cowering before her.[43] In the early eighteenth century, though, where bibles themselves were concerned, England mostly kept its secret to itself. Many representatives of the SPG—which served as the primary missionary organ in the Anglican-dominated South through the revolution—were ambivalent about teaching slaves, free blacks, and Native Americans to read and relied instead on oral catechesis.[44] Writing from South Carolina in 1710, one of the SPG's missionaries reported that at least one slave accepted his distance from literacy: "I asked once a pretty ancient and very fine slave whether he cou'd read," Francis Le Jau wrote. "His answer was he wou'd rather choose hereafter to practice the good he cou'd remember."[45]

The SPG's 1741 "Instructions for Catechists for Instructing Indians, Negroes, &c.," however, does stipulate that every effort should be made to "excite in them an earnest Desire to read the Bible as soon as they can" and even gave voice to the expectation that they have bibles of their own: schoolmasters were to "cause them to carry their Bibles and Prayer Books with them, instructing them how to use them there [at public worship]."[46] Bibles themselves, however, imagined literate readers, and African Americans' access to literacy remained sporadic and fraught; literacy among the enslaved would always be recognized as a risk.[47] The oft-cited trope of the "talking book" in eighteenth-century black Atlantic writing is itself a mark of the foreignness of print. To be scripturalized in the anglophone Atlantic world, as Wimbush argues, was to submit to being, or to learn to be, or to be, English.[48]

Michael Warner has argued that in early America, literacy and printing themselves "constituted and distinguished a specifically white community": "White colonists early learned to think of themselves as inhabiting the pure language of writing and to think of blacks as inhabiting a dialect, a particularized speech, that expressed their racial nature."[49] In this view, any generically English bible imagined a white reader. The print-bible culture notionally addressed to Native Americans in the seventeenth and eighteenth centuries raises more complex questions about imagined bible readers, because English missionaries made an attempt to approach them in their own languages, something that apparently no one considered in approaching the multitudes of African languages present in the New World in the same period. The first bible printed in the Western Hemisphere was not an English bible at all, but a translation in Wampanoag, published in 1663, composed by at least two native translators, James Printer and Job Nesuton, and Puritan missionary John Eliot.[50] The first reader imagined by indigenously American printed bibles, then, was an indigenous reader. Eliot's bible did not spark a larger movement of native translation, though—only two other partial native-language bibles appeared before 1800. Eliot's imagined reader was the exception that proved the rule: the indifference to native translation over the eighteenth century would underscore the white identity of the larger print culture's imagined reader. The translation of bibles and tracts designed specifically for certain groups creates dialect, with its assumptions of a distinguishable norm. The native bible could not be "compleat" or "universal," only particular.[51]

Throughout the colonial period, even for Euro-American residents of the Americas, the "universal" nature of English bibles would be tenuous. Until 1777, reading an English-language bible in the New World meant reading a European book. In the colonial era, all English bibles present in the American colonies came inscribed, on their title pages, with a reminder to colonists that authority resided in some distant other place: bibles originated in Edinburgh or Oxford or, by far most commonly, London.[52] What Warner has observed of all print in the American colonies in the early eighteenth century was true for English bibles until the 1780s, and acutely so: "[P]rint in the early eighteenth century was distinguished for the fact of its distant origins, its ability to cross space and time in a way that made it represent the exotic." Colonial bible readers were always "inscribed in the imperial periphery by a print discourse that everywhere recorded its emanation from distant parts."[53]

Prior to the revolution, the provincialism cast on colonial readers by English bibles did not dampen demand for them. Historians have long noted the "spectacular American demand for English goods during the eighteenth century," and bibles were clearly among such goods.[54] In January of 1774, New York bookseller Samuel Loudon received a shipment which included "Clark's folio bible, quarto bibles, with Ostervald's notes; Burket on the bible, Doddridge's family expositor . . . A large variety of bibles, gilt and plain."[55] Loudon also operated a lending library with over a thousand volumes, including the various bibles he offered for sale, indicating that such books could be known even to those who did not buy them.[56] The effect that English bibles had on the first American domestic bibles is plainly obvious—to printers, anyway, *The Compleat and Universal British Family Bible*, variously titled, was what a bible looked like in the late eighteenth century. The titles of some early American bibles echoed the titles and often repeated the content of earlier imports—*The Self-interpreting Bible* (1792); *The Christian's New and Complete Family Bible* (1790)—even though the need for distinguishing titles was removed since the American printers could patriotically ignore the bible patent. The imagined reader remained "common" in the most-used prefaces: a rhetoric of benevolence persisted in which the Bible was always being given, even when it was being sold. Two major factors, though, conditioned the creation of a distinct American bible reader in the first decades after independence. One was the sheer quantity and variety of bibles, a condition brought about by changing technologies of print and transportation as much as by the advent of domestic production.[57] These changes altered the horizons of print. In sixteenth-century England, Henry VIII mandated that every church have an English bible. In nineteenth-century America, the American Bible Society set out to print and distribute an English bible for every *home*. The other factor that set early national print-bible culture apart was specifically tied to domestic production: American bibles printed in English had to conjure an American, rather than a British reader. These two differences are crucial to understanding early national bible-based authority.

American Bibles

Between 1777 and 1840, American printers and publishers issued at least eleven hundred editions of New Testaments and full bibles.[58] In the late eighteenth century, increased access to the resources necessary for printing and investment capital helped make the market viable, and seemingly every printer who had the resources wanted to be in the bible business.[59] "Everything that can raise type is going to work upon the bible," Weems wrote to Carey in 1800. "You'd take New York for the very town of Man-soul, and its printers the veriest saints on earth."[60]

Those interested in American bible production had to grapple with the established "Britishness" of the English-language bible. In July of 1777, a group of Presbyterian ministers petitioned Congress to endow domestic bible printing, arguing that bibles were in short supply and assuming that bible production should come under the purview of the new government, as it had the old.[61] Specifically, the request was tied to the rhetoric of benevolence that had informed British bible production. "[T]he price of bibles for the use of Families and Schools is greatly advanced beyond what was formerly given for them, thro their scarcity and difficulty in importing them from Europe," the petitioners wrote, reinscribing the old assumption that it is a somehow common reader who is in need of the Bible.[62] The petitioners' interests went beyond simply supplying bibles, however: they assumed that Congress would exert control over the text of this bible and regulate its publication. "Ye most correct Copy of the Bible that can be found [shall] be delivered by ye Congress to the Printer, who shall be bound by solemn Oath not to vary from it know-ingly in his Edition, even in a single Iota, without first laying the proposed Alteration before Congress & obtaining their Approbation."[63] The primary pedagogical voice, as in Henry's day, would be that of the state. The petitioners proposed that a new dedication replace the traditional dedication to King James, and that the title page carry the phrase "Printed by Order of Congress." Codifed and controlled by the state, this was to be the American Authorized Version: "After the Bible is published, no more Bibles of that Kind be imported into the American States by any Person whatsoever."[64] Bids were solicited from Philadelphia printers, but this project never got off the ground—the Continen-tal Congress never subsidized bible production.

In 1777, Philadelphia printer Robert Aitken printed an English New Testa-ment and, in 1782, a full English bible, the first printed in America. If these publications may be thought of as constituting a self-consciously American reader, it is in something of a negative sense: rough and unattractive, their primary claim on the buyer was that they were the proud products of domestic craft. Influenced by the earlier petition, Aitken pursued the project with the desire to sell Congress on the idea of approving and underwriting his bible. He received none of the financial support he requested, but he did get an enthu-siastic if somewhat careful response from the congressional chaplains, recom-mending the work "to the inhabitants of the United States" and celebrating this "instance of the progress of arts in this country."[65] Aitken printed the endorsement with his bible. There, it inhabited the same authorizing space as the dedication to King James—which Aitken left out—underscoring the gen-eral assumption that a bible could and should be authorized by the state, even though, from the perspective of the state, it had not been.

Domestic production of English bibles began in earnest in the 1790s, imag-ining an explicitly American reader in nationalist terms. The first bible printed in New York, in 1792, has at the front a lengthy list of subscribers, headed by George Washington (in outsized type) and other members of the national gov-ernment.[66] The traditional dedication to King James was the most legible evi-dence of American provincialism, and it was the first thing to go. Isaac Collins found it "wholly unnecessary for the purposes of edification, and perhaps on some accounts improper" for American bibles and replaced it with the preface by John Witherspoon.[67]

The subsequent ubiquity of Witherspoon's preface highlights an important fact about the presumption of national identity embedded in the first Ameri-can English bibles. Witherspoon wrote the text while president of Princeton; it first appeared in 1790 in a bible published in Philadelphia; and Collins printed a revised version in his first Trenton bible the next year. This preface, then, found its way into print through local channels (Princeton is about forty miles from Philadelphia, and Trenton is between them). Collins, however, had national aspirations: he headed the text with a statement about the impropriety of using the traditional King James preface in "an American edition." He had his quarto bible stereotyped in 1815, enabling him to sell copies of the printing plates, amplifying the text's reach. Collins's text of the Bible, Witherspoon's preface in tow, became one of the standard texts for American bibles.[68] Witherspoon's preface was also picked up by commentator Hervey Wilbur for use in his annotated bible, and over the next several decades it showed up in bibles published in, at least, Albany; Boston; Brattleboro, Vermont; Buffalo; Dayton, Ohio; and Hartford, Connecticut. In 1876 it shows up, still, in a bible published in Philadelphia, now buried amidst an encyclopedia's worth of images and other parabiblical materials.[69]

The local, northeastern origins of what became a standard national biblical text are indicative of the realities of "American" print-bible culture in the early national period. While early domestic bible producers had national aspirations, the imagined American bible reader was inescapably a northeastern, urban creation. That New York subscriber list from 1792 actually consists of two parts. The main list of subscribers—overwhelmingly from New York—is followed by a supplement, indicating that additional subscriptions were received after the type for the main list had been set. This supplemental list contains several (and the only) subscribers from Georgia, suggesting both the reach of this publishing project and the temporal and geographic distance of the South.[70] American bible production began in Philadelphia, Boston, New York, and their environs in the 1780s, and though these centers of print culture multiplied their production of bibles several times over in the ensuing decades, sites of production spread only slowly and intermittently. The bibliographic record tells a stark tale: in the first thirty years of American bible publishing, no bible or even New Testament was printed *south or west of Baltimore*.[71]

The northeastern dominance of American bible production continued for decades. Editions of a heavily-annotated study bible appeared in the 1820s bearing Cincinnati imprints, and in 1831 the following significant outlier appears—a bible bearing the imprint "Published by Silas Andrus: Hartford, Conn.; Luke Loomis & Co.: Pittsburgh, Penn.; A.B. Roff: Cincinnati, Ohio; and J.S. Kellogg: Mobile, Ala." Examined carefully, though, this geographically-eclectic imprint was another northeastern creation with national aspirations: it was annotated and compiled "for the instruction of youth" by Jesse Olney, widely known as an author of school books and a resident of Hartford, Connecticut.[72] Olney's proximity to Andrus—the first and northeasternmost of the publishers in the imprint—makes it more than likely that Andrus printed the book and coordinated with the farther-flung publishers for distribution.[73] Similar imprints, naming booksellers in Alabama, Charleston, and, in 1850, New Orleans, as distributors appeared during the next few decades. Finally, in 1858, three different New Testaments were published in Nashville. Tellingly, six editions of the New Testament were published in Nashville and Augusta, Georgia, during the Civil War; immediately after the war, this activity ceased. The first full bible printed in the former Confederacy was published under the auspices of the Methodist printing concern in Nashville, in 1874— nearly a century after Aitken published the first American English bible in Philadelphia.[74]

The nation-building aspirations of early American bibles are most readily apparent in the work of the American Bible Society (ABS), founded in 1816.[75] Beginning in the 1810s, the ABS formalized the idea of a national bible. Bible societies in America were originally local affairs—the first, the Bible Society of Philadelphia, was founded in 1808. The Philadelphia Society modeled its goals on those of the British and Foreign Bible Society (BFBS), founded in March of 1804, in organizing to provide bibles to those that might have difficulty buying them, but it explicitly rejected the British Society's sense of national mission. The BFBS wanted a national organization in America, and, in sending the Philadelphia society start-up funds, let it be known that while they were sending two hundred pounds to the "Bible Society of Philadelphia," they would have sent as much as five hundred pounds to the "United States Bible Society."[76] The Philadelphians demurred because they thought local organizations could do the work more efficiently and with greater participation among members. A national organization would have to hold meetings somewhere, and a national membership would find it difficult and expensive to attend. "It was believed, in a word," they wrote, "that such an institution would never be conducted with vigour, and not be likely to continue for a length of time."[77] They concluded that "[i]f as many Bible Societies should be instituted as there are states in the union, the number probably would not be too large."[78]

By the time the American Bible Society formed, there were 108 local societies, six times the number of states in the union. The ABS's founders thought this too many. The founders of the ABS staked their argument for a national society on the question of efficiency: the various state and local societies were "without any common plan of operation" and were failing to meet what they depicted as a dramatic need for bibles in the young nation.[79] The rhetoric they used to justify their consolidation of authority for distributing the Bible clearly imagines a reader in need in terms of education and class. Bible societies expressed particular concern for those too poor to buy bibles and those—such as sailors, convicts, and, eventually, the enslaved—in no position to buy books. The Philadelphia society, likewise, posited the poor as the paradigmatic bible readers: "It was the discriminating character of the gospel at its first publication, that it was preached to the poor; and it is to the poor chiefly that we have it in expectation to send the inspired and authentic records of that gospel."[80]

The imagined recipient of the ABS's bibles was in direct contrast with how the organization imagined itself. The blue-blooded condescension which permeates the rhetoric of the ABS is unmistakable, and, set in the long history of authority for the English Bible, telling. Owing to the state of society and culture in the United States, the ABS claimed that local societies found "it difficult to assemble a respectable audience at their annual meetings." By contrast, "the annual meeting of the British Society is one of the most crowded and interesting assemblies in England, attended by individuals the most distinguished of any in the kingdom for piety, eloquence and rank."[81] The implication was that one benefit of a national organization would be to have a larger set of worthy citizens from whom to select leaders, but in the event the ABS's constitution required that two-thirds of its managers live in Manhattan, again underscoring the conflation of northeastern with national identity.[82] The ABS's founders argued that the group's leadership had to be carefully chosen by a select committee, "and not left to the hasty inconsiderate choice of a promiscuous assembly at a general meeting."[83] This attitude has led historian Peter Wosh to place the ABS at the center of "a massive counteroffensive directed against Jeffersonian values" in the second decade of the nineteenth century.[84] The Philadelphia Society, on the other hand, declined to send delegates to the ABS's founding convention and continued to find ways to invest authority in ever more local organizations just as the ABS was consolidating nationwide power. Their 1816 report outlines the creation of "Bible Assemblies," hyperlocal groups within Philadelphia and the greater area which gave individuals and congregations with little means a stake in the bible society's goals. Membership in these microsocieties was "constituted and continued by the payment of six cents per month, payable monthly, quarterly, semi-annually or annually, at the discretion of the member."[85] Members of these groups took part in running their organizations, voting—in promiscuous assembly—for their fellow members to serve on the operating board.

Along with the arrogation of authority for the Bible on social grounds, the founders of the ABS argued that a national organization was necessary to control the text and form of English bibles in America. Control over the text further belied the local prerogatives embedded in the group's national aspirations. The ABS's directors had intended to distribute plates around the country, and sent plates to the Lexington, Kentucky, auxiliary. Subsequently, though, they changed their minds, opting to maintain centralized control of all bible production in Manhattan.[86] In announcing the "First General Supply" in 1829, the ABS determined to put a bible in every American home, and every one of them was to be printed from stereotype plates in New York City.[87]

For all of their familiar condescension toward their poor, bibleless imagined reader, in eschewing most paratextual materials society bibles evinced a different approach to the pedagogical impulse implicit in all written scripture. The rationale for the "without note or comment" maxim, which all American societies adopted from the BFBS, was that it prevented dissent, ensuring that all denominations could cooperate with the work of bible societies in good faith.[88] "Placing the Good Book in every household, in the minds of many, might lay the foundation for a common Christian social consensus," promoters wrote. The pedagogical impulse nevertheless runs through the way that members of the ABS imagined their books would be used. The ABS's founders assumed that the Bible's importance to America—and, through America, to the world—was pedagogical. The ABS's leaders, John Fea writes, assumed that the "Bible was the source of the laws that kept the United States moral, and it was the means of restraining the passion-driven impulses of democracy that led to licentiousness."[89]

The presentation of the Bible as a singular whole inherently delivering a unifying, "restraining" message to all readers was, at base, a different ideal of "completeness." Incessant touting of the "without note or content" maxim embodied the same pretense used to identify a given printed English bible with the eternal, abstract Bible. By eliminating notes and comments, ABS bibles claimed to be *the* Bible, distinct from the variety of bibles in the market that came with adjectives attached but which also claimed to be complete and universal. Like other claims to universality, though, this one was fictive. In practice, bible societies were widely regarded as Presbyterian affairs, and in 1836 a coalition of Baptists would break from the ABS over translation issues. In any case, the ABS's prohibition on paratexts was not absolute. In 1833 they began printing bibles with marginal references, guide words, and chapter summaries to guide reading, noting in their annual report that they had long intended to do so.[90]

Like other nationalistic organizations of the early nineteenth century, the ABS sought to knit the nation together through print, in their case holding up the Bible as the most essential shared national text. The fiction of a nationally-uniform bible and bible reader would become especially acute in responses to attempted bible distribution among the enslaved. Abolitionists such as Frederick Douglass believed that such efforts allowed sympathetic whites to assuage their consciences while taking focus away from the central problem, and in ridiculing such plans observed both the cognitive and geographical distance between enslaved African Americans and the sort of literate society in which having a bible made a difference in one's life. "Are the men engaged in this movement sane?" he asked, in 1847. "Do they seriously believe that the American Slave can receive the Bible? . . . Do they suppose that Slaveholders, in open violation of their wicked laws, will allow their Slaves to have the Bible? How do they mean to get the Bible among the Slaves? It cannot go itself—it must be carried."[91] The imagined reader conjured by American bibles was still uniformly white, Douglass recognized.

The imagined enslaved reader, or nonreader, devoid of choices with respect to bibles, is in crucial contrast to the reader imagined by early national print-bible culture. The early nineteenth century was a period of economic expansion, involving both the rapidly expanding production of consumer goods and the disruptions attending a capitalist economy, as local economies became subject to distant markets.[92] Bibles entered this market like other consumer goods: as objects intended to find buyers.[93] In 1807, Mathew Carey issued a prospectus advertising more than thirty different iterations of bibles, inviting buyers to specify that their bibles come with or without the Apocrypha, the metered Psalms, or a concordance; with no plates, eleven plates, or thirty plates (the two sets overlapped little); two maps, ten, or none; or any combination of these variables. Beyond the content, buyers could specify the grade of paper used and the type of binding. As James Green has noted, Carey's line of bibles had reached unprecedented variety: "No Bible, in fact, no book of any kind had ever been offered in such a variety of formats, and the innovation was extremely popular with consumers."[94]

To the extent that *shopping*—a word that first appeared in the modern sense in 1764—was from early on gendered as feminine, as ever more diverse commodities in a growing market American bibles came to be oriented toward an imagined reader who was female.[95] In this period women became "highly visible shoppers," in Ellen Hartigan-O'Connor's phrase, and bible sellers took note.[96] Their profit motive meant that they were more open to a fact that scholars of American religion have only come around to in the last few decades, which is that "the numerical dominance of women in all but a few religious groups constitutes one of the most consistent features of American religion," as Ann Braude has put it.[97] While typically barred from formal positions of religious authority, women have always made up the majority of American churchgoers. From the colonial era, moreover, women were identified as the teachers of literacy, and as the teaching of literacy was identified with the Bible, women had a clear stake in choosing among bibles in the market.[98] To be clear, this is not to say that women were necessarily responsible for buying more bibles than men in this period. Subscriber lists bound into early national bibles are overwhelmingly composed of men. What is clear is that many bible producers *thought* that they needed to sell bibles to women, and that their bibles subsequently imagined female readers.

The clearest way in which many early American bibles appealed to women was in their illustrations. Bible illustrations—recognized as important by bible producers both for their pedagogical efficacy and their aesthetic appeal—became much more common in the early nineteenth century. Considering that there are 188 named women in the Christian bible, versus nearly twelve hundred named men, women are vastly overrepresented in early national bible illustrations. Of the eighteen biblical scenes illustrated in ten or more American editions of the bible between 1790 and 1825, at least seven feature women as central figures.[99] Many of these are predictable—scenes involving the Virgin Mary, such as the annunciation and the adoration of the magi—but many are more idiosyncratic. "The Judgment of Solomon," for example, was a particular favorite, featuring two women claiming the same baby (1 Kings 3), as were the woman of Samaria talking with Jesus at the well (John 4) and the widow watching Elijah raising her son from the dead (1 Kings 17). Many other illustrations feature women prominently even when they are not necessarily integral to the biblical passage—the onlookers in renderings of Christ healing the man of Bethesda (John 5) are typically female, for example. Several American bibles of this era contain illustrations of Hagar in the wilderness (Genesis 16), the woman taken in adultery (John 8), and, interestingly, Judith. Protestants relegate the Book of Judith to the Apocrypha, but it was commonly included in early national bibles, and Judith carrying the head of Holofernes (Judith 13) was usually the only illustration in the Apocrypha.[100]

Over all of these stands the image of Bithiah discovering Moses in the reeds (Exodus 2). This scene of a group of young women swooning over an abandoned baby is by far the most common illustrated frontispiece in early national bibles, meaning that it was the first thing many bible producers imagined their readers encountering upon opening their bibles. This scene has interesting resonance with the nationalism that was also an integral part of imagining early national bible readers: Bithiah's raising of Moses is, after all, an act of motherhood in service of the nation.[101]

Weems worried about the illustrations in Carey's bibles. He was obsessed with the visual and tactile appeal of the books he sold and unhappy with the first edition of Carey's bible, the one for which he had recommended the "Bible Dissected" chart; he called the edition "miserable" and "garbled." "[B]ut that's between you & I only," he told Carey. He still wanted to give them as wide a circulation as possible. As much as he didn't care for them himself, Weems was annoyed that many of his provincial customers were not especially interested in the "valuable improvements," such as the illustrations and the "Dissected" chart, that he used to entice them to buy. Explaining concerns raised by his customers to Carey, in a letter Weems narrated a typical conversation with a customer. After Weems elucidates all of the additions and advantages of Carey's bible, the customer replies: "All this is clever, yes, 'tis clever enough indeed, but I wouldn't give a fig the more for all that, for it only sarves to make the Children spoil the book."[102] While Weems and Carey put together a bible for a given imagined reader, customers worried about these bibles facilitating unexpected, ostensibly improper, responses from actual readers.

Those worries were justified. The Mississippi Department of Archives and History, in Jackson, holds a copy of an early Carey quarto bible, one almost certainly sold by Weems himself.[103] Someone—perhaps a child—has indeed "spoiled" many of the illustrations, smudging out the faces of biblical characters in some illustrations, blacking out the eyes of others, doodling on their environments. The prodigal son's homecoming has never been more terrifying (Fig. 1.2).

This bible, then, is an artifact of both imaginary and actual American bible readers. Its crowded family record pages indicate that it was originally owned by the Hewitt family, who bought it when they lived in Washington, DC, in late 1806 and carried it with them to Washington, Mississippi, sometime between

FIGURE 1.2. "The Prodigal Son." Hewitt (James and Caroline Grayson) and Carradine Family Bible. Image courtesy of the Archives and Records Services Division, Mississippi Department of Archives and History.

1817 and 1821.[104] It is now a particularly rough copy of what Weems thought was a rough book to start with: the main title page is gone and the rest of the opening pages have (mostly) survived a fire; one illustration has been ripped in half and stitched back together. While the text and paratextual elements of the book necessarily hailed an imagined reader, its current state indicates its use by actual readers. It is, to my reading, an artifactual demonstration that real and imagined readers exist always in dialogic relationships. In a book market, readers are never completely absent from any stage of the circuit of writing, production, distribution, and reception; producers and consumers are always co-constituted.[105] Chapter 2 will argue that the reader present in this body of print had real consequences, though perhaps not the kind imagined by those responsible for her.

CHAPTER TWO

Taking a Text

READING AND REFERENCING THE BIBLE
IN THE EARLY NINETEENTH CENTURY

EARLY IN 1845, a seventeen-year-old woman named Ellen Harmon reported a vision of scripture. Harmon was by this time developing a reputation as a visionary. She was also, however, developing a reputation as a victim of mesmerism. The latter charge bothered her, and on this occasion, she said, as she felt the spirit of prophecy come upon her she began to suspect mesmerism herself and resisted. She was punished for this doubt by being struck dumb, and then she saw scripture.

> I then saw my sin in doubting the power of God, and that for so doing I had been struck dumb, but that my tongue should be loosed in less than twenty-four hours. A card was held up before me, on which were written in letters of gold the chapter and verse of fifty texts of scripture. After I came out of vision, I beckoned for the slate, and wrote upon it that I was dumb, also what I had seen, and that I wished the large Bible. I took the Bible, and readily turned to all the texts that I had seen upon the card.[1]

Harmon's vision combines two sorts of religious authority; it is a fascinating appearance of scholarly ways of using the Bible in a visionary experience. In one moment she is passively receiving visions from the Spirit; in the next, she is holding open a bible and directing listeners to particular passages, using the conventions of scriptural citation. Harmon's vision might have appeared random or inspired to her onlookers, depending on their dispositions, but at base it was a collation of texts from all over the New Testament around a handful of themes, made possible by the technology of the concordance. The fifty verses Harmon reported seeing are connected by a web of words cited together in contemporary concordances: several passages contain the words "speak," "deceit," "false," "faith," "love," "principalities."

Harmon's vision encapsulates the scripturalized terms of religious authority in the early nineteenth century. The citational possibilities of scripturalization both regulated existing relationships of power and provided for the possibility of new ones. Scripturalized subjects are the products and the wielders of the rhetorical power that comes from having recourse to a scriptural text.

Where the last chapter tracked the emergence of the imagined American bible reader out of eighteenth-century British print-bible culture, this chapter will look at actual American bible readers in the early national period. This requires close consideration of the exact nature of scripturalized texts' privileged differentiation from other texts. That differentiation is accomplished not by abstract ideology—a "belief" that a given text is special—but by intersubjective practices of textual application. Scripturalized texts are texts that are used in ways different from other texts. Scriptures have significance beyond themselves; to treat a text as a scripture is to *apply* it. Scripturalization means that the assumption of citation is implicit in the act of reading. It is the assumption of citation that gives print-bible culture its form.

The scripturalized environment of American print-bible culture was conditioned by a citational environment of increasing plentitude. As documented in the last chapter, bibles proliferated in the early national period. They were only part of the scripturalized print culture of the era, however. They entered a universe of texts that cited and indexed the Bible. Schoolbooks and illustrated children's bibles selected, simplified, and condensed the scriptural text. Cross-references, concordances, and commentaries cited the Bible more explicitly, as texts that were usable only with recourse to actual bibles. All of them encouraged and facilitated bible reading and reference. All of them laid claim to authoritative biblical citation while increasing readers' own access to and facility with scriptural citation.

This proliferation of print expanded the range of late colonial scripturalized culture. It also, however, inevitably asserted particular readings of the Bible: parabiblical texts offered access to the Bible for more readers, but that access was not transparent. Because they carry interpretive meaning and instruct readers in that meaning, paratexts carry scholarly, ecclesiastical, social, or state authority into the text itself. Because they provide a technology for reading a very complicated book, they create lay readers who can assert authority over (and with) the text.[2]

The category of biblical literacy as explored in this study encompasses a range of sense-making abilities and their increasing prevalence among American populations in the first half of the nineteenth century. Jennifer Monaghan places early American readers on a spectrum: "At the least accomplished end of this scale . . . men and women read slowly, and deliberately. . . . 'Reading' was equated with oral reading, an activity shared with others."[3] At the other extreme, she writes, "men and women read as we do today, copiously, intently, and presumably often silently."[4]

In the seventeenth and eighteenth centuries, this hyperliterate extreme was, overwhelmingly, the province of ministers. Becoming a minister was, in fact, defined by attaining this sort of literacy with respect to the Bible, and it was fundamentally construed as a reading act—"reading divinity."[5] The most important products of this literacy were public sermons which enacted authoritative relationships among ministers and audiences. In this environment, even where lay bible reading was widespread, ministers' presumed monopoly on biblical facility cemented their authority. In his study of colonial preaching, Harry Stout assumes that New Englanders across classes read the Bible routinely, but argues forcefully that this reading brought more, not less, authority to ministers. "The vernacular Bible was plain in grammar and syntax but also mysterious," he writes. "Instead of bringing a sense of independence and autonomy characteristic of 'modern' literate societies, Puritan literacy enhanced the public respect for the sermon and for the minster who preached it."[6] This works in service of Stout's equation of the Puritan sermon with "authority incarnate."[7]

There were exceptions to ministerial dominance in the colonial era. The most obvious recorded example is Anne Hutchinson, whose 1637 trial transcript documents her startling facility with the Bible tying even her learned examiners in knots. Michael Ditmore's analysis of a core part of the transcript—Hutchinson's assertion that she heard "an immediate voice"—reveals "three direct Bible quotations with specific chapter and verse, five more direct Bible quotations without chapter and verse, two references to Bible chapter and verse without quotation, and seven allusions to more or less specific Bible passages—a total of seventeen somewhat scattered biblical allusions," all in the span of fewer than eight hundred words.[8] The transcript records a confused exchange between two of her clerical examiners at the end of her speech: "What is the scripture she brings?" one asked. The response tendered by another minister—"Behold I turn away from you"—further underscores the confusion her facility sowed even among the most learned, since it does not appear to actually match any of the references Hutchinson had just spun out.[9]

Ditmore argues that Hutchinson was using three different bibles in her private study. This level of "extensive" bible reading was enough to rival the private reading of any minister; moreover, the composition of Hutchinson's testimony, if accurately reflected in the extant transcript, suggests a clerical level of erudition and reflection in the composition of testimony given more or less off the cuff.[10] But Hutchinson, of course, had no pulpit from which to demonstrate her learning and educate others. Her trial was, partly, about the propriety of the outlet she had found: religious meetings in her home.[11] A hundred and thirty years later, in Newport, Rhode Island, Sara Osborn attracted controversy for presuming to hold prayer meetings and bible studies in her home.[12] Osborn's surviving writings bear witness to her facility with the Bible, gleaned from the culture around her, like Harmon's later, without recourse to formal ministerial training.[13]

Because of such exceptions, it is self-defeating to suggest a hard and fast beginning to the evolution of scripturalization I document here. While I am arguing that the proliferation of print had a great deal to do with the change, too much emphasis on this factor would risk a crass technological determinism as well as a blindness to the realities of print culture: more books need not necessarily have meant more readers, just as relative scarcity did not mean that no one developed biblical facility. As important as the technologies of bible reading that became more widely available in the early national period is the ideological assumption about bible reading that those materials constituted in the print public sphere: the possibility of transparent access to meaning and the skills of application. Those assumptions were fallacious—biblical meaning and use occur only within the matrices of scripturalization, in dialogic relationship with existing authorities and textual habits. Nevertheless, when an entire vast print culture is oriented toward rhetorically enabling a full range of imagined readers, it is bound to have some sort of effect on actual readers.

The first part of this chapter will examine the course of changes in these areas in the early nineteenth century, while the second part will return to Harmon's career—she went on to found the Seventh-day Adventist Church—as an example of the sort of authority for the Bible these changes facilitated. In the seventeenth century, Anne Hutchinson demonstrated a powerful facility with the Bible when interrogated by the ministry. She was clearly capable of formulating bible-based arguments by referencing her bibles. Nevertheless, she found herself in the position of buttressing her demonstration of clerical authority with an appeal to radical, extrabiblical authority. The trajectory of Ellen White's career, more than two hundred years later, went in the other direction: she combined all of the threads of materiality, literacy, and authority as she moved away from visionary authority and toward clerical skill. Access to bibles and indexing materials had fundamentally changed the possibilities of religious authority.

Bibles, Literacy, and Biblical Literacy

Historical literacy rates are notoriously difficult to measure. Various analyses of signatures in eighteenth-century New England suggest a consistent upward trajectory culminating in literacy rates above eighty percent for white women and above ninety percent for men by 1800.[14] In other parts of the colonies, the figure was most likely lower, but with a parallel increase over the same period. Literacy, in any case, is not merely a matter of being able to interpret characters on a page. Cathy Davidson has written that literacy is never simply a rate that may be quantitatively measured, but a complicated social process as well as the embodiment of significant social ideals: "To become literate a person must master, in addition to a set of culturally defined skills, all the cultural information involved in decoding and producing texts, including the frames of reference for comprehending their contents."[15]

Learning to read in early America was synonymous with learning to read the Bible, but it did not necessarily mean reading bibles. In the early colonial era, reading education was built around the "common road," a succession of ever more challenging Christian texts that began with a hornbook, primer, or speller and advanced to the psalter, the New Testament, and finally a full bible.[16] Hornbooks consisted of a single sheet of print mounted to a flat piece of wood and "laminated" with thin, transparent strips of horn.[17] The printed sheet typically bore the alphabet, syllabary, and the Lord's Prayer. Primers contained similar instructional material but a higher percentage of religious content—paraphrases of bible stories and a story from John Foxe's *Book of Martyrs*, for example. Only after these introductory steps would students who were going to advance in their literacy education handle actual texts from the Bible, and at any point on the common road a student's education might be interrupted.

Bibles were therefore the "ultimate goal of reading instruction," but they were not consistently present along the ordinary road to literacy.[18] Although by all accounts the guided reading of the New and Old Testaments would be linear and systematic, this advanced stage of reading was preceded by selective reference to biblical content. Hornbooks, primers, and spelling books taught both reading and reference at the same time: students learned both some biblical content and the notion that these selections cited some other, larger text. The goal was memorization: of ritualized texts (the Lord's Prayer of the hornbook), of narrative moments ("Uriah's beauteous Wife, / Made David seek his Life," in the *New England Primer*), of points of doctrine ("In Adam's Fall / We sinned all," ditto). They rarely included chapter and verse references or actual passages of the Bible: even the Lord's Prayer of hornbooks and primers was the Book of Common Prayer version, which did not match Matt 6:9–13 in either the Authorized Version or the Geneva.[19] This familiarity through memorization meant that once a child turned to the New Testament, certain stories, themes, and the practice of citation itself would be familiar.

Readers' introduction to biblical material was necessarily selective and citational, but once they reached the Bible itself their reading was expected to be sequential and systematic. The *New England Primer* advised young readers that "[b]y reading three Chapters and one Psalm every Day, you will read the whole Bible through in less than a year," which was similar to the plan of reading promoted in Puritan preaching guides.[20] With the increased circulation of bibles at the turn of the nineteenth century, a genre of guides to bible reading likewise became popular, all of them steadfastly against selective forms of reading. These guides are most concerned that readers adopt the proper disposition: attention and diligence are the bywords. Lindley Murray called the proper mode of bible reading a "steady and cordial perseverance."[21] Edward Bickersteth, an English clergyman whose *A Scripture Help* was published in Boston in 1817, advised regular reading that moved through a bible from start to finish: "Read one book through before you begin another, and read the whole bible through."[22] Other writers suggested that it was permissible and sometimes preferable to start somewhere other than at Genesis, but all agreed that there should be some order: "Read in course and instead of beginning the Bible and going regularly through it, take the Psalms, the Gospels and the epistles and make these the first portion your study."[23]

This advice had an effect. Phineas Pratt of Saco, Maine, kept meticulous record of the first time he read the Old Testament to his family in the 1820s.[24] Utilizing blank space at the foot of the book's "To the Reader" essay, Pratt recorded that he "[b]egan to read the old Test in the family in the morning September 10 1821." Subsequent notes record the steady and cordial perseverance of that reading. At the end of the Old Testament, in blank space at the foot of the last page of Malachi, Pratt recorded that he "[e]nded first time thru in family January 25 1824," 868 days after starting. This implies something like a chapter per day with some doubling-up, most likely during the Psalms. There are 929 chapters in the Old Testament—if the family covered a chapter per day in every book except the Psalms, and two psalms per day when they got to them, for example, reading the Old Testament would take 854 days. However it played out, Pratt's markings suggest that he planned his reading schedule in advance. His bible featured a common table listing the books of the Bible and how many chapters are in each one, and Pratt has summed the number of chapters, likely with an eye toward calculating a reading schedule. A chapter a day would have been in keeping with the explicit advice of many reading guides, but it was in accord with all of them in that it was some sort of regular plan, regardless of the exact schedule.

Many of the subsequent dates in Pratt's bible are incomplete and confusing, but he records at least three more cycles of reading the Old Testament to his family; he started again in January of 1824 (apparently right after finishing the first time), June of 1826, and on August 7, 1829. Go-arounds two and three took pretty much the same number of days, according to the finishing dates Pratt dutifully recorded at the end of Malachi. Pratt did not record an end date for the last one, but he did note that he started the New Testament in August of 1829, apparently when he also started the Old Testament for the fourth time.

Adeline Hosner, a farmer in upstate New York in the early nineteenth century, read her bible with similar diligence; however, she read only to herself. Hosner's remoteness from a place of worship and the efforts of her nonbelieving husband to keep her from going to church meant that solitary bible reading was a major part of her religious life.[25] On September 22, 1839, Hosner recorded that she was in the midst of reading her bible through sequentially, from the beginning. By that day she had made it as far as Isaiah 44. On January 19, 1840, she recorded that she was reading Mark 14. This suggests a pace of one chapter per day over the course of the intervening seventeen weeks—similar to Pratt's, except with more consistency.[26]

An earlier moment of Hosner's bible reading was more typical. In September of 1838, she recorded in her diary, she grabbed her bible and went to the barn. She was seven months pregnant with her fourth child and angry after an argument with her emotionally abusive husband, and in the barn she opened her bible at random to 2 Thessalonians 1:4, which she copied out into her journal later that day: "So that we ourselves glory in you in the churches of god for your patience and faith in all your persecutions and tribulations that ye endure[,] which is a manifest token of the righteous judgment of god that ye may be counted worthy of the kingdom of god for which ye also suffer."[27] It seemed to fit, she indicated in her journal.

The consistency of reading guides' objection to selective forms of reading itself suggests that sequential reading was the exception. The vast majority of evidence of bible reading in the early national period confirms this. When individual readers attest to their bible reading— explicitly or by implication, in the ways that they cite the Bible—they mostly attest to indexical, inconsistent, and irregular forms of reading.[28]

Opening her bible at random in the barn, Hosner employed a mode of reading that was probably as old as the codex itself, one of the simplest forms of irregular reading. In the Roman Empire, copies of Virgil were opened at random to answer questions and predict the future, and Augustine famously used a volume of Paul's letters to inquire about the state of his soul, moved by the voice of a child to "pick up and read."[29] Practices known commonly as "bibliomancy" or *sortes biblicae* came to be roundly discouraged by religious authorities—by the Council of Paris in 829, and by the Reformers in the sixteenth century. Martin Luther classed such reading as a form of divination, and later denunciations carry this same charge of the demonic. Cotton Mather equated bibliomancy with "going to the Devil himself" for answers, just like employing astrologers or fortune tellers.[30]

Despite the condemnations, bibliomancy and related practices persisted. Most often, it seems, bibles were merely opened with a finger, at random. Other means of finding a random page relied on letting books "fall open," as Mather indicates, or jabbing a pin or another object between the leaves and opening it from the place where it struck.[31] Famously, Mary Rowlandson recounted her frequent bibliomancy during her captivity and seems to have relied on opening her bible at random.[32]

By the early nineteenth century, random forms of reading were less frequently described as demonic, but they were definitely thought of as sinful.
Thomas Charleton Henry's *Letters to an anxious inquirer*, first published in
1827, made a nuanced distinction between bibliomancy proper and something
closer to the way Hosner would be reading ten years later. Henry found bibliomancy a "baneful trifling with the hidden things of God," recounting a story of
a woman who opened her bible at random hoping for information about the
state of her soul but landed on "a portion of genealogy." Trying again, he
writes, she found another verse "quite as incapable of leading to any decision,"
and then "a word of reproof to the impenitent sinner." In addition to the sinful
presumption in extracting and applying a scriptural passage in a manner "foreign from its original design," Henry finds that the peril in this sort of reading
is that after the third time the woman took this as "a reluctance on the part of
her Maker to disclose her fate," a belief that yielded to despair and then
apathy.[33]

Freewill Baptist preacher William Smyth Babcock recorded a similar failure with indifference in his journal in 1801: "[P]rayed god, that I might know
my standing, by opening to some passage of scripture; opened to the 65 psalm
twice, but not answering my case, I prayed the third time, and opened to the
40th of Ezekiel. I have often heard Christians tell of receiving answers this way
but I never have."[34] Babcock's refusal to take the hint here is at first sort of
amusing—even an unbeliever might wonder if someone were not trying to tell
him something when he landed on Psalm 65 twice. More seriously, though, it
speaks to the significance of the effort required in the *application* of a found
verse. Babcock's journal documents his consuming guilt regarding his sexual
urges, and we can, actually, imagine parts of Psalm 65 answering his need for
solace. Verse three, for example, reads, "Iniquities prevail against me: as for
our transgressions, thou shalt purge them away"—and yet he ignored it. Henry
thought that opening a bible at random expecting that "whatever is adapted
to the condition of his mind will appear so at a glance" ignored both the fact
that "some parts of the Bible are not fitted to meet his cares" and that no part
of the Bible could suit a given purpose "without serious thoughts on the side
of the reader"—that is, there must always be an effort at application.[35]

The most enduring criticism of bibliomancy and related practices has to
do with the careless, unguided use of the Bible. "Unprofitable" reading could
be the product of misdirected enthusiasm as much as apathy. An 1827 pamphlet from the American Sunday School Union— *Eyes and No Eyes and Eyes
that See Not, Or How to Read the Bible Aright*—contained a morality tale of two
young boys given bibles by their uncle, one of whom read the entire thing diligently while the other read his bible "only as a history book," turning excitedly
to battles, voyages, and parables without considering their meaning: "[A]s
for those parts of the Bible which did not contain, what Henry called 'pretty

stories,' he had passed them all very carelessly without thinking about them, or desiring to know their meaning."[36] "I would wish all my little readers to remember that this careless, light way of looking at the word of God is very wrong and sinful, and that they never can expect any good from reading it as Henry did."[37]

The modes of reading placed at odds in these guides are related in interesting ways to the categories that have long framed scholars' discussions of historical reading practices. In the 1970s, Rolf Engelsing advanced the idea that the end of the eighteenth century marked a transition in Western culture from repeated, "intensive" reading of the Bible and a few other religious books to habits of "extensive" reading involving a variety of texts, one after another.[38] Engelsing's argument was not only about enhanced access to both literacy and print at the dawn of the nineteenth century—more people were able to read more books—but also about the effect that this access had on *how* readers read.[39] Given the frequency with which "random" forms of bible reading appear in the seventeenth and eighteenth centuries, though, it is possible to question what exactly "intensive" reading itself might ever have looked like. As readers flipped through their bibles, started and stopped reading, followed cross-references and page headings and indices from one part of a book to another, how different was that from the pace and selectivity of extensive reading?

A better framework, particularly with respect to modes of bible reading, has been suggested by Matthew Brown, who argues that the codex by its very nature promotes what he calls "discontinuous" or "indexical" reading: bound leaves are made to be flipped. Brown posits two modes of reading that are roughly analogous to the intensive and extensive dichotomy: "pilgrimage" reading, in which "readers treat texts as continuous narratives and follow a redemptive journey," and "alvearial," in which "readers, like bees, extract and deposit information discontinuously, treating texts as spatial objects."[40] Brown uses this distinction to make an expansive argument about how the codex helped form the time-structure of Puritan piety (with "its cyclical and teleological modes of anguish and fulfillment"), but at a basic level pilgrim-reading and bee-reading are useful metaphors for thinking about the habits of bible readers.

In acknowledging these different forms of reading the operations of scripturalization loom large. Only scripturalized texts are likely to incite alvearial as well as pilgrimage forms of reading; scripturalization itself might be identified by a text's capacity to bear both sorts.[41] Opening the Bible at random for guidance is the act of a scripturalized subject that enacts and perpetuates the Bible's privileged difference. This privileged difference—and the corollary assumption that bibles could be read indexically—was in no way novel among Euro-Americans in the early national period. What is crucial to note is that the long-standing scripturalization of European culture brought assumptions of indexicality to early national print. For all the protests of bible-reading guides, everything about the scripturalized environment of late colonial and early national America encouraged indexical, discontinuous, ultimately citational bible reading.

Beyond the fact that bibles and parabiblical reference materials were simply more plentiful in this period than ever before, the nature of those materials encouraged indexical reading. Of the editions of bibles and New Testaments printed in America between 1777 and 1840, more than five hundred bore marginal commentary, extensive illustration, full cross-references, or other significant paratextual materials.[42] These books presented themselves as the products of indexical bible work—their compilers, typically named, wore their philological, historical, and theological facility with the Bible like a badge. On another level, they provided the means for bible readers to make use of those indexical resources in their own bible usage.

Margaret Hills's bibliography of American bibles identifies over forty commentators and editors whose names were attached to at least one bible edition published in America through 1840. Many of the same individuals show up repeatedly across the period and across paratextual genres, and when the full sweep of this material is considered it is not difficult to identify those whose work circulated most widely. The names of the best-known bible scholars appeared prominently on the title pages of their various works and became the common way of referring to them: "Brown's Bible," "Scott's Bible," and "Clarke's Bible" are all typical of early national advertisements. These names meant more to early-nineteenth-century book-buyers than they do to us. Doddridge was widely known as the author of the *Rise and Progress of Religion in the Soul*, popular enough to have been the first book stereotyped by the American Tract Society, in 1828.[43] When the first edition of Scott's bible appeared in America in 1804, his autobiography had already gone through at least three American editions, beginning in 1779. Under the titles *The Force of Truth* or *Life of the Rev. Thomas Scott*, it went through more than thirty American editions before 1856. The author's fame supported the sale of his bible, and the success of his bible in America reinforced his fame: an 1848 American Tract Society pamphlet on "Reading the Bible" excerpted from *The Force of Truth* heavily, referring to "Rev. T. Scott, the Commentator."[44]

The first of these massive works published in America was Brown's *Self-Interpreting Bible*, in 1792. Scott's bible was published in parts between 1804 and 1809 in Philadelphia; Doddridge's *Family Expositor* appeared in Massachusetts, 1807–8. Although they still inspire hagiography—a modern biographer of Doddridge calls his subject's testimony to Christ "fragrant"—these names have not attracted sustained scholarly attention, most likely because their work is daunting in its density and, one may say, in its capacity to induce desperate boredom.[45] The pages of these bibles—all of them printed in quarto and larger—contain spiraling, dense commentary. Scott's annotations to theologically-contested books of the Bible such as Romans often leave room on the page for only two or three lines of scripture.[46]

Doddridge's *Family Expositor* contains not just a paraphrase, but three English versions of the New Testament. The main text is a combination of literal translation and paraphrase. Doddridge found paraphrase to be the most effective way to present scripture to common readers, but expressed concern about the possibility of inadvertently misrepresenting the text. His solution was to weave his own direct translation into the main text, in italics, surrounding it with extra words and phrases which he felt made the text easier to read and understand. Acts 2:2, for example, appears as follows: "*And on a Sudden there was a* very extraordinary and surprising *Sound from Heaven, as of a rushing violent Wind*, which shook the very Place, *and* came with such a mighty Force, that *it filled all the House where they were sitting*."[47] Additionally, the King James text runs in the margins, aligned with corresponding verses in Doddridge's own translation/paraphrase. A dizzying mixture of commentary, paraphrase, "improvements" (short sermons on each chapter), and the original text of the Authorized Version, the first American edition ran to six volumes— and Doddridge had only covered the New Testament.[48]

Many scholars have agreed with the American Bible Society's founding principle that "notes and comment" distract from and undermine the biblical text. On another level, the most dizzying commentary—that of Scott, for example, with sometimes only a couple of verses on a quarto page, surrounded by his own small-print commentary—might as likely be said to visually magnify the importance of the line of text on which it hangs. The close-written text of something like a Scott's bible gives an immediate visual impression of both the Bible's scripturalized importance and its complexity. Many contemporary advocates of bible reading emphasized the importance of notes. Lindley Murray advised that "[t]he Holy Scriptures may sometimes be read with advantage, by being accompanied with the appropriate remarks and exhortations of devout and learned men"; he specifically recommended the *Family Expositor* (but also, knowingly, the "Abridgement of it by [Samuel] Palmer").[49] Noting that someone had sent his wife's brother Cruden's Concordance, Mohegan minister Samsom Occom wrote in 1773 that such books were in great demand: "Which are most needful Books for these Young men. . . . Expositors on the Bible are very Needful."[50]

The distracting complexity of these volumes, though, raise legitimate questions about how something other than an uncommonly gifted—or at least uncommonly patient—reader might make use of them. Who, if anyone, followed all of those references? Scott himself worried about this question: "It is a great discouragement, in the laborious task of collecting marginal references, that it is to be feared, but few, in comparison, will take the pains to consult them." He thought that diligently following his cross-references was the least a reader could do, since he "was constrained to spend far more time each day in arranging them" than it would take to read them.[51]

As elaborated in chapter 1, these commentators imagined their readers as "common" and in need of careful, approachable instruction. It is likely, though, that complex bibles like Scott's reached primarily a market of the educated and the wealthy. An early subscriber list for the first American edition of Scott's bible sent to the publishers' Philadelphia office from central Virginia in 1805 is composed overwhelmingly of ministers (three) and titled Southern gentlemen: one "Esqr.," one major, one colonel, one general, and one doctor are identified among the thirteen subscribers.[52] The men were expected to pay twenty-four dollars for the six-volume set. Adam Clark, the Methodist commentator, may have imagined his readers as "comparatively simple people, or those whose avocations prevent them from entering deeply into subjects of this kind," but the first American edition of his bible was published in "about twenty" installments advertised at a very patrician dollar and a half each.[53] Nevertheless, they did sell. Each went through numerous American editions, and the names of the major commentators appear widely in various popular nineteenth-century sources. William J. Gilmore's analysis of probate records from rural New Hampshire and Vermont between 1787 and 1830 found twenty-seven sets of Scott's bible, about eight percent of all bibles recorded, a substantial proportion for a large book in a rural area.[54]

The work of these scholars was most likely to reach audiences through abbreviated or abridged versions that appeared in smaller, cheaper bibles. Sometimes this meant excerpts from these exhaustive biblical commentaries. The *Daily Scripture Expositor*, for example, was a pocket-sized book of scripture passages put together by an unnamed compiler to "furnish those who have not the advantage of a large library, with the substance of the researches of eminent biblical students." Along with scripture texts, it contained notes from Scott, Henry, and Doddridge, among many others.[55] A cheaper, one-volume abridgement of Scott's bible was published in New York in 1812.[56] At least twenty early national editions promised "comprehensive" commentary, composed of annotations by several different scholars. The "large bible" that Ellen Harmon called for to look up the citations in her vision was a long folio published serially in Boston beginning in 1822. It was advertised in the Harmons' local newspapers beginning in early 1821, and they would have been able to subscribe through at least two local bookstores at twelve and a half cents per installment, bringing the final price of the book to $17.50. Advertised as *The Columbian Grand Folio Bible, or Christian's complete Library of Divine Knowledge,* the finished bible actually contained fewer paratextual aids than that original title suggested, but it did have "concise notes" drawn from Brown, Clarke, Scott, Doddridge and several other scholars.[57]

More common than selections from commentaries, though, were extracts and compilations of other aspects of these commentators' works. The same handful of popular bible scholars were responsible for cross-references, concordances, bible dictionaries, and other indexical materials that were essentially ubiquitous in early national bible culture. Canne's cross-references—

superscript letters embedded in the biblical text, corresponding to a list of verses in the margin or in a center column that a given compiler has found relevant to the verse at hand—appeared for decades in countless editions of the stereotyped quarto bibles published by the Phinney Company in Cooperstown, New York, beginning in the 1820s. Brown's concordance—an index of biblical verses based on shared words—was featured in Mathew Carey's cheap, wildly popular quartos.

The increased availability of these reference materials is a key feature of early national bible culture. Concordances had long been an important tool for ministers to cut through the density of the Bible. When Cotton Mather praised a fellow minister as "mighty in the Scriptures" because he could locate any text without a concordance, he underscored the fact that, generally speaking, concordances were essential tools for the ministry.[58] Concordances were not printed in America during the colonial era, and they were not imported at the same rate as bibles—Philadelphia bookseller David Hall ordered more than eight thousand bibles and testaments from Britain in the 1750s, and perhaps a couple hundred concordances.[59] The first concordance to the King James, published by John Downame in 1630, was also the first published in America, in 1791. In the early nineteenth century, the reference skills supplied by concordances were no longer the exclusive province of ministers. Between 1801 and 1819, though, at least thirteen different printers in nine different cities from Boston to Louisville to Charlotte produced editions of seven different types of concordances, at least twenty-two editions in all. Bickersteth summarized the importance of concordances and the available options for the English reader:

> Though a good knowledge of your bible will afford you some help in comparing one part with another, yet, in order to obtain this advantage in any considerable degree, you must have a Concordance, that is, an index of words, and a Bible with marginal references. The Rev. Thos. Scott has carried this mode of illustrating scripture to the greatest extent in his Family Bible. Cruden's Concordance is the best, but Butterworth's is more portable and very useful. Brown's is on a smaller scale, and is therefore much the cheapest, and will be of use to those to whom the others would be too expensive.[60]

Even Bible compilers who were opposed to annotations and marginal commentary allowed concordances and cross-references, viewing them as a case of "Homer interpreting Homer," as the ideal was expressed.[61] Rather than adding anything, the editor supposedly merely folded the biblical text on itself to allow one part to explain another. This is the essence of John Brown's ideal of the "self-interpreting bible." Thomas Chevalier, a British surgeon whose bible preface and cross-references circulated widely in America after 1831 in "Polyglott" bibles, wrote that the selection and arrangement of cross-references was designed only "to exhibit the Scripture as its own Expositor."[62] Even the American Bible Society, founded partly to stem the tide of annotated bibles by presenting the scriptures "without note or comment," added cross-references (along with section headings and dates) to its bibles beginning in 1833. The annual report of 1832 stated that the society had always wished to include these—the ABS, apparently, did not consider these marginal materials to be note or comment.[63]

With a surgeon's care (he also published treatises on gunshot wounds and suicide), Chevalier detailed what he found wrong with other reference bibles and the thinking behind the innovations of his own. The benefit of references, he wrote, required no argument: "The greatness of the advantages that must accrue to a sincere and diligent reader of Sacred Pages, from having constantly before him a reference to similar and illustrative passages, carefully investigated, and suitably applied, must be obvious to every one." He complained (inaccurately) that references had been too exclusive to "the margins of Bibles of a *large* size and the benefit resulting from them has, in consequence, been very much restricted." This was, he felt, not just because large bibles had been less accessible to the masses, but because large formats gave the compiler too much space to work: "If the size of the book were too large, or the page too crowded, so as to be made wearisome to the eye, its convenience would be lessened." His references were confined to a column running down the middle of the page—an innovation that the ABS would adopt when it began printing references in 1833—and "the limits which these considerations imposed," he felt, made for more useful references by forcing him to be judicious. His ability to select only the most relevant passages is, then, part and parcel of making a useful bible.[64]

The only American to publish a complete annotated bible in this period took an idiosyncratic approach. Hervey Wilbur, a Congregational minister born in Massachusetts in 1786, began publishing his reference bible in the 1820s. Wilbur's bible was extremely popular— a new edition appeared, on average, every year between 1823 and 1837. The British commentators discussed here produced cross-references and commentary that accompanied the text of scripture; printed in the margins, the reader encountered this material as he or she read. Rather than offering extensive commentary in the margins, Wilbur placed letters corresponding to questions listed in a "Key" at the front of his bible, which he insisted readers should memorize prior to reading. For example, when encountering a lowercase "s" next to a verse, the reader should immediately think of Wilbur's suggested context for considering that verse: "What affecting SCENE is here exhibited? What feeling should it produce?" An uppercase "L," meanwhile, denoted "What LOFTY FLIGHTS of devotional fervour? What longings after intimate communion with God are here manifested?" The Key—along with several other charts and tables Wilbur included in his bible and insisted that readers become familiar with—was to become the lens through which readers would view the Bible.[65]

Concordances operate according to principles similar to those of cross-references, but are more arbitrary in their arrangement of texts. Concordances in this period were generally arranged around individual words, a technique that put verses together if they contained the same word typographically, even if it had different meanings in the respective passages. Concordance groupings also varied by translation. Alexander Cruden's concordance, for example, lists well over one hundred and fifty verses containing the word "light" in the King James, classified under nine different stock phrases and shades of meaning. Under one heading (verses in which "light" has the sense of "carefree"), only three out of nine verses listed would appear together if the concordance were pegged to the Douay-Rheims rather than the King James.[66]

These types of indexical materials became the primary means of locating scripture texts among all classes of American bible readers. For lay readers looking to inform themselves on scriptural topics or to form arguments regarding the theological disputes of the day, cross-references (along with indices and concordances) were important tools. After hearing Mormon missionaries preach in Illinois in 1831, William McLellin first bought from them a *Book of Mormon*; next, found a store and bought a pocket bible; and then, wishing to "examine for myself," he bought Brown's Concordance, for seventy-five cents.[67] William Miller was an enthusiastic user of Cruden's Concordance, keeping the same copy throughout his career. "He never had a commentary in his house," though, according to one account.[68] Humbly deflecting credit for securing one man's conversion, Miller wrote in 1832 that "I only made him read the Bible, and I held the Concordance."[69] William Smyth Babcock copied from the *Family Expositor* in composing his never-published treatises on religion, and also recorded that he bought "Canne's reference bible" in 1802.[70] Lorenzo Dow made frequent references to "Dr. Clarke," meaning Methodist commentator Adam. The clustering of proof-texts in the first Mormon catechism, drafted by Joseph Smith and Sydney Rigdon in 1834, clearly suggests that they were using Scott's cross-references, and they cited by name Charles Buck's *Theological Dictionary*, another widely-circulated piece of early national biblical scholarship.[71]

Would-be preachers with limited access to a traditional ministerial education made particular use of the resources of biblical citation widely available in print. Nancy Towle, a well-known preacher of the 1820s and 1830s, personified her bible as the "man of my counsel," drawing on Isaiah 46:11.[72] She refers to that bible repeatedly as her "companion" and "only earthly treasure."[73] She footnotes that designation, though, with an addition: that bible, she says, "and sometimes a Bible Dictionary," have been her "only *Library*."[74] In addition to her dictionary, Towle had familiarity with at least one bible commentary, citing

Adam Clarke's commentary on Romans 16:12 in her defense of female preaching.[75] Other female preachers, likewise, demonstrated facility with indexing materials: Fanny Newell, a Methodist exhorter in the 1810s and early 1820s, narrated a part of her conversion account with a cluster of verses that plainly suggests concordance behavior—five New Testament verses all connected by the word "believe."[76] The clustering of citations in some parts of Zilpha Elaw's journal suggests her use of Scott's cross-references.[77] Like other revivalist preachers, these women tended to espouse a "Bible alone" ethic tinged with anti-intellectualism, and their disavowal of learning is belied by their obvious skill with the Bible.[78]

The relationship between private reading and sermons changed little even as eighteenth-century developments in American religious culture unsettled traditional ministerial authority.[79] In the early nineteenth century, preachers who traded on a reputation for simplicity and plainspokenness, such as Lorenzo Dow, nevertheless built their sermons around complex references to the Bible. The difference was that Dow had never "read divinity." Dow relied, rather, on his own reading—including his own reading of others' references. The skills of reference and sermon composition came to him through annotated bibles, concordances, and the sermons of others. At least one of Dow's bibles is extant—his copy of John Wesley's *Notes on the New Testament*, published in New York in 1815, is well-used. Its penciled annotations in Dow's hand include what appear to be sermon outlines.[80]

The fact that these preachers' facility with the Bible was heavily informed by *others'* references to the Bible had important consequences. From James I to the founders of the ABS, bible readers have long agreed that material printed in the margins of bibles is crucially important. The margins of a page literally "frame" the text, so when they are something other than blank, the information they contain takes on a very special role, balancing on—and oscillating across—a porous border separating text and paratext. For that matter, bible margins can have meaning even when they are blank: a now-rare "Students' Bible" published in New York in 1835 consists of large folio pages that each contains only a single narrow column of the King James text, inviting the reader to fill the rest of the space with his or her own notes and reflections.[81] Elias Boudinot was instrumental in the founding of the American Bible Society, with its rejection of biblical paratexts, but he relished creating his own. Boudinot's copy of Isaac Collins's 1791 quarto bible, held by Princeton University, was specially bound with two blank leaves inserted into the volume every four leaves. These pages are filled with Boudinot's own notes on the Bible, including drafts of at least one of his published works.[82]

The American Bible Society was correct to observe that biblical paratexts brought contingent meanings into the Bible. Depending on the decisions of a compiler, even cross-references—ostensibly the least-intrusive form of biblical paratext—enforce a sense that a given verse has some application to another verse elsewhere in the text, helping to form a reader's understanding. Chevalier frankly acknowledged that his work involved judgment on his part, writing that if "great care were not employed in *examining* and *applying* the References, [his work's] utility would, in a great degree, be destroyed."[83] Scott recognized the contingency of cross-referencing, advising readers that his conception of the relationships among some verses "may not at once be perceived by the reader," but he was confident that "if the several places referred to be consulted, it will generally appear."[84]

The rubric under which a compiler brought verses together might be dependent on extrabiblical traditions—the imaginative traditions surrounding the text. Cross-references attached to Genesis 9:25, for example, reified extrabiblical traditions about the connection between the "curse of Ham" and the enslavement of Africans. In the text, Noah curses his son Ham and his descendants, naming them as servants to the descendants of his other sons: "And he said, Cursed be Canaan; a servant of servants shall he be unto his brethren." A long imaginative tradition has identified Ham's descendants as Africans, and Noah's curse as biblical rationale for their enslavement—by the 1670s, at least, Genesis 9:25 was being used to justify the enslavement of Africans in America.[85] The cross-references that American Bible Society bibles associated with this verse can be read to support such an application. They emphasize elements useful to pro-slavery arguments: they maintain a historicized reading of the verse by linking it to 1 Kings 9:20–21, a listing of Canaanite tribes, regarded as descendants of Ham; and to Joshua 9:23, which emphasizes that the curse had to do with physical servitude. Both suggest that the curse would be in effect in perpetuity. The significance of these choices and the contingency of such a gloss is demonstrated by the references attached to the same verse by John Canne, whose links to Deuteronomy 28:18 and John 8:34 spiritualize the meaning of servitude and universalize the role of servant:

> **Deut 28:18** [referring back to verse 15: if thou wilt not hearken unto the voice of the LORD thy God] Cursed shall be the fruit of thy body, and the fruit of thy land, the increase of thy kine, and the flocks of thy sheep.

> **John 8:34** Jesus answered them, Verily, verily, I say unto you, Whosoever committeth sin is the servant of sin.

Read through these verses, Genesis 9:25 means something very different: if one sins, one is a servant to that sin, and this type of servitude is hardly limited to the purported descendants of Ham.

The question of how biblical paratexts affected reading comprehension is difficult to answer, as it requires the historian to observe the line between differences of interpretation and genuine misreading of the Bible, something better left to theologians. It can be said that "aids to reading" published in early national bibles did little to mitigate traditional differences of interpretation, as they often presented diametrically-opposed interpretations of the same passages. Biblical commentary was always polemical in intent. English dissenters were responsible for most biblical annotation throughout the seventeenth and eighteenth centuries, and this material was widely reprinted in early American bibles. John Canne, a seventeenth-century commentator whose work remained popular in the nineteenth century, was a strict Separatist (and likely a full-fledged Anabaptist by the time of his death); Samuel Clark, author of an annotated bible endorsed by George Whitefield, was one of the dissenting ministers ejected after the Act of Uniformity in 1662. Philip Doddridge was an Independent; Matthew Henry and John Brown were Presbyterians; Adam Clarke a Methodist. Among the most prominent names attached to American bibles, only Thomas Scott was an Anglican, and his strong conversionist bent and sharp criticism of his fellow churchmen set him somewhat apart.

In opposing the established church, dissenting scholars recognized the authoritative value of laying claim to the Bible, and their annotations advanced distinct theological positions. The margins of most early national bibles contained guide phrases designed to assist readers in locating and understanding passages, much like guide words found at the tops of dictionary pages. These seem straightforward, yet they are contingent on the way a compiler has understood a given passage. The guide phrases attached to Romans 9, for example, bore the weight of centuries of dispute about these passages. Some American bibles espoused a Calvinist reading of this section, suggesting that the pages containing Romans 9 were about "predestination and election" and the idea that "God hath mercy on whom he will."[86] The ABS's 1842 edition with notes had something moderate: "The ground and assurance of the Christian's hope." And many bibles at least left open the possibility that this chapter endorsed Arminianism and unlimited atonement: "Of God's unmerited mercy" and "[s]alvation to all who believe."[87]

Beyond perpetuating interpretive variety, American bibles may have done little to prevent objective misreading. Both William Smyth Babcock and Adeline Hosner, for example, made reference to a particular passage of Colossians in their private writings, and both appear to have misunderstood it. In Colossians 2:20–22, Paul criticizes ascetic and ritual practices that were apparently being taught in the church at Colossae. Like much in the Pauline letters, the passage is syntactically complex, and the King James translators had resorted to parentheses to clarify Paul's rhetorical quoting of those teachers with whom he was disagreeing: "Wherefore if ye be dead with Christ from the rudiments of the world, why, as though living in the world, are ye subject to ordinances, / (Touch not; taste not; handle not; / Which all are to perish with the using;) after the commandments and doctrines of men?" Both Hosner and Babcock, though, read the parenthetical passage as a New Testament command. Hosner, in condemnation of ministers whom she thought enjoyed the things of the world too much, wrote in her journal that "to be separate from sinners they must touch not, taste not, handle not."[88] Babcock, after documenting his own sins, advises an imagined future reader of his journal not to repeat his errors: "Only my Brother whoever thou art that readeth this do not turn tempter to thine own soul[:] touch not, taste not, handle not any thing whereby thou mayest in any degree expose thyself to be tempted."[89] Although Babcock's primary New Testament at this time, Doddridge's *Family Expositor*, clarified the verse's meaning (albeit with Doddridge's characteristic verbosity), he misapplied it.

Contradictory guide words and the complex punctuation of Colossians point toward the significance of the material circumstances of print-bible culture with respect to reading and comprehension. For all of their promise to provide transparent understanding of the Bible, early national bibles were as likely to multiply interpretations and readings as to reconcile them. This can be attributed to the effects of printed matter in a general sense and also to the particular characteristics of early national bibles. *Writing is mediation*, and mediation ensures variety.[90] While the abstract Bible could be idealized as a singular whole, printed bibles were, by definition, varied. Moreover, while the abstract Bible could exercise an idealized authority that came only from God, printed bibles participated in the creation of other authorities.

When seventeen-year-old Ellen Harmon began slipping into trance states in 1844 she was joining a very old tradition of female visionaries, but she had access to an unprecedented print-bible culture that allowed her to parlay her visionary authority into something enduring: a fully articulated bible-based authority.[91] The fifty verses that Harmon said she saw in her vision were connected in Alexander Cruden's concordance, with which, Harmon's husband James later recorded, he and Ellen began their career.[92] The physical form of Harmon's early trance states would be described in terms very similar to those of earlier young women: "Her eyes are always open, but she does not wink; her head is raised, and she is looking upward, not with a vacant stare, but with a pleasant expression."[93] What she did afterward, though, showed her to be a product of the print culture in which she lived: the next day, Harmon described her vision in exacting, overwhelmingly biblical detail. The first published account of this vision appeared a year later, and in it she loaded her account with biblical metaphors to situate her own calling—"I have tried to bring back a good report, & a few grapes from the heavenly Canaan, for which many would stone me, as the congregation bade stone Caleb and Joshua for their report"—and presented her vision of believers' assent to the heavenly city in a pastiche of imagery and terms from the Book of Revelation, from the 144,000 saints (Revelation 7 and 14) to crowns of stars (Revelation 12) to a sea of glass (Revelation 15 and 16).

Harmon's claim to authority was mediated through printed bibles that surface in her early career in the content of her relentless proof-texting and, more literally, as material objects that she used as symbols of her authority during prophetic events. Born in Portland in 1827, Harmon enjoyed benefits of class and education, but achieved her facility with the Bible against considerable odds. When Harmon was nine, she was struck in the face by a rock by another little girl, sustaining injuries that affected her eyesight, ability to read, and memory. After the injury, her formal schooling ended, but she had already learned to write—she notes that after the rock-throwing incident she had trouble "holding the pen" for some time, a difficulty that she overcame.[94] Many important moments of her prophetic career involve specific acts of writing.

Harmon's attachment to the Book of Revelation demonstrated in the vision above is traceable to her devotion to the teachings of William Miller. The Harmons became involved in the Millerite movement after hearing Miller lecture in Portland in 1840, and spent the next four years waiting for Christ's return, as Miller predicted it. Two months after the "Great Disappointment" of October, 1844, Ellen Harmon had her first vision. The Millerites had been unusually receptive to female authority, and this undoubtedly influenced the response Harmon's visions received.[95] Her level of biblical facility, though, enabled her to quickly cultivate a prophetic reputation that transcended the Millerite message. Her first vision, as discussed above, contained allusions and references to favorite Millerite texts, but her use of the Bible soon expanded beyond the familiar Millerite imagery. In an early vision that would come to define the Seventh-day Adventist Church, Harmon related that it was revealed to her that Christians should be keeping the Sabbath on Saturday. The style of that vision, moreover, heralded White's focus on materiality in her revelations. She explained that she was not just told about the importance of the fourth commandment, but shown in writing: Jesus himself led her to the ark of the covenant and lifted the lid, revealing the stone tablets of the ten commandments, and she saw "the fourth commandment in the very center of the ten precepts, with a soft halo of light encircling it."[96]

Harmon's early bible usage also points to the plurality and variety of print-bible culture in the 1840s that had replaced the relative scarcity of earlier eras. At a basic level her call for the "large" bible tells us that the Harmon family had more than one. An abundance of physical bibles continued to be an essential presence in Harmon's prophetic performances, where they appear both as totems and as sources. In about 1845, a skeptical witness, having heard that "visions of satanic power were arrested by opening the Bible and laying it on the person in vision," decided to test Harmon by laying a bible on her chest while she was inclined against a wall during a trance state. She rose and held the book, and "with her eyes steadily looking upward, declared in a solemn manner, 'The inspired testimony from God.'"[97] Witnesses to Harmon's visionary events reported that later she took to this laying on of bibles. One Frances

Lunt remembered a visionary performance in April of 1847 in which Harmon made similar use of several different bibles which happened to be at hand:

> There was at the side of the room where the meets were held, a table upon which were a number of books of various kinds, among which were several Bibles of ordinary size. While in vision, Mrs. White rose to her feet, went to the table, picked up a Bible without touching another book, and holding it open above her head with her left hand, with the index finger of the right hand pointed to the text of Scripture she was repeating as she stood before the person for whom it was designed, and then placed the open book on the chest of the person before whom she repeated the scripture.

White then repeated this with other bibles and other verses for the people in the room. Another woman remembered the same incident, and even the verse she was given.[98] Here, authority for the location and application of bible verses is enacted in a very literal manner: Harmon found verses and then applied them to her audience members by laying open bibles on their bodies. The laying on of bibles underscores the tactile, totemic aspects of bible reading, but it is also an example of biblical reference: Harmon opened the bibles and pointed her audience members to specific verses.

Over the course of Harmon's long career—she died in 1915—her prophetic style of biblical application came to incorporate more and more clerical skill. In 1846, she married James White, a Millerite minister and former school-teacher. James annotated Ellen's early revelations with bible references for publication, demonstrating again the symbiosis between ministerial and prophetic skill.[99] Ellen's success was in some sense despite James, however, rather than owed to him. Their early division of labor broke down in the early 1850s, due to James's discomfort with accusations that he and other Adventist leaders were putting Ellen's visions above the Bible. James's response to charges that Ellen's visions had become a "test of doctrine and christian fellowship" was to roundly downplay their significance.[100] This, in turn, drew the opposite criticism from the main body of early Adventists, who found James's position that the visions were of God and yet belief in them was optional for the church "inconsistent and absurd."[101] Ellen subsequently published visions and took on a new clerical responsibility toward them. In addition, she expanded her studies and learned to integrate her reading of the Bible into other types of writing. Prophetic access to divine inspiration remained central to her self-presentation and authority, but her biblical fluency manifested in vast, multivolume works of church history, biblical scholarship, and health advice. These works were clerical enterprises—in her later years, teams of editors worked with White to compile this material from her own earlier work and the wider print culture around them. White's bestselling book, *Steps to Christ*, is a biblically-grounded devotional work that was originally published by a non-

Adventist publisher. There, writing for a general Christian readership, she claims only the authority to read and apply the Bible, not the authority of a visionary.[102]

Ellen Harmon White combined all of the threads of materiality, literacy, and authority discussed in this chapter. Her performances owe something to family reading, to preaching, to education, and yet are not reducible to any one of these. Women's access to bibles and indexing materials had changed the possibilities of religious authority. Women of this era who developed facility with the Bible and made authoritative use of it did not all become prophetesses, though. Adeline Hosner's journal shows her engaging with doctrinal and practical questions such as election and the proper mode of baptism, referring to verses that supported her opinions. Hosner often "perused" her bible at random, but she was also able to locate specific verses and apply them to specific purposes, sometimes challenging her ministers' usage of the Bible: "Last Sabbath heard a well constructed sermon on Election and our Elder appeared to draw undisputable evidences from the bible in favour of the sentiment. Yet it had a chilling influence upon my soul. . . . If the doctrine be true why does it produce this effect and why is it kept back in times of revivals[?] . . . For the bible assures us those that seek shall find and likewise enjoins it upon parents to bring up their children in the fear of the Lord."[103]

Hosner claimed bible-based authority for herself and eventually for her family. She believed that her husband should have responsibility for family reading in the home, but he was hostile to religion. After struggling within herself for some time, praying on the matter, and asking her husband ("[t]he bible teaches wifes to be in subjection," she believed), Hosner decided to take family reading upon herself after her sister died unsaved.[104] "The apparent impropriety of reading and praying aloud after my family has retired to rest has long kept my mind a wavering, till I saw the distress of my sister. . . . I became fixed in my resolution to do my duty at all hazards."[105] She began reading the Bible if not precisely to her family at least in situations where they could hear her. She also began to wonder whether her "duty extend[ed] any farther than [her] own family?"[106] In contemplating a public authority, she most likely had in mind becoming a Sunday School teacher, an avenue of religious authority open to women in the early nineteenth century.[107]

Further symbolic of this transition is the first American woman's foray into producing the sort of bible-indexing print that helped make it possible. Novelist Susan Warner's *The Law and the Testimony*, published in 1854, is made up of bible verses which Warner and her sister selected and arranged thematically. Warner's name appears nowhere on the book—the spine and title page say only that it is by "The Author of the Wide Wide World," which was Warner's bestselling novel. It happens that Warner published many of her books this way, to preserve her anonymity, but in this case the title carries special resonance, since "Author of the World" is immediately recognizable as an appellation for God, the presumed source of the scripture Warner has excised and arranged. As source and editor, both God and Warner are responsible for the compilation and here their respective forms of authorship are folded into one tidy phrase.

In her introduction to the work, Warner cites the difficulty of the Bible as the rationale behind it, hoping that through her collation of the Bible's "scattered rays" of wisdom "the truth may be made manifest": "In their ordinary arrangement, the Bible forces may be said to charge in 'dispersed order;' here, they seem to stand as in the old Macedonian phalanx, shoulder to shoulder, with shields locked." In order to create such an army, Warner and her sister went through the Bible, one chapter at a time, several times over, identifying the verses which they felt applied to each of thirty-one topics identified for them by their father (the book started as sort of an edifying parlor game for two very serious children). The topics read like subject headings out of a work of academic theology: "The Divine Nature," "God's Universal Government," "The Nature of Sin." It looks an awful lot, that is, like "learned theology," though Warner and her sister were hardly seminarians. "I don't doubt some heads have been shaken at the idea of such work being done by a woman," Warner wrote in the introduction. "No woman set about it, in the first place; it was but a girl and a child. And they had little knowledge of the theological world."[108] Warner claims authority to present the Bible as a collection of collated verses, by virtue of—rather than despite—being a plain, ordinary, female reader.

When Warner and her sister cut up and rearranged the Bible, they were making a dramatic entry into the culture of biblical citation explored here: like a commentary writer or a compiler of cross references, they were reminding readers that the Bible was a text worth treating in this way. They were also creating a new text, refracting the scripturalized status of the Bible in new directions. As Harmon, Hosner, Warner and others like them applied biblical citations to changing circumstances, they not only conjured different forms of bible-based authority for themselves, but also altered the Bible's own authoritative position in early national culture. The next three chapters will explore the ways in which biblical citation relied on the biblical text for recognition and effectiveness and yet constantly changed that text itself by bringing it into contingent circumstances and meanings.

PART II

Beyond Bibles

{≈≈≈ẉ≈≈≈}

THE ASPECTS OF PRINT BIBLE CULTURE covered in the preceding two chapters involved bibles and more or less explicitly parabiblical material. These are elements of a scripturalized environment that make direct reference to the central privileged text. Hervey Wilbur's bible-reading interface is emblematic: it was designed to facilitate comprehension of the Bible, and without reference to an actual bible it was useless. The next three chapters will address forms of biblical citation in the late colonial and early national period that expanded upon rather than referred specifically back to the Bible itself. To be clear, any sharp distinction between these two aspects of scripturalization is arbitrary and, to the point, false. All moments of biblical citation create new texts; citation changes the text itself. Each moment of citation happens in a dialogic relationship with circumstance, and bringing the biblical text into such contingent relationships necessarily changes it. Wilbur's bible-reading guide is equally emblematic of this aspect of citation: while pointing readers back to the Bible, it also demanded that they reflect imaginatively on the text. "The REFERENCE LETTERS and KEY are adapted," Wilbur wrote, "to exercise the understanding about the ideas contained in each paragraph of the oracles of God, and thus break up a habit lamentably common of reading mechanically or without reflection."[1]

Nevertheless, such a division is useful for organizing this investigation. The citationality requisite in the scripturalization of early national America was not limited to explicit reference to the Bible or bibles themselves: it was widely present as resonant, gestural appeals to the assumptions of early national scripturalized culture. Lorenzo Dow Barnes, who was barely twenty-one when Joseph Smith made him an elder in his church, recorded his life events in a manner that clearly reflected a scripturalized sense of how to signal the gravity of the life of one called of God, headlining the first page of the second notebook of his diary, "The Third Mission of Lorenzo." Similarly, Jedidiah Grant, another early missionary, narrated his travels with the weight of scripture: "Behold it came to pass in 1836 on the 13 of April that I Jedidiah Grant left Kirtland Geauga Co., Ohio, on a mission to the east to proclaim the ever lasting

Gospel of Jesus Christ." Missionary Reynolds Cahoon, meanwhile, went all in: "Wherefore these are the Acts of Reynolds up to August 19th 1832."[2]

These self-identifying gestures cite the Bible in ways akin to all other bible citation—both author and reader are made aware of the Bible as they "get" what this language is doing. But such citations as these actively expand upon the Bible in a distinct way, as well—they create new scriptural texts. The Acts of Reynolds provides a sequel to the Acts of the Apostles. In a scripturalizing environment, the notional core scripture is ever-expanding as it is cited and re-cited. The following three chapters will focus on the performative, rhetorical, and material circumstances and effects of such expansion.

CHAPTER THREE

Joshua, When the Walls Fell

BIBLICAL ROLES IN CHANGING TIMES

ON THE FIRST PAGE of the introduction to their 1822 report on the trial of Denmark Vesey and his co-conspirators, Lionel Henry Kennedy and Thomas Parker identified the ways in which Vesey had "perverted" the Bible in the service of fomenting a slave revolt in Charleston:

> He rendered himself perfectly familiar with all those parts of the Scriptures, which he thought he could pervert to his purpose; and would readily quote them, to prove that slavery was contrary to the laws of God; that slaves were bound to attempt their emancipation, however shocking and bloody might be the consequences, and that such efforts would not only be pleasing to the Almighty, but were absolutely enjoined, and their success predicted in the Scriptures.[1]

Vesey's conspiracy was discovered before any plans could be carried out. The trial on which Kennedy and Parker reported as officers of the court was about the rhetoric used to describe intended actions rather than actions themselves, and biblical rhetoric figured prominently in the construction of this rumored discourse.[2] The three sorts of purported misuse identified by Kennedy and Parker map onto three modes of bible application. In a legalistic mode, Vesey argued that American chattel slavery was "contrary to the laws of God." Reading other biblical texts prophetically, he predicted that a rebellion would be successful. In between, however, Kennedy and Parker identified a sort of biblical application that demanded not the acceptance of a legal argument nor a reading of prophecy, but of a biblical role for the rebels: "Slaves were bound to attempt their emancipation, however shocking and bloody might be the consequences." This referred to the several moments in the trial transcript in which various witnesses noted Vesey's bible-based insistence that *all* white citizens of Charleston be killed in the uprising once the violence began. As one of the accused testified, "He then read in the Bible where God commanded, that all should be cut off, both men, women and children, and said, he believed, it was not sin for us to do so, for the Lord had commanded us to do it."[3] Another reported that Vesey had instructed "that they should kill every man as he came out of his door, and that the servants in the yard should do it, and that it should be done with axes and clubs, and afterwards they should murder women and children, for he said, God had so commanded it in the scriptures."[4]

Vesey's insistence on wholesale slaughter was certainly amplified by the authors of the report, who, as representatives of the slaveholding establishment in Charleston, had a vested interest in making Vesey appear as bloodthirsty and terrifying as possible.[5] Nevertheless, the repeated appeals to biblical violence in the recorded testimony are too integrated into the statements of witnesses to ignore, and, while these textual moments demonize Vesey, they suggest the humanity of many of those in his circle, potential conspirators who objected to the murder of women, children, ministers—a humanizing at odds with Kennedy and Parker's interests.

Vesey's insistence that his followers must "destroy them totally" was grounded in the bible-based role that he was proposing for himself and his people.[6] They were God's chosen, wronged slaves who would undertake violence with His support, and in the Bible God's people do not take half-measures against their enemies. When a people go to war in the Bible with the Lord on their side, abject violence is the rule, not the exception. "Now go and smite Amalek, and utterly destroy all that they have, and spare them not; but slay both man and woman, infant and suckling, ox and sheep, camel and ass" (1 Samuel 15:2–3). For the violence of a slave revolt to be recognizable and authoritative in a biblically-inscribed culture, Vesey argued, it should be enacted on a biblical scale.[7]

Vesey's call for biblical violence was a moment of attempted scripturalized self-creation. Early national self-creation cannot be understood monologically—there is no self-creation outside of a discursive field and a community of recognition that simultaneously constrain and enable speakers. Building on the arguments of part I, this chapter and the next two will elucidate the ways in which would-be authorities interacted with the Bible as the defining part of the early national period's discursive field, imaginatively building on and expanding the text through their applications of it, even as they often insisted on the efficacy of scripture alone and were constrained by the options it provided. Vesey used biblical roles to script eccentric action in the world—in this case, eccentric violence. Plenty of other early national bible users offered audiences biblical scripts for devastating violence. John Corrigan has written evocatively about the Amalekites as an "illustration of the theme of genocide" in the Bible, mobilized by Protestants against Catholics, Native Americans, Jews, and other religious minorities.[8] However, most early national moments of self-creation through *performed biblicism*—as I will here distinguish biblical identifications predicated on action for their application and recognition—went beyond violence.

Performed biblicism offers a way of making sense of the ways in which the Bible participated in the construction of relationships of religious subjectivity as a dynamic aspect of lived circumstance. Would-be authorities extracted roles from the Bible that challenged audiences, real and imagined, to respond with coordinating roles, conjuring relationships that pushed against the limits of early national structures of power and authority.[9] Moments of performative biblical self-identification in the early national archive are not monolithic. Sometimes they recorded explicit physical actions. On March 1, 1832, Mormon missionary Orson Hyde recorded in his journal that after preaching in one small town where he received a cold reception, he "went on from Fairview 6 or 7 miles [and] shook off the dust of [his] feet against almost all." The reference is to Mathew 10:14–15 and Acts 13:50–51.[10] Other bible-based roles were lived in a broader sense. The rhetoric of Southern slaveowning encouraged landed white men to think of themselves as Abraham: patriarchs of vast holdings and responsibilities. Published in 1852, Southerner John Fletcher's fiery defense of slavery relied on biblical arguments and, ultimately, a prediction of bible-based performance. If it came to it, he wrote, "the South, like Abraham in olden time, 'will arm their trained servants,' and go out to the war.'"[11]

Finally, some biblical self-identifications were post hoc rhetorical moves, later descriptions of lived moments that writers represented to themselves and to imagined readers using biblical citation. In their autobiographies, for example, early national preachers routinely related their experiences in Pauline terms.

What all of these modes of performative biblicism share is that they are rhetorical gestures aimed at enacting forms of bible-based authority. This chapter will look at self-characterizations claimed in written descriptions of lived circumstances, culminating in a close look at the bible-based performances of Peggy and Lorenzo Dow, two of the era's most eccentric biblical performers. As this chapter will illustrate, bible-based roles were more or less explicit or implicit, more or less imagined or performed. What distinguishes the moments discussed here under the rubric of performed biblicism is their expansion of the ostensibly static biblical text into the contingency of embodied life. Performed biblicism is biblically-scripted activity that is not repeatable nor defined by its notional repeatability. It is social, contextual, provisional, and, most importantly, ad hoc—behavior in lived circumstances that accords with an assumed biblical identity. Looking hard at biblical performance in the everyday world is a way of maintaining focus on relational religious subjects. Lived, relational performance, moreover, provides a framework for acknowledging the Bible's usage in circumstances of contingency and chance.[12]

When scholars discuss the living of biblical roles, they do so overwhelmingly in the language of typology. "Typology" is a complicated word. In its strictest sense, a type is an Old Testament sign that has its fulfillment (its antitype) in the New Testament, or in a prophesied future. Typologies, technically, pivot on the life of Christ and, once fulfilled, are completed. "Typology" in such a technical sense is a hermeneutic method first articulated in various ways by the earliest Christian thinkers in order to stake a Christian claim on the Jewish scriptures: Israel is a type for the church, Adam is a type of Christ. What are commonly called typologies in contemporary historical and literary scholarship, however, are examples of bible users connecting their own lives and experiences to biblical lives and experiences—*extra*-biblical lives made sense of through biblical characters, scenes, and events. In this way, as Sacvan Bercovitch has articulated at length, Cotton Mather wrote a biography of John Winthrop that made him an antitype of Nehemiah.[13] In American religious history, the most important typology of this sort is the association of the African American experience of bondage and freedom with the Exodus narrative, the terms and stakes of which have been searchingly elaborated by Eddie Glaude.[14] As assertions of identity, they expand the hermeneutical utility of typology (meant at its core as a way of understanding the Bible) to later lived reality (meant as a way of understanding the self).

On its face, using the same word for these two very different modes of bible usage appears benign. Actually, this usage has occluded some important distinctions, because the word brings with it assumptions of the hermeneutical method that do not fit well with its application to contingent, lived circumstances. Typology remains a mode of reading when applied to lived experience, which means it holds or purports to hold lived experience as static as it does the biblical text. Lives are "read into" the Bible, in a typical phrasing; lives are examined—"read"—as the Bible is read so that they can be interpreted in biblical terms. This form of self-reading is unquestionably important in the history of American bible usage.[15] Focus on this sort of self-reading, however, has made self-*creating* bible usage appear abstract, cerebral, and—for all except religious elites—singularly passive. This chapter will develop the notion of performed biblicism as a practice imbricated with, but distinguished from, biblical typology by 1) its sense of historical rather than abstract time; 2) its purpose in claiming relationships of authority rather than furthering homiletic goals that assume those relationships; and 3) its dialogic rather than monologic interaction with the Bible itself. In this chapter I will take each of these differences between typology and performed biblicism in turn, making an historiographical intervention while illustrating the importance of this role-playing in the early national period. What I want to argue is that these performances made these historical actors visible, recognizable, in a culture where the Bible was the textual ground for the constitution of subjects.[16]

In her memoir, first published soon after her death in the spring of 1824, Methodist itinerant Fanny Newell imagined the prophet Isaiah coming to prayer meeting with her. "[I]f the good evangelical prophet Isaiah had been in our little class meeting this evening, he would have said, 'Look in the 12th chapter of my prophecy, and there you will find where I had a view of the happy believers shouting praise to God, while on their way to Zion.'" Isaiah would have been referring to a short song of praise, most notably to the sixth verse: "Cry out and shout, thou inhabitant of Zion: for great is the Holy One of Israel in the midst of thee." Newell reported that her prayer meeting had been so full of the Spirit that they "had a shout in the Camp of Israel." Her connection of their behavior to biblical precedent brought in a New Testament scene as well: "Yea they might have said of us, as they did of the apostles on the day of Pentecost, 'They are drunk with new wine.'"[17]

Scenes like this define the historiography of Protestantism in the early national period. Kinetically emotional Methodist class meetings and related open-air, multiday revivals are the terms in which scholars imagine the Second Great Awakening. Here, Newell makes plain the biblical script on which these moments were performed: shouting made sense in the worship context because of Isaiah, and the erratic, "drunk with new wine" behavior of her group was inspired by the apostles at Pentecost. How her prayer group's behavior is perceived is her primary preoccupation—Isaiah understands it, marks the biblical resonance himself, while Newell imagines scoffers seeing them just as scoffers saw the apostles, declaring themselves confused by the apostles' drunken behavior so early in the morning.

Richard McNemar, one of the key figures in the Kentucky revivals of the first years of the nineteenth century, reported on such competing perceptions of revivalist activity first-hand. The most eccentric behavior was first "looked upon by the generality, even of professors, as wild enthusiasm, or the the [sic] fruits of a disordered brain." Only after the initial shock, he reported, could "a few who understood the disorder, and were ready to fly to their relief" move in to comfort those drunk on the new wine.[18] For his part, McNemar thought that the biblical basis of such performances was obvious, and expressed surprise that the nature of the revivals was "a matter of much debate, even among those who profess to take the scripture for their only guide."[19] In his written accounts of the revivals, he makes explicit connections, not just to Acts but to Numbers 24:5, for example, a vision that he suggests actually incorporated the Kentucky revivals.[20]

The imagination applied in these readings—Newell's imagining of Isaiah as a character in her prayer meeting's story; McNemar's assumption that the behavior of both worshippers and scoffers had biblical precedents—underscores the historicized sense of the Bible that went with these performances. Newell assumes measurable historical distances separating three distinct moments: the lifetime of the prophet Isaiah, "the day of Pentecost," and her class meeting. She isolates Isaiah and the apostles as characters who lived embodied lives in a past continuous with—not abstract from or potentially identical to—her own historical moment. She imagines Isaiah pulling up a chair and commenting on their behavior in light of his own revelation. This characterization of biblical figures was a prominent feature of print-bible culture in Newell's day. In the late eighteenth century both British and American bible readers showed an increasing interest in the biographies of individual biblical characters. These parabiblical materials extracted individual personalities from the Bible and narrativized their lives and actions, drawing on scriptural content, other traditions, and contemporary authors' imaginations.

Seventeenth-century Protestants took a negative view of Catholic saints' lives, charging that they relied on tradition to augment what scripture provided, but their own relentless impulse to explain the Bible extended readily to retellings of biblical stories. John Foxe's *Book of Martyrs*, one of the most popular texts of the seventeenth and eighteenth centuries, put Protestant suffering under Mary I into a tradition of Christian sacrifice, beginning with stories about the New Testament martyrs.[21] Several Protestant collections of the "lives of the ancient fathers" appeared in the seventeenth century, but it was in the eighteenth century that "scripture biography" became a staple genre of English print.[22] Paralleling the development of the novel, these works relished the elaboration of biblical figures as *characters*: *Sacred Biography, Or, Scripture-Characters: Illustrated in Several Discourses* (1712); *Biographical Sermons, Or, A Series of Discourses on the Principal Characters in Scripture* (1791); *Scripture Characters: Or, a Practical Improvement of the Principal Histories in the Old and New Testament* (1800); and *Scripture Characters, by a Parent for His Children* (1811).[23]

These texts aimed to present biblical characters as active historical figures to be imitated in life, not as static icons for worship.[24] John Watkins, in his preface to *Scripture Biography*, first published in London in the 1790s and in several American editions beginning in 1810, argued that scriptural characters were more valuable than those of fiction or hagiographic historiography because the Bible represented them as fully human: "In a moral sense alone the Scripture Characters are the most proper that can be presented for our imitation, because they are represented as they truly were, without any design of extenuating their errors or exaggerating their virtues. No art is made use of to exhibit them to us to the best advantage, but they are shewn in their native simplicity, in a great variety of natural situations, and exactly 'as men of like passions with ourselves.'"[25]

Scripture biography as a genre developed out of the eighteenth-century impulse toward historicizing the Bible. Imagining the lives of biblical characters was part of a larger interest in refining the narrative possibilities of scriptural content: of presenting the Bible in more straightforward narrative form than the traditional arrangement of the canon. Gospel "harmonizations," in which authors distilled the repetitions of the synoptics and the Gospel of John into a single coherent narrative, also proliferated throughout the colonial era, along with "histories of the bible" retelling the historical books of the Old Testament. Growing numbers of illustrations both within bibles and elsewhere in print-bible culture further facilitated an increasing interest in biblical characters as such.

The increasing focus on individualized biblical characters in the early national period is of a piece with literary culture's fascination with literary characters. In *The Afterlife of Character*, David Brewer examines the "imaginative expansion" of diverse literary characters in eighteenth-century Britain. Brewer uses the term "for an array of reading practices . . . by which the characters in broadly successful texts were treated as if they were both fundamentally incomplete and the common property of all."[26] Brewer argues that the widespread cultural knowledge of certain literary characters led readers to treat them as a sort of public property. Readers, that is, imagined characters as real people, with "full possession of a deep interiority and a life which extend[ed] off-page."[27] He explicitly ties this treatment of certain characters to an imagined immateriality that, paradoxically, arose from seemingly limitless material availability: "[T]he more copies or performances of a text there were in circulation, the more the characters who inhabited that text came to be regarded as . . . simultaneously everywhere and nowhere, transcending textual origins."[28] It is difficult to imagine more ubiquitous characters than those of the Bible; moreover, the rhetoric of colonial and early national scripturalization insisted that the Bible was "available to all" in exactly the sense Brewer says gave rise to the imaginative expansion of literary characters.[29]

Scripture biographies cited the Bible. *Bible biography, in the form of questions* (1830) actually contains no biography at all, but a frenetic list of questions about named characters in the Bible with chapter and verse citations pointing readers to their bibles to look up the answers. Scripture biographies are defined, though, by a willingness to apply novelizing imagination to build upon the biblical text. At least by a simple count of editions, the most popular scriptural biography of the early national period was John Macgowan's *The Life of Joseph*. First published in London in the 1770s, it saw at least twenty American editions between 1792 and 1818. *The Life of Joseph* reads like a novel and opens with a scene of biblical storytelling: "It was at the end of autumn, when the bounties of providence were safely gathered in," Macgowan wrote, "that venerable Jacob entertained his convened family with the history of his own life, and the lives of his father Isaac, and Abraham his grandfather." Here, Macgowan humanizes and contextualizes the patriarchs, inviting readers to think of Abraham as Jacob's "grandfather," someone about whom a young Joseph would sit and listen to stories. From the first pages, the reader is invited to imagine a biblical prophet as possible—he obtains knowledge about his family's history, just as the reader is doing, and responds to it: "None was more affected than pious Joseph, who seemed earnestly to catch every syllable in the narration."[30]

Like bibles themselves, these materials imagined a reader in need of instruction. Macgowan explained that he wrote for children and others with "young capacities." In a nod toward women supposedly overly infatuated with the romantic adventures of novel characters, he advised that there was plenty of romance in the Bible: "And rather than one class of readers should want entertainment, let me tell them, that the Bible contains many histories of love affairs. Perhaps this may tend more to recommend it to attention, than all besides which I could say."[31] Other scripture biographies labored to highlight women's roles in the Bible. Francis Cox's *Female Scripture Biography*, published concurrently in London and New York in 1817, corrected for what the author described as the "small proportion" of women in other collections.[32] Henry Hunter made a point of finding some women in the Old Testament: *Sacred Biography: Or, The History of the Patriarchs: To Which Is Added, the History of Deborah, Ruth, and Hannah* (1794).[33]

The title of Frances King's *Female Scripture Characters: Exemplifying Female Virtues* (1816)—one of the few such texts written by a woman—underscored the point of holding up these biblical roles to be imitated. Increasing awareness of and interest in biblical characters multiplied opportunities for biblical self-characterization. In private writings, these appear as fleeting rhetorical moments in which an author or speaker compares themselves to a biblical character by way of personal sense-making. Met with repeated disappointments, William Smyth Babcock made frequent self-identifications in the prayers he wrote into his journal: "[B]y thy grace assisting, [I] do like thine ancient servant Abraham 'believe against hope'"; "Religion dear lord is dying in my soul I am sinking like peter help lord or I perish"; "I often think of alien Jacob, an injured stranger in a distant country, but God blessed Jacob & so he will William, if like Jacob he wrestles with God until he prevails."[34]

In the published memoirs of nontraditional religious authorities, these similes take on more rhetorical weight. In the early national period, biblical self-characterization became crucial for those staking nontraditional claims to relational authority. Newell wrote of various circumstances in which she acted or felt "like young Samuel of old, [not knowing] that it was the Lord" (5); "like Nehemiah of old, my countenance was sad for about one week" (15); she prays "like poor blind Bartimeus of old, 'Jesus, thou son of David, have mercy on me'"; "[l]ike Abraham" she is "surrounded with a body of darkness" (29); she is made new, "like Naaman of old, who dipped himself seven times in Jordan" (32); her congregation sings "[l]ike the inhabitants of Zion" while walking (32); "low on my knees, like Mary, at the footstool of mercy, I besought the Lord's direction" (37); "I, like Isaiah, cry aloud, and spare not my voice or lungs" (59). Similarly, she ventriloquizes versions of the lines of biblical characters in a construction that would become familiar: "[W]e moved on toward home, and as I cast a look toward that most endeared and never to be forgotten spot, I said like Moses of old, O Lord, let thy presence go with me, and I am sure all shall be well" (59; Exodus 33:15). As with her thoughts about Isaiah above, it is important to note Newell's assumption of the historicity of her biblical models and her own temporal distance from their lives; all of those "of olds" are not accidental.[35]

Tellingly, lines quoted this way come most often from Paul. "[A]lmost like Paul I could say, 'Whether in the body or not I cannot tell, but this one thing I will do, forgetting the things that are behind, I will press forward toward the mark of the high calling of God, which is in Christ Jesus" (34; Philippians 3:13–14); "[w]ith the apostle of the Gentiles I can pray, 'may the very God of peace sanctify me wholly;—may my spirit, and soul, and body, be preserved blameless unto the coming of the Lord Jesus Christ'" (76; 1 Thessalonians 5:23; "[A]lthough I see my short comings, yet I can say with Paul, I take the people of this vicinity to record this day, that I am clear of their blood; for I have not shunned to declare unto them the whole counsel of God, so far as he has revealed it to me, and has given me ability to perform it" (88; Acts 20:26). Newell narrates her call to preach—and her resistance to that call—in Pauline terms: "More and more distressing were my feelings, until at length, like Saul of Tarsus, I cried out 'Lord! What wilt thou have me to do?'" (69; Acts 9:6).

Direct self-comparison to biblical figures is a double claim to authority. Newell's repeated written performances of Paul's words are a powerful claim on apostolic authority. Again, both the audience within the text—"the people of this vicinity" of whose blood she declares herself clear—and the audience of the text are crucial to the value and the logic of that claim. Biblical self-characterization conjures a biblical figure of authority to lend authority to the author. At the same time, biblical self-characterization is a demonstration of scriptural facility, deploying the appropriate citation at the appropriate time and suggesting—by context and application—interpretation. In this sense, Newell's citations cultivate readers' understanding of her meaning and offer opportunities to share a sense of community with her to the extent that they "get" them. The very fact that the repeated biblical similes of preachers' memoirs are sprinkled throughout the text blithely and conversationally, usually without chapter and verse references, creates the possibility of identification between reader and author.

Similetic biblical self-characterization provided legibility to authors in ways that both constrained and provided possibilities for expanded spheres of authority. In the preface of her 1846 memoir, African American itinerant Zilpha Elaw likened herself both to characters traditionally read as black (a nod to the biblical roles scripted for her race) and to the apostles on whom she modelled her itinerancy.[36] She offered her memoir as a "portrait of my regenerated constitution—exhibiting, as did the bride of Solomon, comeliness with blackness, and, as did the apostle Paul, riches with poverty, and power in weakness." Demonstrating a focus, typical for her time, on the damning qualifier "but" in Song of Solomon 1:5 ("I am black, but comely"), Elaw folded race into the set of humble qualities that, by Paul's measure, ironically made her more, rather than less, qualified to preach the gospel (iv). The particularity of her choices underscored the need for her preaching to inhabit a legible biblical role. Later, Elaw similizes herself to the "Ethiopic eunuch" (7), and when she recounts that the Holy Spirit called her to be "like another Phoebe, or the matrons of the apostolic societies," she is particular about what that meant she was required to do: "I must employ myself in visiting families, and in speaking personally to the members thereof, of the salvation and eternal interests of their souls, visit the sick, and attend upon other of the errands and services of the Lord" (23). The families and the sick she visited in their homes made Elaw's self-characterization as a woman of the early church legible in its performance, but here in writing she invites the reader to go beyond the circumscribed female roles to claim an emphatically male one: as she went about her labors, she writes, "[l]ike Enoch, I walked and talked with God" (24).

Elaw's biblical self-identifications exploited and expanded upon the ambiguities of biblical roles themselves. "[M]y mind was greatly moved with evangelic interest for this young man: and, like Paul, for the Galatians, I travailed in birth for him" (77). After having an experience of the Holy Spirit calling her to preach, she is pregnant with the Gospel: "I kept these things very reservedly to myself, and pondered them in my heart, as did Mary the mother of Christ" (36). When her Methodist class abandons her for preaching, "[l]ike Joseph, I was hated for my dreams; and like Paul, none stood with me" (49). Her biblical facility shows through in her weaving of disparate verses into her life story: "How often I have said, 'Lord! Send by whom thou wilt send, only send not by me; for thou knowest that I am ignorant: how can I be a mouth for God!— a poor, coloured female: and thou knowest we have many things to endure which others do not.' But the answer was, 'What is that to thee? Follow thou me'" (Exodus 4:13 &c). Elaw's references are often obscure. She declines an offer of a place to live, not daring to, "like Demas, forsake my itinerating ministry, to love this present world"—the reference is to a companion that Paul complained left him to settle down in 2 Timothy 4:9–10.[37]

These moments locate not just these authors but those around them in biblical roles. Elaw's reverence for some of the preachers she knew extended to applying biblical characterizations to them at particularly powerful moments: "On the Lord's day morning the presiding Elder stepped forth in the might of the Holy Spirit, like Joshua, when he went to meet the angelic captain of the Lord's hosts."[38] Newell uses biblical roles to articulate relationships of subjectivity that situate her authority to preach. Referring to Henry Martin, a Methodist itinerant she considered her spiritual father, Newell writes, "I thought on Elijah and Elisha, and was prepared to say, 'behold the handmaid of the Lord, let the mantle of an Henry, or rather Elijah, rest on me.'" When she is determined to set out preaching but lacks money to travel, she records that distant friends "came to me with presents, as did the wise men who came to the infant Jesus and his mother." In another place, she writes bluntly and affectionately about how her supporters regarded her: "Her affection for me was as great as that of Aquila and Priscilla for St. Paul, who would have laid down their own necks upon the block for him."[39]

On the part of authors, the use of biblical characterizations extended to applying them to audiences and readers to homiletic ends, as accusations or goads. Just as Puritan jeremiads used the corporate character of biblical Israel as an exceptionalist identity as well as a lacerating epithet, and African American leaders encouraged their communities to think of themselves as biblical Israel as a grounds for hope, Newell exhorted her readers to adopt appropriate biblical roles. "O, my dear youthful reader! Choose the good part, like Mary, and it will not be taken from you," she writes.[40] Authoritative instructional texts employed biblical characters the same way. Hervey Wilbur's catechism closes with a prayer, to be used by readers, asking God to love contemporary readers as he loved "Martha and her Sister and Lazarus. . . . Bring them like Mary at thy feet." Wilbur continues, "Like Isaac may they love evening pious meditations. Like Nathanael, may they delight in secret devotion."[41]

Among nineteenth-century Protestants, Gregory Jackson ties such applications to an "aesthetics of immediacy" that "cultivates a kind of double vision that allows audiences to perceive themselves as forever in a transhistorical present, or eschatalogical time, bearing the cross with their suffering Savior."[42] These themes are real—Jackson offers a detailed reading of Elaw's autobiography demonstrating the ways in which she "elicits readerly identification with the universal experience of all Christians."[43] They are, however, just one aspect of the "readerly identification" conjured by authors such as Elaw using biblical models. When she discusses her concept of the ideal minister, for example, Elaw's use of these models is firmly historicized: "Such ministers have adorned and blessed the church in all ages; and such ministers occasionally adorn it still. It is an axiom which holds good in Christianity, as well as in common life, that whatever man has borne, been, or done, man may bear, be, or do; and there is no more impossibility of attaining eminent saintship in the present day, than there was two thousands of years since." Significantly, it is partly the possession of the Bible itself that Elaw believed set Christians of later eras apart from the early Church: "[W]ith the Scriptures in our hands and the Holy Spirit in our hearts, we possess advantages even beyond those Christians who enjoyed the living ministry of the apostles."[44] Elaw's biblicism was not beholden to an abstract concept of reentering or experiencing a special sacred past; it was actually grounded in the opposite conviction that that past was not temporally severed from the present. People could be just as holy now as they had been then.[45]

This historicized sense of the Bible is crucial to understanding how the biblical text was expanded and changed by its daily performance. Importantly, one effect of Elaw's historicism is to open up space for her own authority within the biblical model: "[T]he Scriptures in *our* hands and the Holy Spirit in *our* hearts." Relying on homiletic typology and broken time to think about the lived performance of biblical roles isolates the biblical text from the effects of its performance. It also overlooks the need of non-elites to *establish* homiletic authority with the Bible, not merely to exercise it. Viewing biblical identifications through the lens of typology has meant viewing them as abstractions rather than as contingent, dynamic realities. This association of all typologies with homiletic goals has meant that scholarly attention has sought only the major themes of Christian preaching in "typological" appeals to the Bible, ignoring the complexity and nuance of those appeals and flattening a varied topography of biblical characters invoked in particular moments into rote themes of pilgrimage and the imitation of Christ.[46]

Beginning in the late eighteenth century, a vibrant and expanding interest in the details—scriptural and extrascriptural—of biblical lives meant that the topography of biblical self-identification was more varied than ever and that historical particularity in biblical role-playing became both possible and desirable. This mode is most easily seen in the explicit, written moments discussed thus far. Within such texts, though, it can occasionally be observed in accounts of real-time, live-action moments where a biblical self-characterization was claimed more or less bluntly. Near the beginning of her memoir, Newell recounts a kinetic moment in which, feeling convicted by a Methodist itinerant for taking too much care with her appearance, she takes immediate, eccentric action: "As soon as he had done speaking to me, I arose and passed through the kitchen, where the people had began [*sic*] to assemble for meeting—the dread of Jehovah had taken away any fear of the people; for as I passed through the room I took down a pair of shears, and cut off the curls which I had made in my hair, and threw them into the fire in sight of the people."[47] Newell cites no specific biblical text either in the lived moment itself or in her written description of it, but the performative citation is plain enough—burning her hair has resonance with Ezekiel 5, for example. What is crucial is that Newell is clear about the significance of her audience's presence: three times in her short description of the action she notes "the people" present. "The people" are the cause of her shame—"fear of the people" led her to dress up in the first place, created her as a young woman bound to worldly things—as well as the necessary witnesses of her dramatic demonstration of God-fearing. For Newell's God-fearing persona to be realized, the people had to be in the kitchen to see her self-abasement, to smell a young woman's burning hair and make sense of it by dint of its biblical resonance.

Other instances of early national performed biblicism were less fleeting and more explicit. Newell records that Martin, her "spiritual father," at one point headed off to preach on Parker's Island, "at the mouth of Kennebec river," in performance of the biblical injunction that "The Isles shall wait for thy law" (Isaiah 42:4).[48] Islands were disproportionately targeted by preachers of this era because of their prominence in the prophecies of Isaiah; with limited resources in the 1840s, Joseph Smith made Polynesia a priority among the first Mormon missions.

The remainder of this chapter will explore in depth the consequences and stakes of performed biblicism in the early national period through the public lives of two of the era's most eccentric biblical performers: Peggy and Lorenzo Dow. Lorenzo was the most well-known itinerant preacher in America during the first three decades of the nineteenth century, made famous through his sermons and a large body of autobiographical and polemical print material. Peggy was his first wife. She exhorted occasionally and edited a compilation of hymns, but she was best known to the public for her memoir, published in four editions during her lifetime and one after her death. Both Peggy and Lorenzo drew on bible-based performances to cultivate relationships of authority with audiences. Their roles were very different, however, owing to their dispositions, cultural environment, and the constraints imposed by their relationships with audiences and with each other. In particular, Peggy's experiences as a woman looking for a biblical role demonstrate the constraints that the early national scripturalized environment placed on women.

Lorenzo Dow became the most famous itinerant preacher in early national America by playing an apostle. Dow's apostolic performance was both recognized in the world, in immediate, visceral moments of interaction with audiences, and rhetorically constructed after the fact, in his autobiographical writings. His apostolic identity began with his refusal to acknowledge the ecclesial authority of any existing church. Although he credited his conversion to Methodist preaching and started his own career as a preacher in 1795 under Methodist auspices, Dow was not ordained until 1825, when he accepted ordination from a Methodist splinter group, long after his personal authority could have been helped or hurt by it. In the intervening decades he had ignored all ecclesiastical discipline, taking his cues, like the apostles, directly from the Spirit. He refused to keep to a regular circuit, as the Methodist hierarchy demanded, traveling tens of thousands of miles in the United States and the British Isles according to no discernible pattern.[49]

Dow's activities during his travels, likewise, invited apostolic associations: he founded churches, dispensed advice and explained doctrine in lengthy epistles. It was his erratic travel and eccentric personal style, though, that truly set him apart from other itinerants. Following Luke 22:35, he presumed to go about without purse or scrip, depending on those he met for room and board, and he wore apostolic poverty on his body: he was notoriously unkempt, with long hair and an unruly beard, his thin frame wrapped in a perpetually threadbare overcoat. "[H]e has preached to large multitudes—the eccentricity of his manners and the singularity of his appearance, wearing a long flowing beard, in imitation of Apostolic times, are calculated to attract attention," one newspaper wrote.[50] His preaching style earned him the epithet "Crazy Dow," which he accepted with glee.

As important as Dow's embodied performance was the fact that he narrativized his apostolic life, both in speech and in writing. He published at least six editions of his autobiography during his lifetime, along with countless polemical tracts relating to personal grudges and public debates. His accounts of his travels are straight from 1 Corinthians 4:12–13: reviled, he blessed; persecuted, he suffered; defamed, he entreated. He gleefully recounted his Pauline clashes with authorities both civil and satanic. He was, on several occasions, almost in a shipwreck (Acts 27). As his fame grew in the first decade of the nineteenth century, Dow (who made a habit of referring to himself in the third person) started calling himself "Cosmopolite": "a citizen of the world; one who is at home in every place," as defined by a contemporary dictionary.

Sometimes, in his writings, he claimed his apostolic role explicitly. Dow argued in an 1814 publication that there had to be latter-day apostles, because in the Great Commission, Christ told his (first) apostles that He would be with them "alway, even unto the end of the world" (Matthew 28:19–20). "I ask how he could be with his Apostles unto the end of the world, unless he had Apostles to be WITH?" Dow wrote, with his usual logic. "It is evident he could not allude to the twelve only; for he knew they would not live to the end of the world. . . . [H]e must include succeeding ministers, who would step into the Apostles' shoes."

In one matter, though, Lorenzo deviated from playing Paul: he may have abandoned his family for Christ's sake (Matthew 19:29), but he did not "become a eunuch" (Matthew 19:12).[51] In 1804 he married Peggy Holcomb, and it fell to her to create a role that did not exist, strictly speaking, in scripture. Lorenzo was conscious that Paul was ambivalent concerning marriage—"I would that all men were [celibate] even as I myself" (1 Corinthians 7:7)—and that his marriage went against his apostolic persona. In a short essay called "On Matrimony," he defended his choice, pointing out that Matthew 8:14 indicates that Peter was married, as Jesus healed his mother-in-law. In any case, Lorenzo was hardly the first evangelist to admit he was not as Paul was. George Whitefield, according to Harry Stout, agonized over his need for a sexual partner and eventually married.[52]

Lorenzo was already famous for playing an apostle when they met in 1802, in their mid-twenties; Peggy writes that "I was very much afraid of him, as I had heard such *strange things* about him!"[53] Eccentric in marriage as in everything else, Lorenzo proposed during their first conversation. After she accepted Lorenzo's proposal, he left on a preaching tour and was away for two years. When he returned, they were married—Peggy's journal says on September 4; Lorenzo's says September 3, 1804. Peggy was now an apostle's wife, but the only thing the New Testament says about Peter's wife is that she was once sick: if Peggy were to have a biblical role comparable to Lorenzo's, she would have to be creative.

As a condition of marriage, Peggy and Lorenzo agreed that she would never interfere with his call to travel and preach, and she came to regard any such interference as the darkest sort of sin. For the duration of their marriage, Peggy and Lorenzo referred to this agreement as their "contract."[54] The day after they were married, Lorenzo left for the Mississippi Territory and was gone about seven months. Lorenzo preached at five to eight hundred meetings in the year he and Peggy were married, and he traveled ten thousand miles in 1805.[55] Their fifteen-year marriage was punctuated by at least two separations of a year or more, several others lasting as long as ten months.

Peggy traveled with Lorenzo on and off for several years, about which she kept a journal, first published in 1814 as *Vicissitudes Exemplified*. Lorenzo's hand in its publication is manifest—it was printed by New York printer John C. Totten at the same time as some of Lorenzo's works—but his editorial voice appears only lightly in the text. This journal and three subsequent editions published during her lifetime both report on Peggy's attempts to find a role for herself and serve as part of her eventual answer.

Peggy's published journal is not, like Lorenzo's, an account of a single, consistently-pursued role. Its initial focus is her attempt to travel with Lorenzo. At the beginning of their marriage, Peggy continued to live with her sister Hannah Miller and her sister's husband, Smith. The Millers had raised Peggy from the age of six, following the death of Peggy and Hannah's mother. Hannah, Peggy wrote, "was as a mother" to her, and she intended to continue living with the Millers indefinitely after getting married: "I expected to continue to live with my sister, as she had no children—and was much attached to me, or seemed to be so at that time."[56] In 1805, however, the Millers moved to Mississippi from upstate New York, limiting the possibilities for Lorenzo to drop in on Peggy. He gave her the option of staying in the North with acquaintances or, per 1 Corinthians 9:5, following him about. "I chose to go, and take my lot and share with him, of what ever might befall us."[57]

Lorenzo's apostolic life frequently put Peggy in situations which she found difficult. "My heart trembled at the thought of sleeping out in this desert place, with no company but my husband," she wrote of her first wilderness journey. "[W]e stopped for the night, built a fire ... prepared our supper, which consisted of *coffee* and a hard *biscuit*. ... We had no tent to screen us from the inclement weather .... it was a gloomy night to me."[58] She missed her sister and, often, female companionship altogether: "I felt very gloomy to be left among strangers, and to go on board a boat with a company of men, without one woman for a companion."[59] Upon leaving for Britain with Lorenzo, she was nervous, but wrote that "I thought if I might find one real *female* friend, I would be satisfied" and then noted that during the journey and the time in quarantine in port she "never saw a woman for thirty-seven days," with one exception.[60] Despite her misgivings, Peggy continued to travel with Lorenzo for several years. She was frequently ill during these trips and had trouble keeping up on horseback, often necessitating the extra expense of travel by boat or carriage.

Peggy's discomfort underscores the fact that there were no immediately-accepted roles for female itinerants. Itinerant life for women demanded the expansion of biblical models: this is why the biblical self-identification most commonly invoked by women such as Zilpha Elaw and Fanny Newell was *Paul*. The first edition of Peggy's journal evinces none of the desire to transcend or ignore popular conceptions of feminine behavior observable in the writings of many of the notable female preachers who were her contemporaries. Nor was she able to embrace traveling with her husband like a few other itinerants' wives. Rare as they were, the best known example is Mary Orne Tucker, who wrote a memoir in the late 1840s. Tucker relished traveling with her husband, setting out with him on the same horse "young and nimble as a squirrel" for her "first essay in circuit traveling."[61] She continued traveling with her husband through thirty years of marriage.[62]

Peggy's writings, by contrast, are built around the biblical models of Martha and Mary. Peggy longed to be the biblical Martha, glimpsed in Luke 10 in a flurry of domestic activity and in John 11 boldly questioning Jesus after the death of her brother Lazarus. Martha walks to meet Christ and says, "Lord, if you had been here, my brother would not have died," and then essentially asks him to relieve her grief by raising her brother from the dead (John 11:21–2). Peggy lacked both the domestic environment and the boldness to be Martha, however. By the end of her life, Peggy routinely compared herself to Martha's sister Mary, whose inert submission contrasts with Martha's active role in each of those scenes. While Martha is busy serving, Mary sits still and listens to the Savior; where Martha confronts Jesus about their brother's death, Mary drops to Christ's feet and delivers the same line—"Lord, if you had been here, my brother would not have died"—from the ground in front of him, asking for no relief: she states a fact while submitting to Christ's will.

Peggy's scripturalized view of the relationships around her is apparent from the first pages of her published journal. Before she met Lorenzo, she wrote, ministers frequented the Miller home, and she imagined her relationship with them according to the biblical models of both Mary and Martha: "The preachers made our house their home, at that time, and it was my delight to wait on them—I felt I could lie at their feet, and learn instructions from their lips."[63] Here, Peggy combines both sisters' roles—she delighted to wait on the preachers like Martha and to sit at their feet, like Mary.

The first edition of Peggy's journal is a story of her frustrated desire to be like Martha. Lorenzo's penchant for apostolic itinerancy and Peggy's conviction that he was doing the Lord's own work left her with no hope of being domestic in the sense of maintaining a home of her own and nurturing morally upright children. Between September of 1804 and June of 1815, Peggy and Lorenzo kept a home of their own for about three months. Traveling with Lorenzo meant mostly living with strangers. Typically, Lorenzo dropped her off with acquaintances—generally people he barely knew or had just met and whom Peggy did not know at all—and fulfilled preaching commitments in the surrounding area. Like traveling itself, Peggy found her time in strangers' homes trying. "My heart often trembled at what was before me, to be continually among strangers, and not much acquainted with the ways of the world, it made me feel like one at a loss, how to behave, or what to do."[64] Again, she reached for biblical phrases to explain her predicament: "I had neither house nor friends in that country, without the people chose to befriend me. I was a stranger in a strange land" (Exodus 2:22).[65]

Peggy accompanied Lorenzo to Liverpool in November of 1805, and gave birth to a baby girl in Dublin in September of 1806. Lorenzo was away during most of her pregnancy but came back in time for the birth. When the baby was five weeks old, Lorenzo felt called to return to Liverpool with his family. Peggy blamed her behavior during the crossing for her subsequent illness: "The weather was rainy, and tolerable cold; there was no fire in the cabin. . . . I was so much afraid that my little infant would be too much exposed, that I neglected myself, and probably took cold—[we] were two nights and one day on board."[66] She became very ill and their new infant was sent away from her to be nursed while she recovered. At this time Lorenzo left her with acquaintances to return to Ireland to preach, and Peggy struggled to accept the will of God in the matter: "Although I felt willing for him to go and blow the gospel trumpet, yet my heart shrunk at the thought of being left in a strange land, in my present situation, so weak that I could not put on my clothes without help; and my sweet little babe at a considerable distance from me, and amongst strangers. But the Lord was my support, and gave me strength to be, in some considerable degree, resigned to the will of God!"[67] To complete the picture, Peggy recorded that she was at this time lodging in a crowded house full of people she did not know, in a room adjacent to a chair-maker's shop, a source of constant noise—sawing, hammering, the indelicate speech of working men. Lorenzo had not yet returned when the infant, Letitia, died about two months later, while still being kept a few miles from the ailing Peggy. "They kept me in ignorance of her sickness until she was dead," Peggy wrote, in one of the shortest and starkest lines of the journal.[68] Rather than a mother, in her journal Peggy most often compared herself to a child during the next few years.

If her marriage constrained Peggy's ability to perform Martha's domesticity, her sister, Hannah Miller, unsettled its positive associations for her. While Peggy and Lorenzo were in England, Miller—Peggy's living model for Martha's domesticity—left her husband for a younger man. "[T]here was a criminal intercourse between them for several months before it was discovered," Peggy wrote. "[T]he disgrace attending it was almost unbearable."[69]

The period surrounding the publication of Peggy's journal marks a change in her self-characterization. The 1815 edition contains material narrating the publication of the 1814 edition, indicating that the foray into authorship was initially part of an attempt to play a larger role in Lorenzo's ministry. In the summer of 1814, while her journal was in press, crowds had begun to turn out at the promise of getting to see her.[70] Lorenzo was an enthusiastic supporter of female preaching and encouraged Peggy to try her hand—to play Priscilla to his Aquila. The ensuing entries in the published journal note several instances in which Peggy attempted to speak at Lorenzo's meetings—she led closing prayers and occasionally attempted to act as what Methodists called an exhorter: the opening act or closing prayer at a preaching event, someone who would warm up the crowd by speaking from personal experience or exemplify the sermon's points by offering a testimony.[71]

These attempts exposed Peggy to a crippling fear of public speaking. Her entry for Sunday, June 12th, 1814, begins, "This hath been a day of deep trial to my soul." She recorded that she had attempted to lead a prayer after one of Lorenzo's sermons "but the cross was so weighty, I did not fully answer my mind."[72] "I feel many times much distressed on account of my backwardness," she wrote later.[73] Peggy saw this nervousness as yet another sinful reluctance to submit to the will of God: "I left [one of Lorenzo's sermons] condemned in my own mind, for not taking up my cross—may the Lord forgive me, and enable me to be more obedient in future!"[74] The final period of Peggy's life is preceded in the journal by intensified self-criticism arising from her attempts to take a greater role in Lorenzo's public ministry.

Here, too, Hannah Miller provided Peggy with a complicated and ultimately frustrating model: Peggy's sister was not afraid of crowds. Lorenzo recorded that when she and Smith Miller left their community in New York, Hannah "standing upon a log, bade her neighbors farewell."[75] In Mississippi, she became known as a preacher in her own right. One minister recorded that her "zeal, gifts, and abilities" were such that "she attracted the attention of the people as much as any preacher in the territory where she was known."[76] Hannah's "fall" was made all the worse, Peggy thought, by her reputation for godliness: because "she had been a great professor of religion . . . the cause must suffer by her falling so foully."[77]

Peggy continued to struggle with the "cross" of performing as Phoebe or Priscilla over the summer of 1814. During this period of Peggy's journal she began to apply the concept of "usefulness" to herself for the first time. Previously she had talked about not wanting to stand in the way of Lorenzo's "usefulness to souls," but now her writing began to show concern for her own usefulness: "May my heart be filled with love and gratitude to the Great and Beneficent hand that is daily showering down blessings on my unworthy head, and improve my lengthened days, in doing good to myself and others! For why should I be useless in this time of need?" Her life of tagging along with Lorenzo and living with strangers, childless, had left her wondering what it was that she should do, and by the time her journal was first published she saw uselessness as the alternative to taking a role in Lorenzo's ministry. "Why should we desire to live in this world to be useless?" she asked.[78]

Late in her journal, Peggy wrote of catching herself admiring a home she and Lorenzo came to while traveling, reproaching herself for thinking that it would be "a sweet retreat." "[S]top, my fancy! Stay thy soul on God. . . . To him and him alone would I look for comfort . . . my lot appears to be in a peculiar sphere, and I hope in love and mercy the master will enable me to fill it with patience and submission."[79] But she knew by this time that she would never have this for herself; she would never serve table like Martha. In 1815, Lorenzo brought her to stay with his father and sister near Hebron, Connecticut, and she lived out the next few years there while Lorenzo went about preaching—he was probably there a cumulative year and a half, at most two years out of the four and a half years she lived there. It was only the second time in their married life that Peggy had a fixed residence of her own, albeit one which she shared not with her husband but with a father figure.

Denied the role of a nurturing mother and never comfortable with a public life, in her later years Peggy found a different sort of private role symbolized for her in a different New Testament figure. Like Hannah Miller, Martha had a quieter, humbler sister, and Peggy repeatedly stated her desire to have "Mary's place," at the feet of Christ: "O that I could always keep the place of Mary at the feet of Jesus!" she wrote. "May he give me the spirit of a Mary, to lie at his feet, depending only on his mercy. O that I may have a heart of agonizing prayer." [80] In an 1817 letter to Lorenzo, she apologized for missing him too much while aspiring to Mary's role: "I would leave all to the disposal of our great Master—yet I feel my heart too often holding you tight—may Jesus be the greatest and most lovely object in my eyes! I would have Mary's place at his feet, and receive his instructions with submission."[81]

Peggy recognized Martha's role as one that was denied to her, and found solace in the counterposed figure of Mary. "O that I may be prepared for whatever may be the will of God concerning me, whether prosperity or adversity. May I ever lay passive at HIS feet, and feel a disposition to say, Not my will, but thine, be done."[82] Peggy invoked the contrast between Mary and Martha to explain her sister's "fall," citing an inability to "submit to any one" as the core of Hannah's faults.[83] Hannah would have been a blessing and a comfort to everyone, Peggy wrote, "if she had kept at the feet of her Saviour, and attended to the dictates of the Spirit which teaches humility."[84]

After settling in with Lorenzo's father in Connecticut, Peggy's journal became less a travel narrative and more an account of daily solitary devotion focused on the theme of submission. From then on she traveled only locally with Lorenzo during his stays in Connecticut, and she stopped mentioning her fear of speaking, presumably because the point had become moot. Her death in early 1820 was widely reported in connection to Lorenzo's fame, but her obituaries mentioned neither her writing nor her public speaking; the lengthiest one, widely reprinted, identified her as "Peggy Dow, wife of Lorenzo Dow, long distinguished for *his* earnest devotedness to the best of causes" (emphasis mine). "It may safely be declared of her, that she imitated the example of the blessed Saviour, being possessed of an uncommon degree of meekness and humility, sweetly resigned to his will, and left this vale of tears, without a struggle or a groan."[85] Peggy's marriage to Lorenzo may have continued to constrain her choice of biblical self-identity even in death. While she desired a posture of submission at the feet of her Lord, one of the many enduring stories told of Lorenzo's eccentricities is that in order to make it easier for Peggy's body to exit the grave on Judgment Day, he had her buried standing up.

Peggy's performance of biblical roles within a matrix of constraining intimate relationships is an important window on the implicit, embodied, social presence of the Bible in the early nineteenth century. The inscriptions at the front of her memoir—Proverbs 12:4 and 31:10–12—stayed constant throughout all the editions. They stand as a question Peggy was always trying to answer: they extol the value to a man of a "virtuous woman," but they offer no guidance as to what she should do beyond "being virtuous." Like other early national bible readers, Peggy looked to the characters of the Bible to understand, adapt, and create the interpersonal relationships that conditioned her life as a religious subject. Acknowledging the effects of her specific interpersonal circumstances rescues Peggy's biblicism and accompanying religious commitments from abstraction; Peggy's commitment to a biblical role was not abstract or prerelational, but part of a matrix that included intimate relationships themselves not easily given to change.

The intentional creation of biblical resonance within a given contingent context was a claim both on the Bible and on the context. Beyond that, the effect of the widespread similetic and performative use of biblical characters was to rapidly multiply the contexts in which those characters might be found. Each written self-characterization and lived performance was an argument, a statement about an attribute or narrative moment relevant to the biblical character named. Every use of the text was an expansion of the text. Typology in its most formal sense requires that typologies be finite: for every type in the Old Testament, an antitype in the New, marking the fulfilment of Old Testament promises in the Christian dispensation and completing the typology. By contrast, opening biblical comparisons to lived experience meant that the set of antitypes became ever-changing and infinite. Recognizing this dissolves the deterministic time-order demanded by typology, which insists that antitypes merely come to pass. Instead, it permits analysis of the way biblical moments may be perpetually reimagined in light of later applications. This is not folding experience into the Bible as it is; this is extending it to cover present-day experience. The Bible (its perception by readers, its perceived meanings, its other applications) cannot be unchanged by such extension.[86] The next chapter will home in on visionary texts as one form of performed biblicism that made particularly dramatic claims on relationships of authority, highlighting the possibilities and stakes of performed biblicism both for authoritative roles and the place of the Bible itself.

CHAPTER FOUR

"Write These Things in a Book"

SCRIPTURALIZATION AND VISIONARY AUTHORITY

*After these things I sat Silent before the Lord for a time, but durst not
henceforth Question with him any more, for his Word was as fire and as
an hammer in mine heart, and I was broken before him, & humbled with
his goodness, and my heart was Opened and Fingers loosed to Write, to
shew forth to the World that which I have seen in the light of the Lamb.
And be it known to all people to whom these few Lines may come, that
notwithstanding things of this Nature at this time are something
Uncommon among Men, yet I dare not distrust the Wisdom of Heaven
nor disobey the Command thereof.*

—*THE VISION OF ISAAC CHILDS*[1]

One of the most widespread forms of performed biblicism in the early national period consisted of claiming otherwise-inaccessible information from
God. These accounts often transgressed the boundaries of analytic categories—prophecy, revelation, dream—but all shared a distinctive demand for a
uniquely authoritative speaker: they were stories that only one person could
tell. As such, visionary accounts—the generic term I will use here—placed the
authority of a given speaker front and center. Although, textually, these accounts were monologic, they depended on an existing field of discourse shared
among speakers and audiences for their comprehensibility. As texts created
and validated by communities of authors, editors, copyists, and readers, visionary accounts are uniquely useful sites for thinking about the stakes and
effects of scripturalization in the late colonial and early national period.

Visionary accounts are everywhere in early American religion; the major
cultural constellations that shaped early America had strong visionary traditions. As Native American, African, and European cultures mingled, the authority potentially available to visionaries in specific situations ebbed and

flowed.[2] Prophecy is integral to Judeo-Christian traditions, but for Protestants a particularly touchy affair. Protestant rhetoric relied on scripture to "bridle," in John Calvin's metaphor, the potential excesses of the inspiration of the Spirit or ongoing prophetic witness. Yet that insistence itself meant that some form of individualized, immediate sharing of divine knowledge was always potentially present. Because each Christian had to have access to the Holy Spirit to comprehend scripture, a direct line was always open. The line between knowledge observable to all in scripture and knowledge given to some readers specially was by definition so blurred as to hardly be a line at all.

Anglophone print-bible culture, as it developed in the eighteenth century, offered new possibilities not just for seeing, but for showing.[3] Relationships of visionary authority were not about experience, at least as far as the historian is concerned, but about presentation.[4] Access to print-bible culture both enhanced audiences' familiarity with biblical models for visionary roles and allowed would-be visionaries to get their messages out. When the terrain of print-bible culture is taken as a whole, the metaphor of a border, suggesting a sharp line between scripture and nonscripture, canon and apocrypha, becomes much harder to apply. This is not to say that attempting to identify and police that sharp border has not been an obsession of American Protestant authorities, as David Holland has recently shown, but to suggest that we need not adopt our sources' assumptions about what was at stake. Understanding scripture as a genre—a routinized form of text, its material and rhetorical conventions arising out of the expectations of readers and the intentions of speakers—allows for a fuller understanding of how the Bible functioned as a resource for authority in early America.

Early national visionary texts participated in the scripturalized environment of the era. Their words, characters, and material assumptions cited those of the Bible. As with the other forms of citation discussed in this study, visionary accounts' references to the Bible both bolstered its authoritative place and changed it. Material and rhetorical assertions of visionary authority that cited the Bible keyed readers to questions about its own visionary origins. This chapter will examine the mechanisms of this scripturalized environment in early national visionary texts, culminating in a close study of *The Vision of Isaac Childs*, a little-remembered late colonial text that circulated widely in both print and manuscript throughout the nineteenth century. The treatment of Childs's vision—copied, recopied, edited, translated, annotated, and commented upon over the course of well over a century—provides an unusually accessible window on the operations and effects of scripturalization in the early national period.

Undoubtedly, most early American visionary accounts remained oral. Archives overflow with hints of evocative but ultimately lost moments: of ministers recounting their dreams midsermon, of young women walking down the

streets of their towns proclaiming the things God had shown them.[5] Many
other visions, though, entered into early national bible culture more elabo-
rately, as fully-formed written texts. The circulation, and occasional fame, of
visionary accounts was not immediately dependent on print. Catherine Liv-
ingstone Garretson's ecstatic writings were never published in the nineteenth
century, but Lorenzo Dow (himself an accomplished visionary) was familiar
with "some of her meditations now in manuscript" in 1801.[6] Likewise, *The
Vision of Isaac Childs* circulated primarily in manuscript for nearly seventy
years between its creation in 1757 and its first widely-circulated printing in
1826. At least eighteen manuscript copies have survived, a remarkable number
for an eighteenth-century text.[7]

Many early national visionaries, however, were drawn to printing. Richard
Bushman counted thirty-two visionary accounts published in America between just 1783 and 1815.[8] Countless others appeared within other forms of
religious print; biographies and autobiographies, sermons and sermon-
accounts, routinely narrated the visionary experiences of subjects. Because
Dow appreciated Garretson's visions, he reflexively hoped that they would "one
day . . . appear abroad, as bread cast upon the waters, and found after many
days."[9] Childs's vision was printed twice in his lifetime, most likely at his own
instigation. Access to print culture increased the density of bread cast on the
waters. A surprising number of visionary accounts from this period came from
small presses outside of the metropolitan centers of American print—Lyons,
New York; Barnard, Vermont; Stonington, Connecticut—indicating that even
those outside the centers of culture could circulate their visions.[10]

Beyond the practicalities of production and circulation, though, print-bible
culture defined the generic and formal terms of what a visionary text should
look like. To begin with, early American readers thought of the Bible as a
printed object. An increasingly historicized sense of the Bible's origins and the
era's humanizing characterization of its creators meant that readers were able
to imagine Jeremiah dictating to Baruch (Jeremiah 36:4) or John of Patmos
in the act of writing Revelation, but they would have been hard-pressed to
imagine a "manuscript bible." Beyond that, scripture as a genre was signaled
by a variety of visual cues typically associated with print: ruled lines, numbered
margins, varied text sizes for varied text.

Beyond the visual cues of print, late colonial and early national visionary
accounts cited the terms of the scripturalized environment in which they originated through a number of interlocking rhetorical and material characteristics. Print-bible culture provided models for latter-day visionaries. At the most
basic level, this affected what visionaries said they saw and the language in
which they described it. Visionary texts of this era were typically warnings and
promises (mostly warnings), on the model of Jeremiah, Isaiah, Daniel, or Revelation, and they used the language of the Authorized Version, either verbatim
or by implication. Childs's vision figured golden candlesticks as prominent

analogical symbols (Revelation 1:12). *The Visions of a Certain Thomas Say* (1774) was dominated by biblical turns of phrase: the devil was a "roaring Lion" (1 Peter 5:8); Say was tempted to "curse my God and die" (Job 2:9); he determined that he "should glory in nothing, save in the cross of Christ" (Galatians 6:14). Several lines of Say's preface are a pastiche of Isaiah 5:20–23, copied in without quotation marks or verse citations. Say also created bible-sounding material: "Oh! who can count the number of my woes" relied on archaic words and styling that were distinctly drawn from the Authorized Version, emphasizing the extraordinary properties of the visionary text as distinct from vernacular language. Say closed his vision with an explicit invocation of Isaiah 12: "Here I was made to adopt the language of the Prophet. I will praise thee though thou hast been angry with me, thine anger is turned away, and thou comfort me, therefore with joy shall ye draw out the wells of salvation."[11]

What visionaries reported seeing likewise consisted of repeated references to the Bible. *The Vision of John Mills*—published as a two-column broadside in Virginia in 1785—was typical both in the repetition of the authoritative "I saw" and in its description of what was seen: "I saw souls fetching to judgment"; "I saw the devil taking them in a fearful manner, and dragging them down to torment, which kept continually raining, foaming, and stinking with brimstone"; "I saw my oldest sister in that place of torment."[12] Mills's description of Hell—"continually raining, foaming, and stinking with brimstone"— had analogues in many passages of the English Bible; Revelation 21, for example. Mills reported that the damned spoke directly to him, describing their suffering and begging him to warn others, recapitulating the parable of the rich man and Lazarus in Luke 16:19–31.

More important than direct citation of the biblical text, though, is the way in which print-bible culture defined the underlying terms of visionary writing. Bible culture emphasized the intratextually named authors of the Bible—such as the prophets—as *characters* in the Bible. The biblical content attributed to men such as Daniel, Elijah, Isaiah, Jeremiah, and John of Patmos was one thing, but print-bible culture also found ways to emphasize the lives of these writers, as explored in chapter 3. The characterization of biblical figures is occasionally present in visionary texts. Ann Phillips, who published a brief vision in 1812, wrote that during her visit to heaven she asked specifically to see Enoch, Elijah, "and a number of other Scripture Worthies," and was obliged.[13]

Identifying the Bible's authors as characters enabled visionaries to see biblical texts as texts—as products of individuals in circumstances. Visionary lives became performable roles. Say compared himself directly to Paul. Acknowledging that some would scoff at his reports of entering a trance, he insisted on biblical precedent. "Witness Saint Paul; you hear him say, whether in or out of the body he could not tell," Say wrote. "[H]e [Paul] says he both saw and heard things which were not fit to be uttered: and I [Say] say, I both heard and saw at that time those things which I related after I came to myself."[14]

In her visionary account, first published in 1807, Chloe Willey gestured toward or explicitly cited language from Isaiah, Jonah, Revelation, and other biblical texts, but it was the character of Daniel that modeled her prophetic role and her subsequent performance. She began her account by narrating a conventional conversion narrative, chronicling her progress from sinner to penitent to saved. This included an "experience of grace" in which, she wrote, Christ "spake peace to my soul in these words: 'Behold I have found a ransom. I gave my life to redeem such repenting, returning sinners.'"[15] Biblical quotations being laid on the suffering sinner—here, Willey invokes Job 33:24—were frequent parts of such narrations.[16] A few pages later, though, Willey signaled a turn toward something more than a typical conversion account with a specific invocation of the Prophet Daniel: "I thought of Daniel, who said, 'The visions of God are too wonderful for me.'" There is no such line attributed to Daniel—this comes closest to Psalms 139:6: "Such knowledge is too wonderful for me; it is high, I cannot attain unto it." Nevertheless, Willey then recorded her growth into the role of Daniel. She was visited by an angelic guide who "came to let me know, that I was to be in trouble for certain days, and for seven days I must fast as Daniel did, i.e. eat bread and water; and that I should be restored after thirty days."[17] It was this fast—in Daniel 1 and 10, the prophet is seen fasting for ten days at one point and three weeks at another—by which Willey first performed her prophetic identity in front of an audience. "When at breakfast, I told those with me, that I had no appetite for the food then provided; that I must eat nothing but bread and water for seven days; and informed all present, that something special was about to take place."[18]

The reading act that Willey cited as the immediate prompt for her first dream does not involve the Bible directly. Willey recounted constant bible reading in her visionary account, but it was Thomas Newton's *Dissertation on the Prophecies* that overcame her. First published in London in the 1750s, Newton's analysis of biblical prophecy was available in several editions in the eighteenth century and (for a comparatively dry work of biblical scholarship) widely read (William Smyth Babcock took extensive notes from it in the early eighteen-aughts).[19] Newton identified and extracted prophecies from the Bible, relying not on conventional distinctions among the biblical books, but on generic designations. Newton's isolation and elaboration of the biblical prophets can be seen as a guide to prophetic roles, and he spent nearly one hundred and fifty pages on the prophecies of Daniel.

Other visionary accounts similarly underscored the embeddedness of biblical knowledge within the larger scope of parabiblical print culture. Thomas Say anticipated an objection to his claim that he saw the dead looking much like the living, "each in a complete body," and referenced Luke 16 to counter it: "Now some may think that the dead know not each other, to whom I say, did not Dives know Lazarus, yea Abraham, tho' afar off." The rich man of Luke 16 is not named in the biblical text, though. The extrabiblical tradition naming him Dives ("rich man" in Latin) was present in an array of eighteenth-century published sermons along with several other easily accessible texts, such as *History of the Holy Jesus*, one of his era's best-known biblical books for children, and Joseph Alleine's *Alarm to the Unconverted*, a ubiquitous devotional tract. In *The Practice of Piety* (another well-known tract) Lewis Bayly used Dives and Lazarus to make the same point that Say made about how the dead recognize each other.

The discourse-constituting influence of the environment of religious print was most evident, however, in visionary texts' preoccupation with literacy, with writing itself, and, most importantly, with the written presentation of revelation. For texts that relied fundamentally on the possibility of direct, unwritten revelation, written visionary narratives demonstrated an overwhelming concern with writing. Visionaries typically reported a command to, as in the case of John Mills, "tell the people of the world" what they have been shown, and "telling" was equated with writing. Childs, like John of Patmos himself, was commanded to "write in a book"; Norris Stearns testified that he was "an illiterate youth" who nevertheless had been "shown many things, which he [was] commanded to write."[20]

Women's visionary accounts are more likely than men's to identify themselves as scribal productions. Not only were women less likely than men to have had an education that included writing instruction, but there was both precedent and a propensity for men to co-opt female religious authority by co-opting the work of female authors.[21] For her part, the author of *The Vision and Wonderful Experience of Jane Cish*, a well-known English text reprinted several times in America, said that while she was literate, she felt herself "ignorant and incapable of setting forth these things in proper order and stile." She asked readers to "pardon imperfections" and also reminded them that these imperfections in fact made her dictation more like scripture: "[A]s the scriptures of truth are in a plain and humble stile, I hope you will receive these things at the hand of the Lord, in the same manner, for in them you will find no grammatical flourishes, no learned connections, nor any thing designed to please the ear."[22] Audience demands were a large part of these texts' self-authorizations. Ann Phillips wrote that it was only "the desire of many of God's people, and . . . a sincere well wish to a *dying* World" that led her to publish her vision at all.[23]

Dictated visions meant that the first moment of transmission was purely oral, leading editors to emphasize the reliability of that moment. In the grammar of biblical prophecy, the circumstances of visionary accounts were a part of the message, inviting readers to accept visionary authority on terms made familiar by bible culture. As with bible prefaces, the integrity of the author and editors was a primary concern. Cish's tract ended with an affidavit signed by ten men attesting to her good character.[24] The editors of Eliza Thomas's vision, published after her death, made a point of attesting to her respectability, and their own.[25] The unnamed editor of the vision of Sarah Alley, yet another Quaker, underscored the printed text's proximity to its source on the title page: the visionary experience happened February 25, 1798, and was "taken from her own Mouth, the Twenty-seventh of the same Month, in the Hearing of divers Persons."[26] The visions of Rebecca Ashburn, Eliza Thomas, and Jane Cish all use a version of the exact same phrase on their title pages: "[F]rom her own mouth." Sarah Alley's editors explained that they wanted to bring stability to Alley's oral account through the permanence of the press. "[D]ivers copies having been taken of her narrative, which it is likely will be again copied, and probably very erroneously, it has been thought best, to prevent such errors, to commit it to the press."[27] Laboring to establish the authority of the visions by testifying to the reliability of the visionary, the reliability of his or her witnesses, and the self-consciously bible-esque circumstances of the revelation and its recitation, prophets and editors often moved quickly to advance that authority in print. Oral transmission and ad hoc manuscripts seemed too unstable to bear the weight of scripture.

The material reality of print-bible culture appears at crucial moments within visionary accounts themselves. Ashburn said that a minister came to her in a dream, "took a bible out of his pocket, gave it to me, and told me I must read the 8th chapter of St. John's gospel. He then took the book, turned the leaf down at the same chapter, handed it to me again, and told me to read it hereafter."[28] Sometimes these material moments embedded within immaterial visions underscore the expansive, and recursive, nature of print-bible culture. One of the most important moments in Ashburn's dream account happens around a rhyming couplet—"Oh love the Lord, and he will be / A tender father unto thee"—that was a popular part of sampler patterns throughout the eighteenth century.[29] When the minister in her dream recites those lines to her, Ashburn responds "that when I was a girl, I used to work those lines on my sampler, and to write them in my copy book."[30] In another dream, a dove from heaven brings her a scrap of paper with a version of Romans 10:9 written on it.[31] As readers encountered visions that depicted religious reading, they were invited to see a reciprocally reinforcing continuity between the piety of their own practices and those of the character who had been granted religious visions.

Willey's visionary account is suffused with reading moments. At one point she prays for a sign from God, marked by a tellingly complicated mechanism: if a person she has sent to her father's to convey messages from the angel gets back before she can finish singing hymn 146 in the first book of Isaac Watts's hymnal, she will know that the spirit visiting her is of God, not the devil. "When I had sung the greater part of the hymn, the remainder appeared as if covered with a cloud, so that not a word or letter appeared. At first, I was some surprised; but a voice appeared to say, This is the sign, for which you prayed."[32] She was later empowered to read the Bible in the dark and she depicted at length an encounter with Satan in which he was bent on taking her bible away from her.[33]

The last, and perhaps most important, element of biblical print culture affecting early national visionary writings was that the biblical text itself invited the adoption and performance of visionary roles. Visionaries and those around them used explicit biblical precedent to justify and make sense of visionary claims. "In looking over the pages of divine revelation, we find that Jehovah has frequently discovered his will in dreams, and raised up persons to explain them," a minister named William Rogers wrote in a postscript to Ashburn's vision.[34] The Bible's own openness to postscript was an important part of legitimating visionary writings; visionaries echoed the various elisions and lacunae of the Bible itself. When Willey wrote that her angelic guide "spake many more precious words, which, as I thought, concerned me, and which I never told any person," she invoked biblical passages such as John 20:30.[35] "[M]illions of new objects presented to my view, which is impossible for mortal to describe," Say wrote.[36] Norris Stearns, like Say, neatly and explicitly inserted his visions into the biblical canon by invoking 2 Corinthians 12:2: "St. Paul said he knew a man in Christ (so many years ago) such an one, caught up to the third Heaven, and in Paradise heard unspeakable words, which is not lawful for man to utter. But in *this generation* they are to be uttered."[37] Perhaps the scripturalized assumptions of visionaries' written accounts are most apparent in the fact that they declined to foreclose the possibility of yet more revelation.

Chief among the scriptural entry points for visionary activity in this period was Joel 2:28.

> And it shall come to pass afterwards, that I will pour out my spirit upon all flesh, and your sons and your daughters shall prophesy, and your old men dream dreams, and your young men see visions.

Joel 2:28 permeated early national print culture. Zilpha Elaw cited this verse to contextualize her preaching; William Rogers cited it in support of Rebecca Ashburn; it served as an epigraph to the visions of both Caleb Pool and Isaac Childs.[38] Citing the verse in defense of ecstatic religious activity was itself a sort of act of performed biblicism: the apostle Peter cited it in Acts 2, to explain Pentecost. James McNemar cited it in this vein, to explicitly link the Kentucky revivals to their New Testament model.[39]

Joel 2:28 provides the epigraph for all known manuscript and print copies *The Vision of Isaac Childs*, a widely circulated but little-remembered text that offers a particularly rich study of the scripturalized terms of visionary authority in the late colonial and early national periods. The versions of Childs's text are both subtly and not-so-subtly different, but the epigraph is present without fail. Its consistent presence across eighteen surviving manuscripts suggest that Childs himself—a "young man" of twenty-three when he recorded his vision—

(2)

❖✕◇✕◇✕◇✕◇✕◇✕◇✕◇✕◇✕◇✕◇✕◇✕*❖*

And it shall come to pass afterwards, that I will pour out my spirit u on all flesh, and your sons and your daughters shall prophesy, and your old men dream dreams, and your young men see visions. Joel ii. 28.

IN the appearance, which is not of man, nor according to man, I looked, and beheld a great mountain; 1--2 And thereon stood candlesticks of gold, of silver, of brass and iron, and in them were candles, some of them burning bright and clear, and some appeared dull, and almost gone out, and some were gone out quite.

3 And others were covered with vails to defend them from storms, for they were all standing open to the firmament; and whilst I looked, behold, the light of the sun disappeared for a short season, and clouds, and darkness, and storms, and tempests, came and beat upon the mountain; then the candlesticks (which were men) were left in thick darkness, for their candles were beaten out, and some of them overthrown; and whilst I was looking off the walls of the mountain, which was built of pure gold and precious stones,

4 There appeared a numerous company from another country, following *ignus fatus,* and their leader rode a scarlet coloured beast, and his name was Oppression and Defence; and when they that sat in darkness upon the mountain, saw the multitude which came forth, they went forth from the mountain, and broke over the precious walls that were round it, and went to the leader of the multitude, and honoured him with great honour, and some joined with him in his host, and followed *ignus fatus,* and they rejoiced, saying, We will do valiently, for our God is with us, and we will tread down our enemies, and every one that riseth up to oppress us; and others gave him money and many great gifts, saying, Go forth with thy army, and bear down those storms and tempests.

5 So he went forth with his company, and fought against, but could not prevail; and they which remained in darkness upon the mountain (*a*), made war with the golden candlesticks, whose light appeared bright, and ceased not from shining; but they were not able so much as to dim the light thereof neither they nor the tempests that beat against them; for they fled to a great tower, which was in the midst of the mountain.

6 When they who were in darkness, were grievously perplexed and pricked in their hearts, and gathered themselves together, (*a*) and considered one with another, saying, Let us build ourselves places of refuge, whereunto we may flee in time of trouble (*b*); and they took the holy name of the God of heaven in vain,

FIGURE 4.1. Pages 2 (*above*) and 3 (*opposite*) from *The Vision of Isaac Childs* (Philadelphia[?]: n.p., 1766a). Images courtesy of the Library Company of Philadelphia.

most likely wrote it into the original copy. The biblical entry point was integral to the text.

Childs—the family name is also given as Child in eighteenth-century sources—was born to a Quaker family in 1734 in Bucks County, Pennsylvania.[40] He appears in Quaker records as an active but unremarkable member

(3)

vain, faying, He will be with us, and go forth with our armies; and they made themfelves preparations for war (c).

7 And as I looked, one came forth in his glorious appearance, and cried, faying, Ceafe ye to make unto yourfelves martial preparations, and inftruments of war and of defence; for behold, there is in this mountain a fafe hiding place (a); and the walls they are fure (b): But many believed not, for they were in darknefs, and hardnefs of heart overcame them, fo that they gave no heed unto him nor his meffengers, which he fent unto many that remain exercifing themfelves in martial manner; and there came forth a voice from on high, faying to him that appeared, Remove the golden wall and bulwarks from about this mountain, for they have exalted themfelves in their own ftrength (c), and have forgotten the mighty power, which is a place of refuge in the midft thereof (d), who built the walls, and fet the candlefticks, and light the candles that are therein; and he faid, Let the tower remain therein (e), and he that is able to flee unto it, let him flee, and be fafe, for I am determined what I will do unto this place.

8 And fuddenly the walls, which were of gold and precious ftones, were taken away from about the mountain, and the wild boar of the foreft entered into the borders thereof, and raged in his fury, for his chains were loofed (a), and he was releafed out of his prifon, and began to remove many candlefticks, and affayed to deftroy the whole mountain, and the cry of the widow and orphans began to be heard in the land, and they were greatly diftreffed who trufted in the holy name of JESUS, whofe light ftill appeared; and they mourned and wept for the candlefticks that were removed out of their places, and for the golden walls that were taken from about them (b).

9 And there appeared an angel of the Higheft, having in his right hand golden fnuffers, and he paffed through the midft of the mountain, and fnuffed the candles that were dim, and gave of the golden oil, running through the golden pipes, from the two golden olives that ftand before the Lord on high, and he fpake comfortably unto them, and told them, that it was for the curfed fodomy (a), and great forfaking the Lord their God, that they were thus judged; but he faid, Fear ye not, although the ancient walls are removed from about this place, it is but that the wicked may have the reward of their works, and the land be cleanfed from the pollutions thereof, for there is an horrible rebellion in the land, and turning afide from the way of the righteous, provoking the Holy One by fin and tranfgreffion, and breaking the holy covenant of the moft high God (b).

10 Thus faith the Lord, I have turned my hand againft this place for evil, and I will give the people over to the furnace of affliction, and he that cometh forth, fhall be as pure gold tried in the fire, more pure than the golden wedge of Ophir; and he

)(2

that

of monthly meetings within the Philadelphia Yearly Meeting until his death in 1769.[41] All copies of his visionary account indicate that it was first written in 1757; Childs is not known to have written anything else. The manifestly biblical imagery of the vision is a pastiche of allegory: there are candlesticks made of metals of varying values and purity, a mountain, a tower, a rampaging wild

(8)

THE
EXPLANATION.

1 THIS mountain is the Quaker profeffion, or yearly meeting, in Pennfylvania.
2 Shews the members, under the term of candlefticks, and
thofe who were born fons. By candles, and thofe which fhined
bright, were fuch who bore a clear teftimony againft the idol
difcipline : They had not only oil in their lamps, but lighted
alfo, and burning bright.
3 As thofe in this verfe, being covered, fhews fome, who,
in their private opinion, were one with the bright ones ; their
lamps were alfo lighted, but kept under cover, for fear of the
yearly meeting authority, and felect party:——Whofe committees, to deal with fuch who could not conform to difcipline,
were the clouds that carried thofe ftorms which darkened the
light of the Spirit of God in almoft all the members minds;
and as fome were overthrown, it fhews that fome were overcome by thofe ftorms, and their faith failed in the light of
Chrift, in their own hearts ; and they put their truft in, and
depended upon the wall for fecurity, which was difcipline;
being built of, or compofed of fuch laws and rules as was truly
the inward law of God's own Spirit ; that is, where men truly,
by the dictates of God's own Spirit, made confcience of things,
and according as they walked, as to outward actions, by the
leading of that Spirit;—this was collected into writing, and
made into a law of difcipline; thus was this idol, or wall, in
which they trufted, made of precious ftones.
4 But this company, from another country, fhews the natural
man acting, exactly in all outward appearance, to this law,
while yet ftrangers to the work of converfion; following the direction of this difcipline and orders, fenfe, judgments and ap-
pointments of the meetings of bufinefs, which is *ignus fatus* ;
for every man and woman that ever acted in any fervice of a
religious nature, by virtue of their appointment from a meeting, fo far as that appointment was their warrant, or motive of
inducement, fo far they followed *ignus fatus*, whofe prime
leader to all the inferior meetings, is the authority of the yearly
meeting. This authority is the fcarlet coloured beaft ; becaufe
fcarlet is the kingly colour here in the kingdom of England ;
and it is to fignify, that it has a fhew of kingly or royal authority: And as in its very nature it oppreffes, which begets
defence, fo oppreffion and defence is its proper name. (That
its very nature is to opprefs, will be fhewn at large in a work
now preparing for the prefs, wherein the myftery of *Babylon* will
be

FIGURE 4.2. Pages 8 (*above*) and 9 (*opposite*) from *The Vision of Isaac Childs* (Philadelphia[?]: n.p., 1766a). Images courtesy of the Library Company of Philadelphia.

boar, and savior figures both true and false. The text conjures visions of biblical objects and scenes indirectly (e.g., the "golden candlesticks" appeared in Revelation; an angel descends bearing a live coal from the altar of God, invoking Isaiah 6:6), and with direct quotations (e.g., an injunction to "incline your hearts to wisdom, and learn understanding" [Proverbs 2:2]).[42]

(9)

be fully ſhewn and demonſtrated to be moſt compleat in the
Quakers.) The natural man, thus acting according to the
very exact copy of the living world, while yet entire ſtrangers
to it, deceived thoſe who had once known it, and were darkened
again by this great outward ſhew; ſo that they went forth from
the true living word of God, in their own heart, which was
going out of the very profeſſion: Omitting juſtice and judgment, is alſo breaking over the rule, becauſe this is the end
and deſign; and breaking over the very wall, whoſe very firſt
foundation was laid by the firſt Quakers, not to ſtir or act but in
God's power only; but inſtead thereof, their eyes are turned
to the leader of this multitude, namely, the orders and authority of the yearly meeting; him they honour, and in that they
truſt, and alſo rejoice; yea, alſo ſay, that we will do valiantly,
for our God is with us. It is high time to riſe againſt the
mighty, (has been a common ſaying in meetings of buſineſs,
by the ſelect party) meaning ſuch who call the authority of the
body of friends in queſtion, and the authority of the yearly
meeting. Let the diſcipline be put in practice, and compare
this with the latter part of this verſe; as alſo, the yearly collections to print epiſtles, with private gifts to traveling friends,
who are valiant for this cauſe; obſerve alſo by the way, that
though, as hinted in (3), thoſe committees were the very
clouds, ſet to work by this authority, which carried or occa-
ſioned all contention, tempeſts and ſtorms, or ſtrife; yet they
themſelves aſſigned the cauſe to an oppoſite ſpirit.—Having ſet
the reader on the tract or true ſent of the meaning of this viſion,
ſhall now but juſt give a hint of matters in ſhort, in order to
leſſen the bulk of the book,

5 (a) Such who had known the truth, made war alſo againſt
thoſe whoſe light ſhined to diſcover this falſe idol diſcipline;
but could not dim it. Witneſs that nine years ago the authority of the yearly meeting was ſcarce queſtioned; Quakers were
ſtartled, (as I remember J-n C-n ſaid, I marveled at it) if any
drop'd ſuch an expreſſion: And now it is become a fire ſide
and table talk. Thoſe tempeſts here relate to the diſcourage-
ments thrown in the way, as calling us heathens, ranters, ſe-
paratiſts; and the works (or uſe made of them) of *Barclay's*
Anarchy, *Ellwood's* works, and others, on or touching this
point, who had once known the truth. This proves a hard
labour, even if it were poſſible to deceive the very elect; yet
a number has witneſſed all this, not ſo much as able to dim the
light, for they laboured diligently, and found the pearl of great
price; that is, appealed only to the witneſs of truth in their
own hearts; this is the tower againſt the moſt plauſible outward appearance.

6 (a) Meetings, conferences, &c. (b), let us make a new
rule of diſcipline; (now began the diſcipline to vary from being
a true

The gist of it is that the inhabitants of the mountain (the candlesticks)
believe it to be secure, but it is not. Only the "great tower, which was in the
midst of the mountain" provides unbreachable safety from the various perils
that threaten the candlesticks. Only some of the candlesticks, moreover, can
take refuge in the tower—for many, it is closed. In the course of the vision those
barred from the tower suffer a variety of afflictions, culminating in being cast

into "a great furnace," where they are either destroyed or purified into candle-sticks "all of pure gold set round with precious stones."[43] In all versions the basic position of the speaker remains the same; Childs's voice comes through in the insistent "I saw" of the visionary.

The text as written was a familiar type of open-ended allegory that invited application. For example, readers could identify an elect people and a not-so-elect people, some portion of whom realized redemption only through suffer-ing. In contrast to most of the visionary texts discussed above, Childs's symbol-laden, obscurant vision had no internally prescribed meaning. The title page of Caleb Pool's *News from Heaven*, for example, proclaimed that the message was "communicated miraculously to, and explained by, Caleb Pool," and throughout the text Pool pipes up to explain the meaning of the symbols in his visions.[44] In its original form, by contrast, the allegorical sweep of Childs's text keyed the reader to Revelation and invited application without offering guidance. However, while most contemporary English editions of Revelation offered readers annotated guidance in interpreting the imagery, the first readers of Childs's vision had no recourse to paratextual materials that would have suggested any particular applications of the text's symbols. The first manuscripts bore no commentary, and no studies of *The Vision of Isaac Childs* were floating around popular print culture. Over the course of more than a century and a half after its writing, though, a bevy of commenta-tors, editors, and readers created paratextual material that facilitated the ap-plication of the text to their own circumstances. This history offers a rare chance to witness the ways that scripturalization affected both texts and read-ers as it unfolded.

To start (appropriately for a process of scripturalization) in the middle: *The Vision of Isaac Childs* achieved its greatest popularity in the two decades or so after 1826. In that year it was printed for what was at least the fifth time, but accompanied by brand-new and extensive paratextual materials that both shored up the authority of the text and applied it very specifically to the Hick-site controversy, a dispute then raging among American Quakers. Elias Hicks, an elderly Long Island Quaker minister, had been for years exhorting Friends to reemphasize the ideal of the Inner Light, leaving off what he considered sinful outward forms and worldly things. In 1826, Hicks's movement—sharply critical of the Quaker status quo—had precipitated a breaking point that would eventually result in permanent schism and the creation of parallel Hick-site and "Orthodox" arms of American Quakerism. Some supporters of Hicks latched onto Childs's vision as a prophecy of their moment.[45]

The 1826 edition was published in Philadelphia as a twenty-four-page pamphlet by bookseller John Simmons. It was advertised for sale in a general-audience (not strictly Quaker) newspaper at least as early as February of 1826.[46] The new extra material was unsigned, but the title page made clear that it was not by Childs but "from another hand." This other hand instrumentalized the scripturalized assumptions of the early national period by orienting Childs's text toward the religious controversies of his or her own day. While the text remained more or less consistent with a manuscript tradition going back more than seventy years, the novel annotations demonstrated the flexible terms for making meaning in a scripturalized environment.

First, the preface reiterated concern for the reliability of the text. The editor added material from two affidavits about Childs originally published in 1787, in a collective biography of notable Quakers.[47] These, the editor insisted, demonstrated Childs to have been "a man of large natural capacity" and, importantly, "of sound mind and understanding."[48] With respect to the text itself, as advertised in the preface, the editor of the 1826 edition described "considerable pains" endured to "obtain a correct copy" of Childs's vision—fetishizing the integrity of the text and rhetorically emphasizing his or her fidelity to it.

As a means of establishing Childs's visionary authority, the editor of the 1826 edition elaborated on the text's history. This became the first written account of the originating moment of Childs's text, and it linked the reliability of the oral revelation to the immediacy of its first writing: "At the time of the revelation thus made to his mental view, he was in his harvest field; and that his labourers perceived he was under some very serious impression, by his standing still for some time. After which he went to the house, and wrote the vision that he had seen, for the purpose of publishing it."[49] This story was likely gleaned from Childs's youngest daughter, who—according to a subsequent 1830 edition clearly based on the 1826—kept the original manuscript and had a hand in its printing. She would have been very young when Childs died, however, and no surviving contemporary sources attest to this story.

The 1826 editorial preface went on to say that Childs was "discouraged or prevented, by some of his friends, from having it published," and that he resented this. The same preface, though, says that numerous copies were made and spread among Childs's "friends and others." This much, at least, is confirmed by the survival of at least eighteen manuscripts with varied transcription and circulation histories.

After emphasizing Childs's credibility, the prefatory materials of the 1826 edition argued for its own textual reliability by explaining discrepancies with earlier editions. The editor remarked dismissively on the rumor of an eighteenth-century printed edition: "[I]t is said, a small edition was printed about the time of the American Revolution; with some attempts to explain it, as a prediction of that event."[50] This likely refers to the first printings of the text in 1766. The editor of the 1826 edition was more explicit about rejecting the textual integrity of the edition nearest his or her own. "Another small edition was published," the preface says, "from an incorrect copy, in the year 1814."[51] The 1814 edition is, indeed, markedly different from all but one other known copy of the text, a manuscript with edits and corrections that suggest it may have served as a source for the 1814 printing.[52]

The 1826 editor argued for both this edition's definitive identity as the *Vision of Isaac Childs,* and for the importance of having a definitive text, by invoking the same formulas of originality used by contemporary bible publishers, editors, and translators. "To obtain a correct copy of the original," the editor wrote, "considerable pains have been taken; and the publisher believes the following to be such a one." Just as with bibles themselves, the reliability of the text could be established vis-à-vis an imagined ideal even while paratextual materials oriented reading and inflected meaning. While establishing a reliable base text, this editor adapted it to new purposes by overlaying it with paratexts that applied it to the Hicksite controversy. Indeed, the more distant the application from the original revelation, the more important it became that the original revelation was recorded precisely and transmitted reliably. The 1826 editor avers that it was the text's perceived prophetic relevance to events seventy years removed from its original writing that drove him or her to seek out a precisely accurate copy to reissue: "Many friends apprehending the vision to have some particular reference to the present time, or state of the Religious World, have expressed a wish that a correct edition might be presented to the public; in order that the important doctrine and council therein contained may be spread, for the instruction and benefit of those who have 'ears to hear what the Spirit saith unto the Churches.'"[53] The last bit—a line repeated like a challenge in Revelation—notably reinscribed Childs's own appropriations of the biblical text.

The text of the 1826 edition does conform to the bulk of the manuscript tradition. This editor's commentary, however, brought it a novel relevance to the Hicksite controversy. The reapplication of the text begins on the title page. Many earlier print and manuscript versions of the *Vision* have a line following the title indicating that it was presented to Childs with reference to "the land of his nativity." In the first published versions and a few of the existing manuscripts this is identified simply as Pennsylvania, but in the 1826 edition the "land" is a metaphor, not a statement about geography: it is identified as "[t]he spiritual profession of Christianity, particularly as held by the Society of Friends, of which he was a member." Likewise, the commentator identified the mountain in the text as the "profession of the spirituality of the Christian religion," and here added a biblical flourish of his or her own by citing Isaiah 3, associating the marks of pride in that text (fancy clothes and jewelry) with a prideful but ultimately empty "great and exalted profession of the spirituality of the Christian religion."[54]

The Hicksite appropriation of the text continues throughout the footnotes. As opposition to external forms and discipline in favor of the Inner Light was the essence of Hicksite complaints, Childs's vision offered a skeleton on which to hang theological critique.[55] The "vails" which cover some of the candlesticks "to defend them from storms" were glossed as "[c]arnal or fleshly ideas of spiritual things—human policy, and human reason for defence of the faith, derived through the external senses—traditions and prejudices."[56] The "numerous company from another country" who caused unrest in Childs's vision were glossed in this version as "[p]rofessors of Christianity, having other views less spiritual." Notably, this included not just "observers of days, of outward ordinances, and external forms and ceremonies," but also "trinitarians," a telltale nod to the author's Hicksite positions.[57] (Hicks taught that Christ was an exemplary man who achieved divinity, rejecting the Trinitarian assumptions of traditional Quakers.)[58] Amidst the Hicksite challenge to the wealthy Quaker elite, the 1826 edition claimed that the "cursed sodomy" for which some of the candlesticks are judged harshly by God represented "[p]ride, spiritual pride, or self-exaltation—fullness of bread and abundance of idleness, is sodomy or the sin of Sodom."[59]

Interestingly, the footnotes in the 1826 edition end abruptly not quite halfway through the text. Material evidence suggests, though, that their effect was realized. Two copies of the 1826 edition at the Friends Historical Library at Swarthmore College and one at the Library Company of Philadelphia have been bound into nineteenth-century collections of Hicksite polemical pamphlets.[60] A copy at the American Antiquarian Society has a penciled comment in a margin endorsing the commentator's application of the *Vision* to contemporary affairs: "[V]ery applicable at the present."[61]

The text of the 1826 edition became the standard version of the *Vision of Isaac Childs* for the next few decades. It was published next in Baltimore in 1830 and again in 1837 at Sandy Hill, New York, in the Hudson Valley. The text and paratexts of these editions were identical to the 1826 version, except that the 1830 edition was more specific in shoring up readers' confidence in the source manuscript: on the title page and in a line inserted into the preface, Childs's daughter, Rachel Atkinson, was named as the bearer of the "original manuscript" from which this edition had been printed. The 1830 edition's publisher, William Wooddy, was Atkinson's son-in-law and a well-known Hicksite printer.

John Simmons, the publisher of the 1826 edition, put out a new edition in 1840 with an expanded version of the 1826 notes covering more of the text. In the 1840 edition, the notes were refined again to make explicit connections to both Hicksite Quakerism and the American Revolution. For example, a footnote told readers that the "numerous company from another country" signified British troops and that those who "sat in darkness"—disaffected Quakers in 1826, "full of bitterness and envy"—were American Loyalists.[62] The 1840 footnotes also added another new adversary to the vision: "Creaturely and officious efforts of such who were unsanctified."[63] Some well-meaning candlesticks, that is, "opened a door to the formation of popular societies to put down evil, such as Abolition, Tract, Bible, Peace, Anti-slavery, Temperance societies, &c. &c.," that were both sinful and doomed to fail. This reflects midcentury objections, from Hicksite Quakers and others, that voluntary societies drew

The Vision of Isaac Childs, which he saw concerning the Land of his Nativity —

And it shall come to pass afterward that I will pour out my Spirit upon all flesh, and your sons and your daughters shall prophecy, your old men shall dream dreams, and your young men shall see visions:

Isaiah 2nd Chapt. 28 Verse —

In that appearance that is not of man nor accountable to man, I looked and behold a great and high mountain and thereon stood candlesticks of gold, of silver, of brass and of iron, and there were candles in them. Three or some of them burning very bright and clear, and some appeared dull and almost gone out, and others were covered with vails to defend them from storms, for they were all standing open to the firmament. And whilst I looked the candlesticks became men and walked up and down in the mountain, and I looked and behold the light of the sun disappeared for a short season and clouds of darkness and storms and tempests came and beat upon the mountain, then the candlesticks over which were veils had the veils rent from over them and the candlesticks which were men were left in thick darkness, for their candles were beaten out, and some of them were overthrown, and whilst I looked off the wall of the mountain, which was built of gold and precious stones, there appeared a numerous company from another country following Ignis Fatuus, and their leader rode upon a scarlet coloured beast and his mind was opposition and defence. And when they which sat in darkness upon the mountain saw the multitude which came forth from the mountain and broke over the precious wall that was round about, and went to the leader of the multitude and honoured him with great honour, and some of them joined him with his host and followed Ignis Fatuus with him, and they rejoiced saying, we will do valiantly for our God is with us, and will tread down our enemies even every one that riseth up to oppose us. And others gave him much money and other great gifts saying, go forth with thine armey and beat down those storms and tempests whereby we are so tormented, so he went forth with his armey and beat against them but could not prevail. And they which remained in darkness upon the mountain made war with the golden candlesticks whose light appeared bright and ceased not from shining, but they were not able so much as to dim the light thereof, neither they nor the tempests that beat against them, for they fled to a tower that was in the midst of the mountain. Then they which were in darkness were grievously perplexed & pruned in their hearts, and they gathered themselves together and conspired with one another saying let us build ourselves places of refuge whereunto we may flie in the time of trouble. And they took the name of the great Eye of Heaven in vain saying, he will be with us as we go forth with our armies, and they made themselves martial preparations for war. And as I looked one came forth in his glorious appearance I cried cease to make unto your selves martial preparations and instruments of war & defence, for behold there is in this mountain a safe hiding place and the walls thereof are sure. But many believed not for they were in darkness and hardness of heart overcame them, so that they gave no heed unto him or his messengers which he sent unto many that remained exercising themselves in a martial manner. Then there came a voice from on high saying unto him that appeared.

Remove

yourselves in the time of trouble. And it shall be as long as ye remain faithful & keep my commandments, I will
bless & preserve you & your generations; And ye shall be as a mountain that cannot be removed. But if at any time your
sons or your daughters refuse or rebell & provoke you with judgments to humble you & you lift up your
heel against me in my rebuke as your fathers have done, I will surely cut you off from the land
& you shall have a name among men no more, & I will break down the precious walls that I
have set up about you & they shall never be rebuilt from now henceforth & forever. ~~and~~ For
behold, I brought your fathers from a land wherein they were oppressed & could not serve me
freely & I moved the heathen back for their sakes, tho' not by the power of the sword nor
strength of battle, but I myself rebuked them that they should not destroy mine anointed,
nor do my people any harm. And I fed your fathers in the wilderness many days & I
gave them strength to cultivate the land & blessed their labours with success, I gave them
corn in abundance & many goodly things & they increased in the land & their generations
were in prosperity & waxed fat & did not highly esteem the rock of their Salvation
& rebelled & in the time of correction they kicked. nevertheless I did not inhale their
sins unto their children neither will I, but every man shall suffer for his own
sins. And he called unto them & taught them many excellent things & commanded them to go forth & publish this doctrine wheresoever he should send them even
the glad tidings of peace & salvation to as many as believed in the name of him that
sent them & received his law & obeyed it, promising to be with them from thence-
forth & forever and evermore.

And the Lord said unto me behold I have shewed thee these things that thou
mightest make them known unto the people of this land, for I determined to do unto
it according to all thou hast seen; therefore now write these things in a book that
if any will hear and understand & be converted (if they are not) that I may heal
them & save them from the great hour of temptation that cometh upon all flesh.

And the Lord said unto me all these things are true & many more also, nthless
that which I have commanded thee to write, write, for I will be clear of the blood of all
men, & have them without excuse & because people are forsaking the measure of
the grace of God & departing from the Holy light of Jesus in their own hearts, there still
remains a necessity to prophesy & to preach the Gospel. — And as thou sawest
that judgment was to continue untill none of the Candlesticks appeared remaining
but a few gold with lights burning in them, neither shall my judgment depart
from this land untill all the inhabitants thereof learn righteousness; for I
declare to the world this day that I desire not the death of him that dieth, nor
that the sinner should die in his sins, whereby the Kingdom of Satan may be advanced; for I created man for the purpose of my own glory & have visited all
men with the light of the Son of my bosom for the complete redemption thereof
& I have waited long for the spiritual ~~destruction~~ return of fallen mankind.

And be it known to all People to whom these few Lines may
come, that notwithstanding things of this nature are something uncommon with Men, yet I dare not distrust the Wisdom of the Highest, nor disobey his Commands, nor be so much biassed by any thing carnal as to
hide the Revelation of the Son of God, as I shall answer the same at the
peril of my Soul. ———

(Copy)

Original wrote by Isaac Childs of the Province of Pennsylvania, in the
seventh Month 1757.

FIGURE 4.4. Another page from "The Vision of Isaac Childs." Undated, unsigned
manuscript copy (after 1757). Image courtesy of the Manuscripts Division, Department
of Rare Books and Special Collections, Princeton University Library.

resources, attention, and authority away from the churches and their proper concerns. That is, as new points of theological dispute arose, editors produced paratexts that continually reapplied the text. In the 1840 edition, the footnotes—crammed with quotations from other popular religious texts and with the number of exegetical suggestions growing—expanded to crowd out the text on some pages, very much like a nineteenth-century annotated bible.

The first copies of the *Vision*, however, had no footnotes. Though none of the versions before 1826 tells the story of Childs's visionary moment, all complete copies indicate that he first wrote the vision down in July of 1757. It is unclear how Childs himself initially publicized the work, but it is clear that it became well known among Quakers in Philadelphia and beyond. All eighteen existing manuscripts are more or less the same in terms of text. The number and consistency of manuscripts that circulated indicate that readers took this biblically resonant text seriously, treating it with the significance of scripture. Only a few have the names of their copyists or owners attached, but those that do indicate that copies of the vision were passed down through families.[64] Some are written on folded foolscap; others are folded and sewn into manuscript booklets. Two copies are elegantly written and tightly bound in heavy blue papers, one with the title written across the front cover. Many copies, including one owned by George Dillwyn, a Quaker minister and contemporary of Childs, contain marginal comments and other marks of close reading.[65]

The manuscripts reveal audiences' responses to Childs's biblically resonant performance. The Dillwyn copy has marginal numbering written in, allowing for discrete parts of the text to be identified. A reader's notes (most likely Dillwyn's) augment Childs's biblical allusions with references to chapter and verse, and verbatim quotes. Here and there they also offer glosses on Childs's allegories specific to the context in which the reader thought they applied: where the text discusses those who gave "much Money and many great gifts" to a false leader, one reader wrote, "[S]ides with them, voted for them," making plain this reader's conclusion that this referred to support rendered in the democratic context of a Quaker meeting.[66]

Dillwyn was active in the Philadelphia Quaker community when Childs first wrote his vision, and his reading was conditioned by events in that setting. Childs's vision first appeared smack in the middle of a time of significant controversy in the Quaker community. Childs came of age during a period of reformation among American Quakers beginning in the late 1740s, in the Philadelphia Yearly Meeting, of which he was a member in good standing for his entire life. Initially spurred by a handful of particularly serious ministers, between 1748 and the American Revolution the Society of Friends largely withdrew from what had been an active presence in American politics and society. Quaker meetings raised their standards for membership, subjecting members to rigorous and frequent review of their behavior. The Quaker "Discipline" was reemphasized and "disownings" became commonplace. Reformers placed particular emphasis on sexual misconduct, improper relations with non-Friends, and violations of Quaker pacifism. These measures had especially serious repercussions for well-to-do Quakers, who moved easily within elite colonial society and often held civil or financial positions that implicated them in military affairs.[67]

Childs was active among the reformers.[68] He himself married properly, according to strict Quaker requirements, and served frequently on disciplinary committees, as documented along with his other activities as a minister during the last eleven years of his life. Because of the level of behavioral oversight that tight-knit Quaker communities demanded for their members, Quakers kept particularly good records, and nowhere in the records of the Philadelphia Yearly Meeting is there a mention of Childs's visionary activities. A posthumous endorsement of his character from the Abington meeting may allude to his writing, noting that God "called him forth when but young, to publish the glad tidings," but in Quaker parlance that likely just referred to his becoming a minister.[69] Childs could have been subject to censure for publishing a vision—seven Quakers in the Philadelphia Yearly Meeting were investigated for "printing" between 1682 and 1776.[70] Writing was further fraught for Quakers because of the very things reformers like Childs were concerned about: their emphasis on discipline went hand-in-hand with an ambivalent relationship with written scripture. The Quakers who passed around these written scriptures privileged the spiritual inspiration of the Inner Light, unwritten and untransferable, but not even they could escape the scripturalized terms of religious authority.[71]

In the vision's lengthy coda, Childs struggled with the paradox he was presenting. After being commanded by God to "write all these things in a book," he asks why. Given that Christ has "come to teach his People himself" through the direct impression of the Spirit, Childs recounts himself suggesting to God, "[T]here may be no more Occasion for any man to teach his neighbors[,] his Neighbor[,] or his brother the knowledge of the Lord." God responds that he wishes to be "Clear of the Blood of all Men and have them without excuse": the written text is intended to make things as explicit as possible. Childs then acknowledges that though "things of this Nature at this time are something Uncommon among Men," he could not disobey a direct command of heaven. Childs's text marks the tension that Quakers faced in a scripturalized culture. Quakers' openness to direct inspiration made them simultaneously less dependent on written scripture while being more likely to have visions that they and their audiences would feel compelled to publish.

Childs himself, finally, is a case study in this tension. The 1826 preface depicted him as an anxious visionary frustrated that his fellow Quakers discouraged him from printing his vision. As noted, though, that preface also reported on the rumor of a "small edition . . . printed about the time of the American Revolution." This most likely refers to two printings of the text in 1766, in which Childs almost certainly had a hand.[72] One notable aspect of these two editions is that they have nothing to do with the American Revolution, as would later be rumored. The most significant thing about them, however, is that they have an extensive set of endnotes, most likely written by Childs himself.

Underscoring the potential repercussions of printing a visionary text, neither 1766 edition bears a publisher's name, a place of publication, or the name of an editor. It is likely, though, that Childs, who lived until 1769, oversaw at least one of these printings and wrote the annotations himself. If the later prefatory account is to be believed, Childs nurtured a wish to have the vision printed, in recognition of the advantages of increased circulation. The minutes of Childs's monthly meeting show him travelling to and through Philadelphia a handful of times in 1765 and 1766. The idiosyncratic capitalization of one of the impressions, moreover, resembles work done by the print shop of Joseph Crukshank, who was responsible for a variety of contemporary Quaker publications by noted Quaker abolitionist Anthony Benezdet, with whom Childs preached and traveled.[73]

Like many of the manuscripts, these first printed editions demonstrate assumptions about what "scripture" looks like. Again, the epigraph from Joel sets the tone and invites the reader to place what follows into a biblical context. Also, like some of the manuscripts, these first printed editions have numbering in the margins, but it is more regular; each paragraph is numbered. The commentary appended to these first print editions is substantial—about eighty percent as long as the text itself. Lowercase letters have been introduced into the text, nestled in parentheses, and these correspond to lengthy explanations of the symbols and events, in a clear echo of contemporary biblical annotations. If this commentary was not written by Childs himself, it was written by someone else taking responsibility for explaining and applying the text in very specific ways. It does not, as the 1826 preface would suggest, attempt to make a connection between the vision and the revolution. The commentary offers a precise explanation of the allegories used in the text, applying them to the struggles within the Philadelphia Yearly Meeting during Childs's time: the candlesticks are people, the wall is the Quaker Discipline, and the Mountain is the Philadelphia Yearly Meeting.

This localization of the text's relevance begins on the title pages of both editions, which stipulate that Childs saw a vision "concerning Pennsylvania, the land of his nativity," the same "land" that Hicksite commentary would turn into "spiritual Christianity." A handful of casual asides in the commentary further localize the text; the author refers blithely to "J-n C-n," almost certainly John Churchman, a leading reformer, and to the "dry unnatural seasons and Indian war" that Philadelphia Quakers routinely referred to in their local controversies as deserved scourges sent by God for their sins.[74]

What is most interesting about the commentary is the work the annotations do to legitimate the text as revelation and identify its readers in a scripturalized culture. In these editions, Childs entirely eliminated the conversation with God about the appropriateness of circulating written revelation. Instead, the commentary—which elsewhere chastises the Philadelphia Yearly Meeting for its devotion to "paper gods"—explains that the "mighty river" that features in the vision's imagery is a promise of "the voice of God, sent out in writing, as well as verbal testimonies." These testimonies, the commentary promises, "will come out so thick, as to overflow and sweep away all tradition, sense and judgment of weighty friends (so called) out of men's minds, to serve the living God, and not idols, composed of a body of men and women."[75]

Even as a Quaker devoted to the authority of the Inner Light, Childs—and all of those Quakers who copied out his vision—could not escape the importance of written scripture in a culture that expected it. In annotating a text that he himself had written, Childs actually subordinated *his own* visionary authority to the written scripture. The text of the 1766 printings bears only cosmetic differences from the manuscript tradition; Childs, if he was the editor, did not significantly alter what he had written, but he did refine his word choice. Tellingly, the most significant textual edit that Childs made to his own written revelation was removing the coda in which he questioned God about the value of written revelation. Where he wanted to suggest how his vision should be read, he took recourse only to the tools of annotation at his disposal in the scripturalized environment of late colonial America.

Ultimately, however, the 1766 editions underscore the contingency of scriptural authority and the uncertain relationship between manuscript and print in the late eighteenth century. In the refinements to word choice, the removal of the coda, and the commentary, the 1766 editions differ from all other copies, print or manuscript. Though they do not match any extant manuscripts, they most likely represent Childs's own final version of his vision. Moreover, they appear to have had no influence on any of the known nine subsequent printed editions. Only a few of the extant manuscripts are dated, and all of those were copied after 1766. For whatever reason, the 1766 printings did not circulate widely, and the manuscript tradition passed them by. The next printing of the text was a 1791 German edition, and this and all subsequent editions drew on a manuscript tradition that ignored the 1766 printing—the earliest commentary and the textual revisions were lost. The German version includes the manuscript coda in which Childs questions God about publishing his vision. It also includes yet another unique set of annotations that alter the application of the text; here the "other country" from which a warring company comes is identified as New England, for example.[76]

By the time of the 1826 edition, the 1766 printings were just a rumor. After 1840, *The Vision of Isaac Childs* next appeared in upstate New York during the

Civil War. Over a century after it was written, the original local context was lost. The title page was carefully reworked to include all of the typical parts, but in a different order. Childs, as the author, is given historical specificity as a resident of "Plumstead, Bucks County, Pennsylvania," but this geographic specificity is now separated from "the land of his Nativity," which now clearly becomes America itself. When the text was next published, in 1883, it was in Emporia, Kansas. While the publisher himself had Pennsylvania Quaker ties, it is difficult to imagine that many local readers knew where exactly Plumstead, Bucks County, was. The vision was last printed in 1929. Though there is no evidence that this tiny pamphlet had much of a readership, a copy at Haverford College has been carefully corrected against the Kansas edition. The text is now an object of Quaker history: the editor of this last version added a new epigraphic prayer that places Childs among Quaker "forefathers."

Early national visionary accounts—written and oral, hand-copied and printed, treasured and forgotten—were the products of scripturalized subjects. Their pretension to novelty, by conjuring both new, extrabiblical seers and communities of audience members identified by their attention to that novel seer, makes them ideal windows onto the scripturalized terms of religious authority in the early national period. Each one was, immediately, an author's bid for authority: a claim to special access to the divine on a biblical model and a demonstration of biblical facility. They hailed audiences as those to whom a special message was addressed. In a larger sense, they intervened in the same discursive field that made them possible. They were sites of complex negotiations of authority, between scriptures and their margins, among authors and their sources, audiences, and texts.

What, though, were the stakes of visionary authority? Later editors and readers of Childs's vision found it authoritative and tried to make it so for others in different contexts. If he is the author of the 1766 notes, this would suggest that Childs at least aspired to intervene in the controversies in his own community. Childs's relationship to embodied, personal authority is ambivalent, but other visionaries were more explicit about their personal assumption of authority. Chloe Willey did not preach, but she did seek to directly inform the praying and preaching of others. During her thirty-day fast, she told every minister she saw to preach from Luke 21:36: "Watch, and pray." She tried to get those around her "to send for two godly ministers to fast and pray for three days, for the out-powering [sic] of God's Spirit, and the conversion of the wicked."[77] They did not listen. In other contexts she was more successful. Based on nothing but the authority she claimed accrued to her as a prophetess, Willey took on the disciplinary role occupied by ministers. While fasting, Willey declared that she could discern the saved from the damned: "[D]istinguish[,] in any company[,] saints from sinners."[78] This is a dangerous claim for anyone, especially for a woman, but at least occasionally it bore weight. "A person came to see me. I observed to him, that I had often heard him pray in public, but not from the heart; and that he partook no more of the good spiritual prayer, than the vine, that climbs around the tree, partakes of the sap and virtues of the tree itself."[79] Her chastised subject, she reported, was constrained to agree.

The next chapter will look at the scripturalized community around the most successful visionary authority of the early national period, Joseph Smith Jr., in order to clearly articulate the stakes of these claims and their effects on the status of the Bible. What distinguished Smith from other claimants to visionary authority was the way that a discursive community formed around him and his scriptural productions to extend and amplify a universe of biblical citations and performed roles.

CHAPTER FIVE

The Many Bibles of Joseph Smith

SCRIPTURALIZATION IN EARLY NATIONAL AMERICA

Therefore he caused that the words which he spake should be written and sent forth among those that were not under the sound of his voice, that they might also receive his words.

—MOSIAH 2:8[1]

On June 14, 1829, Oliver Cowdery wrote to Hyrum Smith, expressing concern for his friend's soul: "I write unto you feeling anxious for your steadfastness in the great cause of which you have been called to advocate." The specifics of that "great cause" were still in development, but it ended up as the founding of the Church of Jesus Christ of Latter-day Saints; Hyrum Smith's younger brother, Joseph, had declared himself a prophet. Though previously one of Joseph's most steadfast supporters, in the early summer of 1829 Hyrum was having doubts. Cowdery wrote to admonish him in language and symbolism that would have sounded familiar to any reader of the King James Bible:

> remember the worth of souls is great in the sight of God[;] behold the Lord Your God suffered death upon the cross after the manner of the flesh wherefore he suffered the pains of all men that all men might repent and come unto him and he hath risen again from the dead that he might bring all men unto him upon conditions of repentance, and how great is his joy in the soul that repents and behold he commandeth all men to every where to repent and [be] baptized[.][2]

Part of the letter's interest lies in the fact that Cowdery copied these lines— and about half of this letter's total content, overall—not from the Bible but from a revelation dictated by Joseph Smith sometime in the two weeks prior to June 14. Cowdery, that is, was using Smith's revelations as scripture as quickly as they were issued. Cowdery's citation of the revelation was an act of scripturalization: it created a privileged distinction between this text and other texts. As Cowdery cited the prophet's dictation to support his admonition of Hyrum, he was both making the rhetorical claim *that it was* authoritative and sending it off into the discursive space of early Mormonism *as if it were* authoritative. He invited Hyrum to accept the implicit assertion of the statement's inspired origin, an acceptance which identified Hyrum with the community of believers.

Citation is necessarily selective, though, and this selective use is further constitutive of scripturalization—it inflects meaning. Cowdery's other surviving texts indicate that he was given to a much more sentimental form of Protestantism than Joseph Smith, who emphasized God's justice much more than his love. Cowdery excerpted the portions of Smith's revelation that suited him best, but the full text had much more to say about the commandments of God than about Christ's love (some variation of "command" appears eight times in the brief revelation).

Cowdery's use of the revelation signaled his acceptance of the role in which Smith had cast himself: that of a prophet capable of issuing scripture. At the same time, the writing of the letter itself was part of Cowdery's performance of the role Smith had given him. The revelation in early June had made that role clear: "I speak unto you, even as unto Paul mine apostle, for you are called even with that same calling with which he was called." Cowdery's performance of an apostolic role is manifest not just in the general nature of an epistolary exhortation to Christian faith that quotes from scripture, but in specific features such as Cowdery's elaborate closing to the hortatory part of the letter: "I have many things to write but if the Lord will I shall shortly come unto you" (see, for example, I Timothy 3:14). Accepting the role in which Smith cast him, that is, and finding a fellow believer troubled, Cowdery did what an apostle would do, according to the biblical script: compose an epistolary encouragement. Later, he set off with a fellow apostle to preach the gospel, reported that he performed miracles, and founded churches—all the things that apostles do.[3]

This type of bible-based performance was especially pronounced in the scripturalized environment of early Mormonism, but, as chapter 3 showed, it was not at all unusual among early national Protestants. What *was* unusual was the extent to which early Mormons scripturalized, and became the scripturalized subjects of, new texts. This chapter explores the place of print-bible culture, citationality, performance, and the scripturalization of biblically-resonant visionary texts in earliest Mormonism. Facility with the Bible defined the early Mormon community, and this chapter argues that this skill drew on the full character of the era's print-bible culture: not just the diction of the Authorized Version, but the formats, paratextual apparatus, and translational variety of early national bibles.

In the absence of any formal ministerial training, Smith's own ability to signify on the Bible—to synthesize, compile, rearrange, allude to, and play with biblical texts—was aided by specific elements of his era's print-bible culture.[4] These include the family quarto and the carry-to-church duodecimo as bible formats; at least one published alternative (non-King-James) bible translation; and paratextual materials written by British commentators such as John Canne, Thomas Scott, and Adam Clarke. Smith drew not only from his own participation in this print environment, but chose collaborators with whom he pooled his own considerable skills and knowledge.

Beyond the content and textual apparatus they provided, moreover, the variety of biblical and parabiblical material that defined print-bible culture in Smith's era cultivated an attitude toward the Bible that made his career possible. This chapter will home in on the question of how the ongoing process of scripturalization in an environment of rapidly diversifying bible-related print affected the biblical text itself. Biblical citation changes the Bible. The proliferation of bibles and bible-related print in this era, coupled with a popular awareness of the Bible's history that had developed over the course of the eighteenth century, brought questions about the Bible's material reliability to the fore. These questions are evident in the ways Smith and his early circle approached the Bible and the scripturalization of their new texts. The rhetorical ways in which Smith's texts seek to be accepted as scriptures reflect both the material concerns of early national bible culture and the ways in which that culture dealt with those concerns. Smith's texts display an overwhelming anxiety for their own material reliability, allayed by a multiplicity of intratextual and paratextual voices vouching for that reliability. These voices cite the proliferation of similar editorial and authorial voices in contemporary print-bible culture. Late eighteenth- and early nineteenth-century bibles contained prefatory accounts of the Bible's transmission history and publishers' accounts of the care with which their bibles had been proofread and typeset, all intended to assure readers that the particular bible they were holding was *the* Bible. Translators, editors, and the authors of marginal commentaries all appealed to readers with assertions of fidelity to an ideal biblical text.[5] This chapter will argue that Smith's texts reflect the same impulse, culminating in an examination of Smith's effort, early in his career, to perfect the text of the Bible itself.

Smith voiced deep ambivalence about language and specifically about writing. "Oh Lord God deliver us in thy due time from the little narrow prison, almost . . . total darkness of paper, pen and ink; and a crooked, broken, scattered and imperfect language," he wrote to an associate in 1832.[6] At the same time, he knew that his own career was dependent on writing: like King Benjamin in the *Book of Mormon* passage that heads this chapter, he depended on publishing in order to spread his message. Smith's texts and his persona are clothed in the rhetoric of seership and prophecy, but he was obsessed with the material aspect of scriptural authority.

In the early 1820s, Joseph Smith Jr., part of a farming family in upstate New York, began telling family and acquaintants that he had been visited by an angel who promised him access to new revelation from God. This eventuated in the story of the golden plates, which, Smith reported, he dug out of a hill near his home under the angel's direction in 1827. Beginning in the spring of 1828, Smith dictated a narrative to a series of scribes that he said was translated from the text inscribed on the plates. This work culminated in the publication of the *Book of Mormon* and the founding of the Church of Jesus Christ of Latter-day Saints (originally known as the Church of Christ) in the spring of 1830.[7]

Smith laid the foundation for his church with two types of texts: ostensible translations from ancient texts, beginning with the *Book of Mormon*, and direct revelations from God. Though different in tone, scope, and effect, both sorts of texts are demonstrative of Smith's facility with the Bible and his immersion in early national print-bible culture.

Smith had learned the Bible the way a lot of people did in the early nineteenth century: from his parents. Smith's formal education amounted to little, but his mother Lucy Mack Smith—who had received most of her own education from her mother in turn—read with her children at home. Lucy was, one of her other sons recorded, "a very pious woman and much interested in the welfare of her children, both here and hereafter."[8] The modern editors of her autobiography, dictated in the winter of 1844–45, observe that Lucy herself "had an impressive gift for spontaneous sermonizing" and bible quotation.[9] Smith's father, moreover, had once been a teacher, and contemporaries in Palmyra, New York, where Smith was raised, remembered that the family held school in their home for a time, where they "studied the Bible."[10]

Nevertheless, Lucy recorded that when Joseph started having visions and teaching the family, her youngest son was not particularly literate—she remembered him some years later as "a boy sixteen years of age who had never read the Bible through by course in his life." The phrase "through by course" is significant because it juxtaposes two primary modes of bible reading: discontinuous and indexical, and diligent and systematic. Lucy measured her son's proficiency as a mother was supposed to, according to the standard of continuous, systematic reading promoted by contemporary published reading guides.[11]

While continuous reading was the stated ideal of such works, indexical reading was the practical norm encouraged by the bible culture of Smith's day. Heavily-annotated bibles and parabiblical materials such as concordances encourage flipping—hunting through a bible, following cross-references from one verse to another, "searching the scriptures," as enjoined by John 5:39. In contemporary Mormonism, the story of Smith's career begins with the First Vision, itself an account of indexical reading. While typically associated with James 1:5, the earliest written account of the First Vision—one of the few early

Mormon documents written in Smith's own hand—highlights his impulse to "search the scriptures": "At about the age of twelve years my mind become seriously imprest with regard to the all importent concerns of for the well fare of my immortal Soul which led me to searching the scriptures believeing as I was taught, that they contained the word of God. . . . By searching the scriptures I found that mand <mankind> did not come unto the Lord."[12]

Smith's bible reading is apparent in his first revelation, recorded at a time of crisis in his young career. He had been dictating the *Book of Mormon* for about two months in June of 1828 when everything fell apart. He had been reading, he said, from the golden plates, while Martin Harris, a moderately wealthy landowner who was bankrolling the project, served as scribe. In June, Harris managed to lose everything that had been written so far. During the same month, Smith's wife Emma gave birth to their first child, a boy, who died the day he was born.[13]

The only direct written evidence of Smith's reaction to this time of trouble is a revelation from God he recorded in July. It was to be the first of about a hundred and seventy such written revelations, and like all of those afterwards it is redolent of words and phrases from the King James Bible. Smith's textual productions are often thought of as pastiches of such phrases, but they are not random arrangements. Read carefully in the context of the events in his life, the content of that first revelation suggests that Smith, faced with tremendous grief both professional and personal, had done what many Christians would have: he went to his bible and read the wisdom literature. The signature phrases of that revelation, now preserved by the Church of Jesus Christ of Latter-day Saints as Doctrine and Covenants 3, echo the advice, most clearly, of Proverbs: warnings to him who "sets at naught the counsels of God" (D&C 3:4, 7, 13; Proverbs 1:25) and to those who "despise his words" (D&C 3:7; Proverbs 23:9), along with echoes made out of other distinctive words and phrases from Proverbs: "crooked paths" (D&C 3:2; Proverbs 2:15); "to the right hand nor to the left" (D&C 3:2; Proverbs 4:27); "time of trouble" (D&C 3:8; Proverbs 25:19); and "boasted in his own wisdom" (D&C 3:13; Proverbs 25:14, 23:4).[14]

Smith overcame this early setback, and the *Book of Mormon* was first published in a print run of five thousand duodecimo copies in 1830.[15] Bound in calf, from the outside it was almost indistinguishable from some of the most common bibles of the day, the brick-like duodecimos turned out in massive print runs by the American Bible Society. Between the covers, moreover, it conformed to the genre conventions of early national bibles. As many critics noted at the time, it cites the Authorized Version extensively. This is true both at the level of diction and general feel and in the fact that several often lengthy passages are copied directly from the Authorized Version. The *Book of Mormon* contains 478 verses quoted from the King James translation of Isaiah, for example, including fifteen entire chapters almost verbatim. The variations between the Isaiah of the *Book of Mormon* and that of the King James strongly suggest that Smith had a bible at hand for the insertion of these lengthy passages, because he paid careful attention to the words and phrases that are italicized in the King James Version.[16] While fewer than four percent of the words in those fifteen chapters of Isaiah are italicized, changes to italicized words account for about a fifth of the edits made to the Isaiah text as it is found in the *Book of Mormon*: about forty percent of the italicized words have been removed, replaced, or given contextualizing words and phrases, a much higher rate than applies to nonitalicized words.[17]

When they have taken up the issue of Smith's biblicism, scholars have highlighted matters of diction and of narrative form. Scholars of all stripes have noted that Smith's texts both follow the patterns of biblical narratives and read like the Authorized Version, emphasizing that the "thees" and "thous" and "it came to passes" of the *Book of Mormon*, woven into an Old-Testament-like story of warring peoples and God's justice, resonated with Smith's first audiences, "steeped in the words and rhythms of the Authorized Version."[18] There is of course something to this. Incorporating elements of the King James Version into the *Book of Mormon* is a variety of what Wimbush calls "signifying on" scripture: "[I]ndirect, deflecting, sometimes ironic, exaggerated speech" that plays off of a scriptural text and a community's recognition of that text.[19] "It is all written in imitation of the scripture style," one of its first reviewers wrote.[20]

Signifying is much more complicated than diction, though, and Smith's was no exception. Analyses that highlight only general similarities between Smith's texts and contemporary English bibles assume that Smith's bible knowledge was absorbed and that his usage of that knowledge was habitual—both radical simplifications of his engagement with the specific bible culture of his era. The bible passages inserted into the *Book of Mormon* have amazed believers and allowed critics to regard Smith as the most banal sort of plagiarist. Only a handful of scholars have looked at them from the standpoint of Smith's compositional skill. Mark D. Thomas sees in the clustering of Smith's bible references a "serious playfulness": "These phrases from the Bible interpret each other and resonate against each other in both predictable and surprising fashions."[21] Thomas identifies "clusters" of biblical phrases in the *Book of Mormon* linked by common themes and often by individual words. Ether 13:9–10, for example—"And there shall be a new heaven and a new earth; / and they shall be like unto the old, / save the old have passed away and all things have become new. / And then cometh the New Jerusalem"—contains direct quotations from Revelation 21:1–2 ("a new heaven and a new earth") and 2 Corinthians 5:17 ("old things"), verses that both contain the word "new" and the phrase "passed away." Such clustering strongly suggests the use of a concordance, where the two verses would have been listed together under the word "new"; they are so listed in Alexander Cruden's concordance, for example, the favorite of Smith's contemporary and fellow student of the Bible, William Miller.[22] Marginal cross-references might also have connected the verses for Smith. Using a bible with John Canne's marginal references (which Smith owned later, at least), it is possible to follow a path from 2 Corinthians 5:17 to Revelation 21 to Isaiah 65:17–18, another verse that is connected to the *Book of Mormon*'s Ether 13:9–10.

Combining verses from all over the Bible to create what Thomas calls a "mosaic" signifies on the Bible, cites it glancingly to conjure a new text in its interaction with a reader who gets the citation. It also echoes traditional forms of authoritative biblical reference. Smith used the same tools—concordances and indices—used by learned ministers and theologians, applying an indexical mode of reading to pull out and combine passages from the different authors, periods, and genres contained between a bible's covers. What he did with those pieces, though, was create a story rather than an argumentative sermon. Kathleen Flake has argued for a fundamentally narrative understanding of Smith's methods, observing how his texts "leverage the form, substance, and authority of the biblical myth to subvert definitive aspects of traditional Christianity." Smith, she says, "deployed the formal attributes of narrative to challenge the Christian tradition in ways not possible through discursive debate or speculative theology."[23] The methods he used to process the source material for his narratives, though—methods learned and enabled in his print-bible environment—were perfectly traditional.

Apart from Smith's use of bibles in the composition of his texts, the print-bible culture in which he lived affected his work on a conceptual level. Michael Warner details the significance of print in the founding of the new nation, arguing that a perception of print emerged in the late seventeenth and early eighteenth centuries that permitted it to be taken as "normally impersonal."[24] This perception made possible an impersonal public sphere distinguishable from the state in which political arguments could claim an authority grounded in disinterest and general accessibility to an imagined public.[25] Others have argued, however, that the impersonality of print that Warner finds essential raised its own questions of legitimacy. In his study of oral forms in the revolutionary and early national era, Christopher Looby grants the significance of the textual foundations of American political authority on which Warner fixates but argues that such a focus ignores "the widespread cultural investment of authority in vocal forms like political oration and sermons."[26] Looby observes a "basic legitimacy deficit" in the new nation and argues that public speech of various types represented "a counterpoint of anxiety about the sufficiency of textuality as a ground of authority" by offering visceral, personal forms of attachment.[27]

Anxiety about print as a source of authority extended to bibles as much as to the American founding documents, and responses to that anxiety played out both orally, as Looby suggests, and in "voices" inserted into printed bibles themselves. Viewed in this light, anxieties about written scripture as an essential part of an internalized religious experience—an anxiety as old as the Reformation itself, amplified by the expansive postrevolutionary print market— gave new importance to both oral and written forms of biblical mediation that validated, explained, and codified scripture. Explanatory and prefatory materials bound into early national bibles—voices incorporated into an otherwise impersonal text—were expressions of a desire to allay anxiety about the reliability of bibles as authorities.[28]

The Bible's reliability was specifically challenged by questions about its material transmission, translation, and interpretation. The first two of these concerns began with the increasingly historicized sense of the Bible elaborated in chapter 1. Eighteenth-century print-bible culture cultivated an awareness of the Bible's historical contingencies. In terms of translation, any reader of a King James Bible was alerted to the linguistic distance between the English Bible and the original texts when its title page declared it to be "newly translated out of the original tongues."[29] Many bibles contained articles and essays discussing translation issues in ways intended to be accessible to the lay reader, including "To the Reader" essays that specifically discussed the transmission of the Bible's source documents. Jonathan Sheehan discusses a process of "double canonization" taking place over the centuries after the Reformation, in which first select vernacular versions became the standards in their respective languages, and then Hebrew and Greek originals were collected, evaluated, and arranged by scholars to constitute the definitive original-language versions.[30] Because the vernacular standards were established first and difficult to unseat from the public consciousness, scholars cognizant of subsequent work in the original languages were required to explain that distance in the margins of their work, arguing for better translations but rarely venturing to actually alter the text of the English standard. In this way, marginal commentary brought a sense of indeterminacy and variability to the Bible just as it was trying to bring certainty and clarity.

The variety of early national bibles further contributed to this sense of textual indeterminacy. Many books intended as bibles and recognizable as such were not, or not simply, called bibles. The reader is told only secondarily that Philip Doddridge's *Family Expositor* is a paraphrase of the New Testament. As discussed in chapter 1, many bibles of this period, particularly quartos, were not simply "Holy," but bore other descriptors: "Self-interpreting," "Comprehensive," "Polyglott." In addition to hailing a particular type of reader, these words told that potential reader something about the book in question, something that was in fact often open for interpretation. "Self-interpreting" is meant to refer to the way that cross-references are used to explain verses, but this is obviously a bible interpreted by John Brown. The "Comprehensive" bible in fact contains a selection of commentaries and references from various compilers, chosen by an editor.

As discussed in chapter 1, these words are tools for conjuring particular sorts of readers: they actually do more to describe a certain kind of reader than they do to describe the book itself. They nevertheless lend something extra that promises special access to the scriptures. Popular rhetoric may have declared full understanding available to everyone who could read the scriptures, pray and ponder over them; in practice, an entire industry subsisted on formatting bibles to facilitate access and understanding, fueled by—and eliciting—readers' desires to be brought closer to scripture.

Beyond proper names, other adjectives found their way into titles: "Family" and "Pulpit" were common, along with words suggesting bibles meant for particular demographics or, rarely, denominations or even political parties. A "Baptist" edition was a King James text revised to suit that denomination; the "Right-Aim School" bible was annotated to advocate "freedebtism."[31] What all of these particularizing titles helped to accomplish, in company with the other paratexts they preceded in a given volume, was to open a space for *bibles* within the ideal of "the Bible." David Holland has written about how seventeenth and eighteenth century Protestants saw "a new Bible" in every threat.[32] Referring to a some presumably nefarious source as someone's "new Bible" was a way of charging them with having found some other ultimate authority, some other text that they allowed to function as a bible. The "revelations" of Anne Hutchinson; the writings of Deists; an anatomy book that Jonathan Edwards found to be circulating among his congregation—all, Holland writes, were charged with having become someone's bible. By the 1820s, though, a flurry of books under varied titles and with varied content functioned as bibles and *were* bibles, despite their obvious differences, obscuring the nature of the abstract text they all claimed to represent.

The nineteenth century's most famous "new Bible" provides an important example of the effect of all of this variety. When Alexander Campbell referred to the *Book of Mormon* as "their [Mormons'] bible" in 1831, he was applying a charge and an insult that no longer stung.[33] The recognition of biblical variety underlay detractors' designation of the *Book of Mormon* as the "Gold Bible," but the same awareness led Joseph Smith himself to embrace that designation. In what is likely one of the last portions of the *Book of Mormon* dictated by Smith, Nephi predicts that people will oppose it as a new Bible: "A Bible, a Bible, we have got a Bible! / And there cannot be any more Bible!" (2 Nephi 29:3). The myriad incarnations of the traditional Christian canon claimed to be representing the same underlying text in more accurate or more pleasing ways: in shortened form, clearer language, or with variant translations appealing to one doctrinal disposition rather than another. Nephi applies the same logic to acceptance of the *Book of Mormon*, explaining that God has told him that there are as many bibles as there are nations of the earth: "For Behold, I shall speak unto the Jews, and they shall write it; / and I shall also speak unto the Nephites, and they shall write it; / and I shall speak unto the other tribes of the house of Israel / which I have led away, / and they shall write it; / and I shall speak unto all the nations of the earth, / and they shall write it" (2 Nephi 29:12). Moreover, these bibles are all essentially the same and infinitely combinable, merging together like streams: "Wherefore I speak the same words unto one nation like unto another; / and when the two nations shall run together, / the testimony of the two nations shall run together also" (2 Nephi 29:8). The *Book of Mormon* capitalized on the idea of a plurality of distinguishable bibles, discrete texts that had their unique characteristics but were imagined to be acting upon the same underlying text. Despite its novelty, the *Book of Mormon* could be made another instantiation of that same, known text.

The early national bible market came to reflect and perpetuate anxieties of transmission and translation. Such a textual environment also provided a sense of how the distance between the ideal and material texts was to be bridged: through scholarship and personal testimony. Countless bible editions of Smith's day contained materials attesting to the validity of the biblical text in general or of the particular edition at hand. Typically, this took the form of prefatory "To the Reader" essays in which commentators possessing historical, philological, or archaeological knowledge assured readers of the validity of the text, demonstrating their knowledge as a means of shoring up their authority as commentators and the authority of the Bible itself.

The primary preoccupation of the *Book of Mormon*, from the original preface to the closing lines, is its own material reliability. While the vicissitudes of the Nephites and Lamanites and the appearance of the resurrected Christ in the New World are the ostensible subjects of the text, the story of the text itself is given nearly as much ink—a significant portion of the *Book of Mormon* is taken up with telling the story of the *Book of Mormon*. The text's framing narrative holds that it was drawn from a set of ancient plates written, edited, and preserved by twenty-four different record keepers over the course of about a thousand years (about 600 BCE to 421 CE). Each author and editor addresses the reader directly, each one asserting his (they are all male) confidence that the record is meticulously accurate and attesting to his own efforts to preserve and faithfully add to it.[34] Often the authors overtly affirm the veracity of the story—"I know that [*sic*] the record which I make to be true" (1 Nephi 1:3); "We know our record to be true / for behold, it was a just man who did keep the record" (3 Nephi 8:1). The truth of the record is tied to the exhaustively documented trail of authorship that multiplies the voices able to attest to the text's reliability, culminating in two primary editorial presences: Mormon (the ancient editor of most of the plates) and Smith himself, their translator. These two *Book of Mormon* figures signify on a ubiquitous presence in early national bible culture: the academic editor. Just as learned editors and translators allayed contemporary concerns about the Bible's material reliability, Mormon and Smith assured readers that the *Book of Mormon* was a scriptural text to be treated as such.[35]

The first moment of this sort of assurance in the 1830 *Book of Mormon* was Smith's original preface to the work, which has been left out of subsequent editions. The original preface was the direct product of a concern about the material reliability of the text: it grew out of Harris's loss of the first pages of dictation. After resuming work, Smith issued the revelation from God— informed by the biblical wisdom literature—that chastised him for losing the manuscript and instructed him not to play into the hands of his detractors by redictating the lost passages. To explain this circumstance to readers of the *Book of Mormon*, Smith inserted a page-and-a-half preface into the front of the first edition, headed "Preface" and then "To the Reader." While ostensibly intended to defuse an awkward situation—Smith's critics asserted that he was simply unable to reproduce the lost text, since he was making up the story as he went along—the short text's most significant effect was to establish a material link among the book in a reader's hands, the ancient plates from which it was taken, and Smith's own credibility. In a single short address to the reader, Smith explains his power as a translator ("I translated, by the gift and power of God, and caused to be written, one hundred and sixteen pages"); the nature of the ancient plates ("the which I took from the Book of Lehi, which was an account abridged from the plates of Lehi, by the hand of Mormon"); and his sincerity as God's agent ("Wherefore, to be obedient unto the commandments of God, I have, through his grace and mercy, accomplished that which he hath commanded me respecting this thing"). The last line of the preface, finally, provides another layer of textual assurance by giving the plates geographical specificity: "I would also inform you that the plates of which hath been spoken, were found in the township of Manchester, Ontario county, New-York."[36]

Far from undercutting the authenticity of the *Book of Mormon*, the 1830 preface signified its status as scripture in a print environment in which readers were accustomed to explanatory prefaces and "To the Reader" essays in which an editorial voice vouched for the validity of the text. Nearly all early nineteenth-century quarto bibles bore some sort of preface; as with other paratexts, smaller bibles were less likely to have them, although many did. While many early national bible prefaces were narrowly focused on an individual commentator's work, the most common (Witherspoon's) was focused on the value of the King James text itself.[37] The common goal of bible prefaces was to demonstrate the particular efficacy of a given edition of the King James and, often, of a named editor's relationship to that edition and to the paratextual material bound within it. The prefaces of the most common heavily annotated bibles of Smith's day—those by scholars such as Adam Clarke, John Brown, and Thomas Scott—center on the sincerity and honesty of the author.[38] In his preface, Adam Clarke disparages his own talent and style while vaunting his sincere motivations: "I have at length brought this part of my work to its conclusion; and now send it to the Public, not without a measure of anxiety; for though perfectly satisfied with the *purity* of my *motives*, and the *simplicity* of my *intention*, I am far from being pleased with the work itself."[39]

Evidence from Smith's texts and career suggests that he had direct knowledge of at least four different examples of this type of editorial preface. Several of Smith's alterations to the King James Bible—both as transcribed into the *Book of Mormon* and in the bible-correction project he began later—suggest a familiarity with biblical commentaries, including those of John Wesley, Thomas Scott, and Adam Clarke, each of whom brought his editorial voice to the biblical text.[40] Two bibles which Smith is known for certain to have personally owned feature John Witherspoon's "To the Reader" essay.[41] Smith's preface shares the preoccupations of Witherspoon's, taking pains to make a material link between scripture's original texts and the version in the reader's hands. Hyrum Smith, moreover, copied information from Witherspoon's "Account of the Dates or Time of Writing the Books of the New Testament" into his journal in the 1840s.[42]

Smith's preface is paralleled within the text of the *Book of Mormon* by another editorial statement, also related to Harris's loss of the first pages of the manuscript. As explained in the preface, God had commanded Smith not to retranslate the lost passages, but to translate an account of the same historical events from a second set of plates (the specific injunction against retranslation is found in D&C 10). The existence of these plates—essentially, a redundant account—is explained briefly in 2 Nephi 5, and Mormon discusses their inclusion in his record in an editorial address known as the Words of Mormon. Here, Mormon is introduced as the editor and compiler of the source texts for the book that would bear his name, and, addressing the reader directly, he explains the complicated nature of those source texts: "I shall take these plates, which contain these prophesyings and revelations, and put them with the remainder of my record, for they are choice unto me; and I know they will be choice unto my brethren" (Words of Mormon 1:6). While individual keepers of the narrative introduce themselves to the reader successively throughout the text, Mormon stands over all of them as the editorial voice that, like Smith, vouches for the integrity of the source documents and the reliability of the narrative. Also like Smith, Mormon's personal sincerity and care are central to his attempt to vouch for the text. "And I do this for a wise purpose; for thus it whispereth me, according to the workings of the Spirit of the Lord which is in me. And now, I do not know all things; but the Lord knoweth all things which are to come; wherefore, he worketh in me to do according to his will" (Words of Mormon 1:7).

The print-bible culture of Smith's day offered another possible inspiration for intratextual explanations of a scriptural text's origins. The texts of the Old Testament Apocrypha are uniformly associated with Catholicism, but they were included in both the Geneva Bible and the 1611 Authorized Version, and into the 1840s they were almost as likely as not to be found in American Protestant bibles. The two quarto bibles known to have been owned by Smith both included the Apocrypha. The *Book of Mormon* appears to cite texts from the Apocrypha alongside its other biblical references.[43] The text's most significant gesture toward a part of the Apocrypha might be in the complex textual history, explained in prefatory direct addresses to readers, that frames the entire text. The apocryphal book known as Ecclesiasticus opens with not one but two prefaces that are immediately familiar to any reader of the *Book of Mormon* and which meditate on several of the questions and themes of print-bible culture with which Smith grappled: for example, citational facility, the need for publication, and the perils of translation.

The first preface to Ecclesiasticus—titled, in a later bible owned by Smith, "A Prologue made by an uncertain Author"—presents the text as a collection of "grave and short sentences of wise men" collected and partially written, first, by a wise man named Jesus. It then proceeds to tell a specific story about the transmission and collection of the text: "When as therefore the first Jesus died, leaving this book almost perfected, Sirach his son receiving it after him, left it to his own son Jesus, who having gotten it into his hands, compiled it all orderly into one volume, and called it Wisdom." The second preface is written in the first-person voice of the second Jesus, the grandson responsible—like Mormon—for compiling and arranging a text that has been handed down through his family.

Notably, Jesus's stated reason for completing and compiling his grandfather's text is explicitly about cultivating biblical facility and the circulation of scripture. "Whereas many and great things have been delivered unto us by the law and the prophets, and by others that have followed their steps . . . whereof not only the readers must needs become skilful themselves, but also they that desire to learn be able to profit them which are without, both by speaking and writing."

The first preface, further, provides a way of understanding and accepting why Ecclesiasticus looks like the Old Testament book of Ecclesiastes: "This Jesus did imitate Solomon, and was no less famous for wisdom and learning, both being indeed a man of great learning, and so reputed also." Here is an intratextual justification for biblical citation grounded in biblical facility: this text looks like another text because its author intended it to and was skilled enough to do it. Facile concerns about "plagiarism" have no bearing in a scripturalized environment.

Finally, Jesus—who has ostensibly translated his grandfather's text from Hebrew to Greek—also laments the complications of translation. "[P]ardon us, wherein we may seem to come short of some words which we have labored to interpret. For the same things uttered in Hebrew, and translated into another tongue, have not the same force in them: and not only these things, but the law itself, and the prophets, and the rest of the books, have no small difference, when they are spoken in their own language." This acknowledgement of both the necessity and the perils of translation echoes all over Smith's textual corpus.

In the 1837 second edition of the *Book of Mormon*, Joseph Smith's original explanatory preface was removed and replaced with a preface signed by two of his followers, Parley P. Pratt and John Goodson, who had taken responsibility for preparing the second edition. Smith remained central—he is named, twice, as the text's translator, and his participation in preparing the second edition is noted—but now the voices validating the text are multiplied. The two men vouched for Smith ("the translator of the Book of Mormon"), this new edition of the text ("the whole has been carefully re-examined and compared with the original manuscripts"), and the *Book of Mormon* in the abstract ("we cannot consistently let the opportunity pass, without expressing our sincere conviction of its truth, and the great and glorious purposes it must effect"). Pratt and Goodson explained the inclusion of their personal endorsements by way of their awareness of the impersonal nature of print. "This book will be conveyed to places which circumstances will render it impossible for us to visit, and be perused by thousands whose faces we may never see on this side of eternity," they imagined.[44]

By including these direct addresses to the reader asserting providential preservation of the ancient text and editorial fidelity to that text, Smith (and, later, Pratt and Goodson) signified on the Bible; the prefaces invited readers to "get" that the book participated in a scriptural genre. Beyond that, prefaces were spaces for Smith to establish his own credibility, just as they were for biblical commentators. Though Smith couched his work in terms of his reception of direct revelation and has been widely recognized as a product of an anti-intellectual, antiprofessional trend of his time, he had a respect for learning that is often overlooked. The first of the many monikers he adopted during his lifetime—the one that identified him on the title page of the first edition of the *Book of Mormon*—was *Translator*, an essentially academic rather than spiritual title. In 1828, while working on the *Book of Mormon*, he famously sent a sample of the "Reformed Egyptian" characters from the golden plates to scholars in New York for validation. He pursued education sporadically throughout his life, returning to school at the age of nineteen and hiring a Hebrew tutor in the 1830s, all the while affirming his ability to read ancient languages through divine revelation.[45]

Although scholars have tended to underplay Smith's importance to the original reception of the *Book of Mormon*, its first readers were inescapably aware of where the book in their hands came from. Smith's claim that the *Book of Mormon* existed on golden plates that he found and translated into his own language is *part* of the *Book of Mormon*. The diaries of the earliest Mormon missionaries repeatedly reference the story of the book's "coming forth," centered around the New York farm boy, as a proselytizing tool.[46] People who were touched by this preaching could not wait to meet the man himself: after hearing two missionaries in 1831, William McLellin closed the school he was running and set off to find the Prophet the next day.[47] The *Book of Mormon* was initially transmitted—sold—by Smith and his close associates in face-to-face interactions involving verbal, personal explanation of the book's contents and provenance. Smith was inescapably present in these moments of transmission. If there were situations in which he was not—if it were possible for a person to pick up a first edition of the *Book of Mormon* without having heard the first thing about it—Smith was immediately present when the book was opened. His name is prominent on the title page and in the copyright statement on the reverse. The text opens with "I, Nephi . . . ," but before that opening line Smith's name appears on the title page, and the *first* first-person singular pronoun in the 1830 *Book of Mormon* actually refers to Smith himself: it appears in the original preface.[48] Readers were conscious of Smith's authorial presence in the book's framing materials. An early owner of a first-edition *Book of Mormon* in the Beinecke Library at Yale University has marked, apparently with the sarcasm of a nonbeliever, every reference in the prefatory materials to Smith as the book's author. In 1834, Jedediah Grant, one of Smith's first missionaries, recorded in his journal that an audience member raised a challenge to the *Book of Mormon* based on Smith's seemingly incongruous claim to a copyright.[49]

In a bible culture accustomed to explanatory prefaces and "To the Reader" essays, though, Smith's personal statement about the loss of the first pages was successful and meaningful for many readers. Smith's direct presence allayed concerns about the reliability of his text. David W. Patten lived in southeastern Michigan in 1830, but he heard about the *Book of Mormon* soon after it was published. He managed to handle one in the summer of 1830, but, as he recorded later, "had no opertunity of reading it eny further then to read the prefece and the witnesses."[50] The "witnesses" are the final legitimizing voices in the 1830 *Book of Mormon*: two affidavits signed by eleven of Smith's associates affirm that they had seen the plates, another demonstration of the text's concern for its material reliability. These affidavits appear in every edition of the *Book of Mormon* and were subsequently moved to the front of the book. In 1830, however, they were bound at the back, which means that Patten, holding a *Book of Mormon* for the first time, opened it to the front and then flipped to the back, learning quickly what the book had to say about its own origins. Patten joined the church two years later and became a leading missionary and eventually an apostle; he died amidst anti-Mormon violence in Missouri in 1838.

The overtly asserted material efficacy of the text extended to Smith's other scriptures. Smith participated enthusiastically in his era's enhanced propensity to imagine biblical figures as characters—at various points in his career, he reported that he had received information from God and Christ; John the Baptist; the apostles Peter, James, and John; Moses; Elias; Elijah; Adam; and Noah during personal, embodied visits. "He seemed to be as familiar with these people as we are with one another," an early follower remembered.[51] Smith translated a text from Egyptian papyri that he said declared itself to have been written by Abraham, "by his own hand, upon papyrus" (Book of Abraham, preface) and dictated by revelation a lengthy preface to Genesis in which Moses relates, in the first person, a dialogue with God about Creation (Book of Moses).

Though lacking posited ancient source texts, Smith's direct revelations also display concern for material reliability reflective of the scriptural culture in which Smith worked. Smith's revelatory moments were not sudden lightning strikes: they typically came during planned moments in which he sat with a scribe and prayed for answers to questions or guidance on particular issues.[52] As Smith dictated the Word of the Lord that he said came to him in these moments, it was written down: unlike Jemima Wilkinson, Ann Lee, Robert Matthews, and other early national prophetic figures with whom Smith is often compared, there was no revelation without the artifact produced by the act of writing.[53] The dictated revelations were carefully preserved, copied into a special record book beginning in 1830 or 1831; the first attempt to publish them came in 1833.[54] Like the *Book of Mormon*, the Book of Commandments, as the first collection was known, contained prefatory material vouching for the authenticity of the text: a preface in the form of a revelation from God. "Behold, this is mine authority, and the authority of my servants, and my Preface unto the Book of my Commandments, which I have given them to publish unto you, O inhabitants of the earth." The preface marked these texts as scripture by echoing the "search the scriptures" command of James 1:5: "Search these commandments, for they are true and faithful."[55] Smith made much of his access to direct revelation, but the bible culture of his time taught him that scriptural efficacy came from writing—from paper, pen, and ink; from styluses and metal plates.[56]

Even as he swam in the stream of print-bible culture's inherent destabilizing of the text, though, Smith sought to bring certainty to the Bible itself. Smith's respect for the learning of biblical commentators and translators is further apparent in his own attempt to edit and annotate the King James text. While his primary mode of bible reading throughout his life was indexical—he dipped into the Bible for things that he needed, aided by concordances and cross-references—immediately after the completion of the *Book of Mormon* he undertook a more systematic reading.

An 1833 editorial in the church's organ argued that "any man possessed of common understanding, knows, that both the old and new testaments are filled with errors, obscurities, italics and contradictions, which must be the work of men" and looked forward to a time when "the church of Christ will soon have the scriptures, in their original purity."[57] The editorial gave a few citations from Smith's translation as an example of what the new translation was going to look like, an assurance that the space between the idealized Bible and a printed bible could be bridged. Smith was both vocal about the flaws of the Bible's written transmission history and intent on producing a copy of the scriptures "in their original purity." No one was more conscious of the gulf between the ideal and the material, and yet no one was more confident that it could be overcome.

On October 8, 1829, Cowdery bought a large bible from E. B. Grandin in Palmyra, New York. Grandin was typesetting the *Book of Mormon* at the time, and Cowdery, as Smith's scribe, was spending a lot of time in Grandin's shop. Cowdery inscribed it as "The Book of the Jews and the property of Joseph Smith, Jr., and Oliver Cowdery." In June of 1830, Smith and Cowdery began marking it up with corrections and additions. The work proceeded, on and off and with multiple scribes, over the course of about three years.

When Smith began the bible revision, he dictated a new text the way he had the *Book of Mormon*: Smith and Cowdery opened to the beginning of their Phinney bible, and Smith dictated a new Genesis. The text—known to Mormons today as the Book of Moses—bears scant resemblance to the Genesis of the King James Bible. Smith turned the creation story into a first-person narrative told by God to Moses with frequent and explicit reference to Christ.[58] He elaborated at length on the story of Enoch, which in Genesis says only that "God took him," so that it accords better with Hebrews 11:5 ("[b]y faith Enoch was translated that he should not see death; and was not found, because God had translated him"). Suggestively, Hebrews 11:5 is cross-referenced to Genesis 5:23 in the margins of the Phinney bible.

Like many readers before him attempting to read a bible through from the beginning, Smith skipped ahead to the New Testament after finishing Genesis. His changes became more strictly editorial, involving fewer lengthy additions. The shift in style may have had something to do with a shift in scribe. In December of 1830, Smith had met Rigdon, who quickly took over as scribe for the project. Although ultimate authority for changes to the Bible naturally rested with Smith, Rigdon had a clear hand in the resulting text.[59] The manuscripts are filled with cross-outs and deletions, and Smith and Rigdon returned to the text many times after declaring the work finished in 1833.

Beyond questions of translation and transmission, Smith's bible editing seeks to answer the problems of the Bible's complexity. Smith's changes range from lengthy augmentations to the text to minor tweaks of grammar and syntax, of the sort that he had already carried out on the passages of Isaiah inserted into the *Book of Mormon*.[60] The influence of early national bible culture on Smith's bible redaction is clear. Much of Smith's editing consisted of rearranging words already found in or near a particular verse—Romans 9:32, for example: "Wherefore ~~Because~~ *they* ~~sought it~~ **stumbled at that stumbling stone,** not by faith, but as it were by the works of the law ~~For they stumbled at that stumblingstone~~." At several points, though, Smith and Rigdon inserted words that do not appear in the verse at hand but to which commentators had made connections. The addition of "subdue" to Romans 7:24 suggests a connection to Micah 7:19 ("He will turn again, he will have compassion upon us; he will subdue our iniquities; and thou wilt cast all their sins into the depths of the sea"), which appeared in Thomas Scott's cross-references to that verse. The texts known as the "Lectures on Faith"—the first Mormon catechism, composed by Smith and Rigdon and included in the 1835 edition of *Doctrine and Covenants*—suggest that they knew Scott's cross-references: the proof texts in the answers to the questions in the catechism cluster among those used by Scott.[61]

Rigdon was Smith's scribe for most of the bible-editing project. Rigdon was not, by his own standards, an educated man, but he had been a respected preacher in Alexander Campbell's Christian movement, and was known to his Campbellite colleagues as a "walking bible."[62] He also knew Campbell's New Testament, which had been published in two editions by the time Rigdon joined Smith.[63] The Campbell New Testament's influence on Smith's bible is evident in small turns of phrase—John the Baptist's locusts are called "food" rather than "meat," for example, and the Gospel of John is retitled his "Testimony."[64]

Isaiah 2:16 is one of the verses copied into the *Book of Mormon* that has received particular attention. In the King James—which was translated directly from the Hebrew—the line reads, "And upon all the ships of Tarshish, and upon all pleasant pictures." The Septuagint, however, has that line as "ships of the sea," its translators having recognized that to the original writers "Tarshish" just meant any trading ship, not those of a particular place.[65] The *Book of Mormon* uses both: "[A]nd upon all the ships of the sea and upon all the ships of Tarshish and upon all the pleasant pictures"—a change that Smith kept later when he turned to editing the Bible itself. Some scholars have claimed the presence of an alternate but legitimate translation of Isaiah in the *Book of Mormon* as evidence for the latter's antiquity, but Smith's reference for this reading need not have been any older than contemporary annotated bibles and commentaries by Thomas Scott and John Wesley.[66]

Another suggestive difference between a text shared by the King James and the *Book of Mormon* is Matthew 5:22. This line from the Sermon on the Mount—"But I say unto you, That whosoever is angry with his brother without a cause shall be in danger of the judgment," in the King James—appears in the *Book of Mormon* as part of Christ's sermon to the Nephites (a reprise of the Sermon on the Mount that LDS scholars refer to as the Sermon at the Temple). In the *Book of Mormon*, the clause "without a cause" is removed, a change that accords with scholarship on the Greek manuscripts going back to Erasmus and

Tyndale: work that was, again, widely disseminated in Smith's day.[67] The most notable of these outlets is Adam Clarke's annotated bible, with which Smith was at least moderately familiar. Clarke was a Methodist, and his work was widely known in those circles in America. Smith married into a Methodist family, and his wife's uncle told a story of once challenging Smith to let him use the divine spectacles by which he was translating the *Book of Mormon* in order to read some of the foreign characters printed in Clarke's bible.[68]

Smith never published his revision of the Bible. A journal entry from 1833 records that he felt the work had been finished and he wrote often of plans to publish it, but he was still making changes in the year of his death, eleven years later. Shortages of time and money are usually cited as the reasons for this failure, but those are not easily accepted excuses from a man who failed in so few similar endeavors. I think because of the monumental importance he gave to this project, Smith regarded his bible the way Tyndale did his own, "as a thing begun rather than finished."[69] Scripturalization is an ongoing process. "We believe the Bible to be the word of God," Smith wrote in 1842, "as far as it is translated correctly."

Smith's approach to claiming bible-based authority—the production of new texts that claimed the status of scripture—may have been idiosyncratic, but it was made possible by skills gleaned from the print-bible culture around him and by the attitude toward and access to bibles that defined his era. Such evidence of thoughtful, collaborative engagement with the print culture of his era makes Smith a premier nineteenth-century example of lay biblical facility in signifying on the Bible. At the same time, his new scripturalized texts— which point back to, change, and reorient attention to the Bible—also dramatically illustrate the long-term effects of early national print-bible culture on the place of the Bible in America. In an environment of diversifying and widespread bible citation, the Bible's own place simply could not remain unchanged. The Bible that Joseph Smith read and imagined is not the same as that of subsequent Mormons, precisely because he put it into a mutually constitutive relationship with the *Book of Mormon*. In February of 1832—less than two years after the *Book of Mormon* was published—Orson Hyde, an early Mormon missionary, was making recourse to it just as he would have the Bible. Annoyed after warning an audience member to repent and being treated "rather lightly," Hyde recorded that he and his missionary companions had done they best they could. "We were like Nephi[:] we talked plainly."[70]

Abandoned Quarries

W. P. STRICKLAND'S 1849 *History of the American Bible Society* is riddled with factual errors. Strickland miscounted the years between the first publication of the Authorized Version and the arrival of the pilgrims in New England (nine, not seventeen); wrote that William Tyndale translated the entire Bible (he didn't); and had the Eliot bible appearing in 1635 (about thirty years too early).[1]

These errors and several others were pointed out as gently as possible in a lengthy, careful review of Strickland's work by George Livermore, a noted businessman, bible collector, and pillar of the Massachusetts Historical Society.[2] Livermore took particular issue with another of Strickland's false assertions, namely "that the first Congress printed and circulated the Bible." Strickland had made this claim by way of insulting a Catholic bishop. The middle of the nineteenth century saw sometimes violent public controversy about the place of the Bible in publicly-funded schools. Catholics led the opposition, arguing that it was up to them to determine if and how their children read bibles, and which ones.[3] Writing in the midst of the controversy, Strickland painted Catholics as anti-Bible and (therefore) anti-American. Thus, the false assertion about the Continental Congress: when he opposed the use of the Bible in schools, Strickland suggests, the bishop in question (he appears to be alluding to Bishop John Hughes of New York) "might have been ignorant of the fact that the first Congress printed and circulated the Bible."[4] "Now, in fact," Livermore wrote in his review, "neither the first Congress, nor any subsequent one, has ever printed and circulated the Bible." Livermore was careful, nevertheless, to shield himself from the charge of sympathy with the papists, averring that "[p]robably no denomination of Christians in our country has less sympathy with the Church of Rome than that to which we belong." (He was a Unitarian.)[5]

The 1856 revised edition of Strickland's history did not mention Livermore's review, but it made plain that his criticisms had been heard. The bits about the pilgrims, Tyndale, and the Eliot bible were duly corrected. The lie about the Continental Congress, though, was left entirely unchanged.[6]

Strickland made this reference to a nonexistent bible in the middle of his chronicle of the ABS's production and distribution of a bewildering number of actual bibles. This study has argued, in part, that the scripturalized environment of early national America was distinguished from that of the colonial era by the volume and variety of its print-bible culture, and cultural developments that changed the terms of the Bible's authoritative use. Over the course of the nineteenth century, these developments accelerated. Corporatization and technology made bible production—something so resource-intense that it kept colonial-era printers from even trying—into a nonissue.[7] Strickland reported in 1856 that in the forty years since its founding the ABS had circulated 10.6 million bibles. In 1880, charts published by the ABS reported that its circulation was 37.4 million; by 1900, 67.4 million.[8] In one sense, there is a deep irony in Strickland's invention of an imaginary bible amidst all these actual bibles. In another sense, though, the abstract volume of these numbers makes all of those printed bibles as unreal as the Continental Congress bible. More stultifying even than the numbers in these charts is Strickland's paragraph by paragraph, year by year record of bibles distributed, a chronicle worthy of the Book of Numbers in its unadorned narrative march:

> In 1844 the number printed was two hundred and ninety-three thousand. Issued, three hundred and fourteen thousand five hundred and eighty-two. Gratuitously distributed, twenty-three thousand eight hundred.
>
> In 1845 the number was four hundred and seventeen thousand three hundred and fifty. Issued, four hundred and twenty-nine thousand and ninety-two. Gratuitously distributed, forty thousand six hundred and fifty-six.
>
> In 1846 the number was four hundred and eighty two thousand. Issued, four hundred and eighty-three thousand eight hundred and seventy-three. Gratuitously distributed, forty-seven thousand one hundred and fifty-nine.[9]

These numbers are abstractions; their particularity does not matter—ten thousand, a hundred thousand, a million.[10] Indeed, there is an understandable, if at first glance paradoxical, scholarly tendency to see in this mass proliferation of American bible culture a diminution of the Bible's actual presence or importance. With print-bible culture everywhere, this argument goes, the Bible was effectively nowhere. Gutjahr, for example, argues that though the Bible's "core text could be invoked" in this abundant print environment, "one need not necessarily grapple with that text because pictures, marginal commentary, encyclopedic introductions, and now fictionalized bible stories all created ways in which readers might access the Bible without having to confront the Bible itself."[11]

There is something to this reading of later nineteenth-century bible culture. A primary argument of this book is that citation of the Bible affects all the circumstances of citation, including the Bible itself. As the Bible is cited and re-cited through the universe of written and oral culture, each citation alters the Bible, connecting it in ever-evolving but specific ways to a universe of personal, religious, political meanings. How could biblical citation possibly mean the same thing in this environment that it meant a hundred, two hundred years before, in environments of relative textual scarcity? In the nineteenth century, Colossians 2:21—"touch not, taste not, handle not"—became associated with temperance. Using Lincoln Mullen's *America's Public Bible* database, it is possible to watch newspaper references to the verse proliferate, from Boston to Texas to the Washington Territory, their density peaking in 1880 (possibly related to the founding, the year before, of the Women's Temperance Publishing Association) and then trailing off. This application of the text was a historical contingency, as was the ubiquity of its cultural presence and acceptance.[12]

The corporatization of religious printing, more than probably any other factor, amplified the Bible's status as an abstract commodity. The American Bible Society, the American Sunday School Union, and the American Tract Society—all founded during the period of this study, in the early nineteenth century—adopted and, in many cases, actually innovated the practices of industrial printing, mixing religious interests and market savviness. The company described by Strickland's Chapter Four, as far as the table of contents goes, could be making and distributing pretty much anything.

> Officers known to the Constitution—Number of Managers—Ex-officio Members of the Board—Powers vested in the Board by the Constitution—Officers of the Society—Special and Standing Committees—By-Laws—First Officers all deceased—Only two or three surviving Managers—Scrupulous Economy—Society has no permanent Funds—Managers and Officers perform their Duties gratuitously—Present Officers of the Society [viii]

Gutjahr has calculated that by 1855 the collective output of the three major religious publishers amounted to sixteen percent of all books published in the United States.[13] In this vein, the obscuring of the Bible brought on by its ubiquity can be seen as an aspect of nineteenth-century secularization, which contemporary scholars, such as Tracy Fessenden and John Modern, imagine as a fundamentally Protestant, rather than a-religious, phenomenon.[14] This is the type of thinking in play when Eran Shalev, for example, argues that "[b]y the late 19th century biblicism can no longer be considered a major component of national political discussions," despite the fact that the Bible was still cited obsessively by politicians and others in the public sphere.[15]

The arguments I have advanced here regarding the early national period frame the Bible's mass-media presence at the end of the nineteenth century as just another moment in the never-ending dialogic processes of scripturalization. By this reading, the most misleading characteristic of Strickland's abstractions—the fictional Continental Congress bible and the millions of ABS bibles—is not that they are imaginary but that they are imagined as monologic and static: unchanging, dehistoricized icons of the Bible's importance. As this study has shown, though, scripturalization means that the Bible is never static. All citation alters its meanings and its position relative to other cultural texts, other cultural formations. In this view, questions about the Bible's importance and the relative degree and quality of attention paid to it are simply the wrong sorts of questions to be asking.

It is easy to say that by placing the Bible prominently among the concerns of the Founders, Strickland intended to say something about America. In the midst of the "Bible Wars," Protestants labored to construct an image of America as a bible-reading—therefore Protestant— nation. On the other hand, Strickland's lie was not just in service of shoring up the identity of the nation by appealing to the authority of the Bible: it also shored up the Bible's importance by associating it with the nation. Strickland effectively turned the Continental Congress into the first bible society. "Who will charge the government with indifference to religion, when the *first* Congress of the States assumed all the rights and performed all the duties of a *Bible Society long before such an institution had an existence in the world!*"[16] By Strickland's day, reverence for the Founders and the efficacy of American nationhood meant that insisting on their interest in bible distribution was a statement about the Bible's enduring value, not just a statement about the Founders' piety.

Attaching the Bible's importance to American national identity could not leave the Bible unchanged, because that is not how scripturalization works. Noll summarizes the elements of this "Americanized" bible. "By 1860," he writes,

> a substantial majority of articulate Americans had come to hold a number of corollary beliefs about the Bible—specifically, that besides its religious uses, it also promoted republican political theory, that it was accessible to every sentient person, that it defined the glories of liberty, that it opposed the tyranny of inherited religious authority, that it forecast the providential destiny of the United States, and that it was best interpreted by the common sense of ordinary people.[17]

Americans, that is, attached the Bible to commitments associated with American national identity. In the first part of this book, I have shown how American print-bible culture both cultivated these beliefs and was constituted by them. This culture told readers about the Bible and about themselves as Americans. It wasn't the only reason they read and used the Bible the way they did—no such hail is guaranteed a response, and it is a fallacy to conflate public culture with a public—but I have argued here that the reader imagined by early national print-bible culture did have an effect on real readers.

Noll focuses on the theological crisis that resulted from Americans' being forced to face the fact that rhetorical appeal to "the authority of the Bible" would not, actually, solve the problem of America's founding sin.[18] The extensiveness of nineteenth-century print-bible culture made things worse. It wasn't just the Bible that had to be confronted as endorsing slavery, but also the broad range of parabiblical material. "Such men as Matthew Henry, Dr. Scott, Dr. Doddridge, Dr. McKnight, Dr. Chalmers, and many others, teach us that God did permit the Jews to hold slaves, and that the Apostles did admit slaveholders into their churches as faithful brethren, and, of course, that slaveholding is not in itself sinful," Presbyterian minister Nathanial Rice observed in an 1845 debate over slavery in Cincinnati. "Now, one of two things is true, viz: either the abolitionists are in most serious error on this subject, or the great body of the wisest and best men, with the Bible in their hands, have been blind to the fundamental principles of morality, and most profoundly stupid and degraded." His opponent and fellow Presbyterian, Jonathan Blanchard, preferred to distinguish sharply between commentators and the Bible, but admitted it was a losing game: "They have turned our Bible into a smith shop whence consecrated hands bring fetters for the feet and manacles for the mind. They make the Old and New Testaments a pair of hand cuffs; and the whole book a straight jacket for the soul!"[19]

As this study has demonstrated, specifically exegetical uses of the Bible are only a small aspect of scripturalization. The broader point indicated by the exchange between Rice and Blanchard is the assumption that the Bible was a source for argumentation, for aesthetic resonances—the assumption that it could be a straitjacket. This is the defining characteristic of midcentury scripturalized subjects, and it did not go anywhere in the ensuing decades. Writing a century after the end of the Civil War, Nation of Islam leader Elijah Muhammad—an accomplished user of the Bible's characters and tropes who nevertheless kept it at arms' length—summarized what he saw as the effect of its scripturalization on African Americans: "The Bible is the graveyard of my poor people."[20]

The parabiblical material that became widespread in the early United States knew no bounds by the end of the nineteenth century. If the proposition of the "the Bible alone" was facetious in the period covered in this study, the later nineteenth century's signature development in bible usage—dispensationalism—rendered it completely farcical. Just as earlier "unlearned" bible users like Zilpha Elaw, Joseph Smith, and Nancy Towle drew heavily on learned bible culture, late-century dispensationalists participated in the intellectual currents of their time. The Scofield Bible first appeared in 1909, redolent with marginalia. As B. M. Pietsch has shown, dispensationalist approaches to the Bible required intertextual readings and recourse to a wide array of scholarly aids to understanding. Dispensationalists, Pietsch shows, "held that authoritative biblical knowledge required years of specialized study, study that made use of engineering methods, such as classification, enumeration, cross-referencing, and taxonomic comparison of literary units." Dispensationalism as an ideology and a method was "developed and disseminated among conservative and interdenominational Protestants in new networks of texts, people, and institutions."[21]

The material, rhetorical, and performative elements that enabled and constrained new subjectivities in the early republic effected not the "decline" of the Bible's importance in America, but an evolution in the nature of its persistent authoritative presence. This persistence is evident in the behavior of mid-century American Catholics with respect to the Bible. While the supposed polarization of the "Bible Wars" typically structures scholarly discussions of American Catholic biblicism, in his 1850 essay Livermore noted a curious development: "[s]ome recent evidences of a disposition amongst the Roman Catholics to furnish the Bible to all who desired to possess copies."[22] He was referring to a new English translation of the gospels by the bishop of Philadelphia, which had recently joined a number of new American editions of the Douay-Rheims. An article in the Unitarian magazine for which Livermore wrote had recently celebrated these developments with careful Protestant optimism and latent Protestant condescension: "These things indicate an interest in the sacred Scriptures, which it is generally, and probably justly supposed, has not heretofore existed in the Catholic Church." Tellingly, the author of this unsigned review of the new translation declined to remark on its merits as a version of the gospels; he or she was just glad to see Catholics coming in from the cold. By embracing the proliferation of bibles, American Catholics, as this writer put it, evinced the "willingness or necessity which that church has felt to comply with the demands of the times. We welcome, therefore, this volume, not only as a valuable acquisition to the Biblical literature of the country, but still more, as one of the auspicious signs of the times."[23] At the very moment when scholars have been inclined to say that the Bible's relevance in America was peaking, the sources show us that scripturalization could not be beaten, only joined.

The bible printed and authorized by the Continental Congress is, actually, the archetypal American bible: nonexistent, but everywhere present. Near the end of *In Search of Lost Time*, Marcel Proust describes the experience of picking up as a grown man a book that he had loved as a child. The book, he discovers, conjures both the child he was and precise moments of that child's reading: "If in the library I take down *Francois le Champi*, a child immediately rises up within me and takes my place, the only one who has the right to read the title *Francois le Champi* and who reads it as he read it then, with the same impression of the weather outside in the garden, the same dreams as he formed then about other countries and about life, the same anxiety about the future." We think of our selves as simple, single entities, but in fact we are legion—harboring, Proust suggests, an infinite number of these other beings, distinctive selves tied to various experiences, times of life, moments. "My character today is nothing but an abandoned quarry, thinking everything it contains to be monotonous and identical, but out of which each memory, like a sculptor of genius, makes countless statues."[24]

I find the abandoned quarry—empty because it has filled other places—to be a figure for the themes of citation, performance, and identity with which this study is absorbed. While the Bible's cultural presence in the early national period has been treated as flat and simple, the identities quarried from it were of infinite diversity and particularity. The Bible's presence in the conjuring of those identities was at the nexus of religious authority in the early national period, and that presence persists. Americans, even those who regard the quarry as abandoned, continue to live among the statues.

Introduction

1. Lucy Hurlbut journal, May 20, 1807, New London County Historical Society, New London, Connecticut.

2. While this book will trade in the language of "subjectivity," I do not intend by this to evoke solitary, atomized individuals. My approach to the relational subject is influenced, most immediately, by Constance Furey's argument for the importance of treating relationships—embodied, intimate relationships—as essential points of analysis for understanding religious subjectivity. Furey laments that while scholars' "attention to practice, performance, authorizing discourse, and subjectifying power" has begun to account for the relationship between the body and society, this same work has occluded the intimate relationships that structure the relational subject (9). Too often, she writes, "the religious subject stands alone in a crowd. Yes, we find that subject participating in communal rituals, subject to religious authorities and disciplinary practices, a pious supplicant or abject lover of the divine. But few studies of religion track this subject as a participant in intimate relationships, defined by the problems and pleasures of kinship, friendship, patronage, marriage, and other relationships less easily named. In our quest to better understand subjectivity, we have isolated the subject" (10). Furey, "Body, Society, and Subjectivity in Religious Studies."

Beyond that, as will become apparent, my thinking about subjectivity is influenced most strongly by rhetorical theory, particularly thinkers such as Mikhail Bakhtin and Julia Kristeva. Such work insists on an expansive, dynamic understanding of discursive exchange that necessarily obscures distinctions between an individual speaker or utterance and the universe of other speakers, utterances, and material conditions to which they respond and which will, one way or another, respond to them. Dialogism, Bakhtin's philosophical model, insists on the mutual constitution of utterance and response. Subjects, in this view, are necessarily intersubjective, every text an intertext. See Bakhtin, *The Dialogic Imagination: Four Essays* and *Art and Answerability*; Holquist, *Dialogism*; Kristeva, "The System and the Speaking Subject" and "Word, Dialogue, and Novel."

3. *America's God*, 373.

4. Charles Nisbet to William Young, October 21, 1791, William Young Correspondence, 1792–1827, Historical Society of Pennsylvania, Philadelphia.

5. Noll, *In the Beginning was the Word*, 3.

6. These elements of society "lost their secure foundations in reality," as David Waldstreicher puts it. *In the Midst of Perpetual Fetes*, 12. See also Beeman, *The Varieties of Political Experience in Eighteenth-Century America*; Pasley, Robertson, and Walstreicher, eds., *Beyond the Founders*.

7. On the religious environment of the early republic, see Brekus, *Strangers and Pilgrims*; Butler, *Awash in a Sea of Faith*; Cayton, "The Expanding World of Jacob Norton"; Hatch, *The Democratization of American Christianity*; C. Johnson, *Islands of Holiness*; P. Johnson, *A Shopkeeper's Millennium*; Porterfield, *Conceived in Doubt*; Roth, *The Democratic Dilemma*; Spangler, *Virginians Reborn*; Wigger, *Taking Heaven by Storm*.

8. Studies of the Bible in American history that have informed my thinking include Byrd, *Sacred Scripture, Sacred War*; Callahan, *The Talking Book*; the essays in Frerichs, ed.,

The Bible and Bibles in America; Gutjahr, *An American Bible*; Hatch and Noll, eds., *The Bible in America*; Kling, "A Contested Legacy"; Noll, *In the Beginning Was the Word*; Shalev, *American Zion*; Smith, *Conjuring Culture*; Thuesen, *In Discordance with the Scriptures*; Wimbush, ed., *African Americans and the Bible*.

9. Hatch, *Democratization*, 133.

10. Greenblatt, *Renaissance Self-fashioning*, 97.

11. Contemporary approaches to history, rhetoric, textuality, and religious studies—all of the fields with which I am concerned—place a heavy emphasis on materiality that I find crucial. Many such studies, however, insist on elaborating the "agency" of things in ways that I think are unhelpful. The model of early national biblicism developed in this study incorporates Thomas Rickert's charge, in *Ambient Rhetoric*, to displace the sovereign subject as the solitary agent of historical action by accounting, to the extent possible, for the universe of environmental factors that affect something like, say, authoritative biblical citation. Such a "change in perspective is crucial," Rickert writes, because it paints a truer picture of the world, one described not by the activities of individual, atomized, willing subjects, but by "a dynamic interchange of powers and actions in complex feedback loops; a multiplication of agencies that in turn transform, to varying degrees, the agents; a distribution of varied powers and agencies." It is crucial, further, that this change in perspective makes the material world constitutive of human action, not merely a "backdrop, stage, or exigence" for "cognitive agents wielding symbolic power via language" (*Ambient Rhetoric*, 10–11). However, I cannot make the further step—demanded by Rickert and other theorists influenced by "thing theory" and Latourian sociology—of claiming a desire to sunder this universe of things from a referent in human activity and, most fundamentally, in discourse. Bibles as print objects are constitutive elements of the relationships and responses human beings create around them, often in ways distinct from or even counter to the intentions of their creators as well as of their users. I do not see the value of calling this "agency," however. Moreover, I remain convinced that historical inquiry is necessarily concerned, at the end of the day, with the activity of creators and users, even as it must acknowledge that their being is transubjective, mediated, and constituted by ever-evolving relationships among objects in the world.

12. "Introduction," Vincent Wimbush, ed., *Theorizing Scriptures*, 3.

13. Ibid., 4. See also Wimbush, *White Men's Magic*. For pioneering an approach to scriptural status that counts it not as the possession of a text but as a relationship among readers and texts, Wimbush credits Cantwell Smith's *What is Scripture?* (see Wimbush 2008, 9–11). I follow Wimbush here in pushing beyond Cantwell Smith's comparative-world-religions approach to examine the processes by which scripturalization operates and its constellation of effects on both texts and readers.

14. Bell, *Ritual Theory, Ritual Practice*, 90.

15. My approach to scripturalization has evolved among a vibrant community of scholars affiliated with the Institute for Signifying Scriptures. The essays in James Bielo's edited volume, *The Social Life of Scriptures*, are insightful anthropological studies that have helped me think through the historical questions with which I am concerned. Bielo's introduction, in particular, offers an erudite framework for anthropological approaches to biblicism.

My use of the term "scripturalization" is somewhat narrower than Wimbush's own. Embedded in Wimbush's theorizing on scripturalization is a hesitancy toward literacy itself, which I do not share. Confining, colonizing, and complicated as it may be in some circumstances, I regard sign-making and sign-reading as human impulses. The privileging of some texts over others is one contingent way that these impulses manifest, and this happens to be the manifestation that I am interested in.

16. Ibid., 91.

17. Wimbush 2012, 110. Pierre Bourdieu identified something like this as "symbolic power": "a power of constituting the given through utterances, of making people see and believe, of confirming or transforming the vision of the world and, thereby, action on the world and thus the world itself." *Language and Symbolic Power*, 170. For an elaboration of the implications of "symbolic power" for culture and authority, see Guillory, *Cultural Capital* and, with particular focus on reading and American history, Robbins, *Managing Literacy, Mothering America*.

18. In the 1950s, Hannah Arendt wrote of authority as a relationship grounded in tradition, something that she thought the modern world had lost. Arendt's definition of authority was modeled on an idealized parent-child relationship and precluded both persuasion and force as aspects of this relationship; an authority could not explain itself or exert effort of any sort in the service of maintaining its status. "[A]uthority precludes the use of external means of coercion; where force is used, authority itself has failed. Authority, on the other hand, is [also] incompatible with persuasion, which presupposes equality and works through a process of argumentation. Where arguments are used, authority is left in abeyance." ("What is Authority?", 93.) My definition more closely follows that of religious studies scholar Bruce Lincoln, who emphasizes the fundamentally relational, dialogic nature of authority: authority, he argues, is "(1) an effect; (2) the capacity for producing that effect; and (3) the commonly shared opinion that a given actor has the capacity for producing that effect." This effect is produced in a given situation by a confluence of factors that implicate both an authority and those subject to it: "the right speaker, the right speech and delivery, the right staging and props, the right time and place, and an audience whose historically and culturally conditioned expectations establish the parameters of what is judged 'right' in all these instances." *Authority*, 10–11. See also Sennett, *Authority* and Harris, ed., *Authority*.

19. Miller, "Genre as Social Action," 152. See also three crucial essays by Anne Freadman: "Anyone for Tennis," "Uptake," and "The Traps and Trappings of Genre Theory."

My thinking about materiality, intention, and rhetoric has been further influenced by thinking through the questions raised by Rickert's *Ambient Rhetoric: The Attunements of Rhetorical Being*. Rickert pushes beyond notions of relational, contextualized subjectivity to offer new purchase on the "ensemble of variables, forces, and elements that shape things in ways difficult to quantify or specify" (7). Ambience here refers to "the active role that the material and informational environment takes in human development, dwelling, and culture," with emphasis on *active*. Rather than positioning environmental factors as a backdrop or even as a conditioning factor relative to rhetorical action, Rickert looks to dissolve "the assumed separation between what is (privileged) human doing and what is passively material" (3). As I will discuss later, this emphasis on active environments is enlightening for studies like this one, that take materiality seriously. From the perspective of dialogic approaches, though, there can be no exchange without actors who are in some final sense distinct from one another and from their environments. Dialogism is predicated on "outsidedness" (see Holquist 32–35). This separation is what compels discourse, Bakhtin says, and it does so precisely because there *is* no being in solitude. For Bakhtin, as Holquist puts it, "self/other is a relationship of simultaneity" (19). One does not exist without the other— and yet they are distinct.

Further, dialogism requires some notion of intentionality to be placed at the core of rhetoric, something with which approaches to ambience and materiality are deeply uncomfortable. Utterances, Bakhtin's basic unit of discourse, are always meant to do something. This intentionality, though, is never that of the oft-caricatured uninhibited, self-willing, solitary, self-conscious subject. Bakhtin explains:

The living utterance, having taken meaning and shape at a particular historical moment in a socially specific environment, cannot fail to brush up against thousands of living dialogic threads, woven by socio-ideological consciousness around the given object of an utterance; it cannot fail to become an active participant in social dialogue. After all, the utterance arises out of this dialogue as a continuation of it and as a rejoinder to it—it does not approach the object from the sidelines. ("Discourse in the Novel," in *The Dialogic Imagination*, 276–7.)

Rickert objects that when rhetorical studies is organized around intention it implicitly endorses "a model of human being as an autonomous, self-knowing, subjective agent" (36), but this does not seem to give credit to genre theorists such as Freadman, influenced by Bakhtin, who are preoccupied with the co-constitutive nature of discourse and action. Ultimately, Rickert's emphasis on the active role of ambient factors is important, but it risks leaving little room for "human doing" at all, privileged or not. Human action cannot be separated from environmental factors, but neither can it be completely constituted by them, because if it were it could not be in dialogue with them.

Nevertheless, attention to the full range of factors that inflect rhetoric is essential, and *Ambient Rhetoric* offers crucial considerations for such an approach. For an enlightening, more measured approach to ambience with specific application to religious studies, see Matthew Engelke, "Angels in Swindon."

20. Wimbush's approach to scripturalization emphasizes its constraining, pernicious effects. In this, he expresses a great deal of confidence in the effective operation of scripturalized power, particularly political power (see, for example, *White Men's Magic*, 19). Acknowledging the realities of power, I am inclined to the deconstructive attitude toward citationality advanced by Amy Hollywood, which is not so much optimistic as, I think, realistic about the effectiveness of language itself. Appealing to Jacques Derrida and Judith Butler in addition to ritual theorists including Bell, Hollywood highlights the potential for misfiring inherent in cultural performance:

> In changed conditions, performatives constitute new kinds of subjects and communities. Seen in this way, misfiring looks less like a danger than a possibility, one that opens room for improvisation and resistance within the very authoritarian structures (e.g., of child rearing, education, and religion) in which subjects are constituted. We do not freely choose ourselves or our communities, nor are the worlds into which we are born absolutely determinative ones in which no new meanings can be performed. Instead, subjects and communities are created and sustained by the complex interplay of sameness and difference constitutive of repetition itself. (Hollywood, "Performativity, Citationality, Ritualization," 115.)

As this study will demonstrate, the potential for "misfiring" (as defined from the perspective of inherited authority) certainly applies to the citationality inherent in scripturalization.

21. Green, "The Rise of Book Publishing," 75.

22. Noll, *America's God*, 372.

23. Warner, *The Letters of the Republic*, xiv.

24. Shalev, *American Zion*, 14.

25. *Blessed are the Organized*, 94. The mechanisms by which authority is earned and enacted in a democratic environment, moreover, need not be left to abstractions or accidents. "Charisma"—"a term that more often mystifies than instructs," Stout observes—was Hatch's most common explanation for new authorities. I maintain, by contrast, that the

mechanisms of bible-based authority can be unpacked. As Stout writes of his "charismatic" subjects, leaders of grassroots democratic movements: "I have no doubt that [they] are gifted in ways that contribute to their authority, but their gifts can be described. . . . I want to take seriously the thought that the authority of a grassroots leader needs to be earned, that the sort of authority that such leaders ideally, or even typically, possess is not merely a matter of natural talents" (95).

26. See Fessenden, *Culture and Redemption,* chapter three.

27. Stanwood, "Catholics, Protestants, and the Clash of Civilizations in Early America," 219.

28. For a wide-ranging analysis of early-American anti-Catholicism focused specifically on the rhetorical value of Catholicism to the Protestant imagination, see Franchot, *Roads to Rome,* and Mercado, " 'Have You Ever Read?' "

29. See Martin, *A Discouerie of the Manifold Corruptions of the Holy Scriptures . . .* and Gebarowski-Shafer, "Catholics and the King James Bible: Stories from England, Ireland and America," 254.

30. See, for example, Carroll to Mathew Carey, April 1789 and February 1790, in *The John Carroll Papers,* 355, 425.

31. "Address to the Subscribers for the Doway Translation of the Vulgate Bible," 2.

32. See Mathew Carey to Frederick Craig, December 30, 1790; January 12, 1791; January 14, February 3, February 22, and Craig to Carey, February 12, 1791. Lea & Febiger Records, Historical Society of Pennsylvania. For Carey's later reflections on the episode see Carey, "Miscellanies," 281, Library Company of Philadelphia. See also Green, "The Rise of Book Publishing," 82–3.

33. Gebarowski-Shafer, 256. See also Green, "The Rise of Book Publishing," 97–8.

34. Neuman, *Jeremiah's Scribes,* x.

35. Nord 2004, 136.

Part I: Print-Bible Culture in the Early United States

1. See Satlow, *How the Bible Became Holy.*

2. Witherspoon, "To the Reader," 1793, unpaged.

3. This combination of a historicized sense of the Bible's transmission and faith in its providential purity was common among early national Protestants. Richard McNemar, an important figure in the early revivals of the Second Great Awakening, wrote that "however great the contention has been about the copy; and however much these presumers have altered, amended, expounded and paraphrased upon it, yet the original has remained unsullied. God is of one mind; and his promises in Christ, are Yea and Amen" (*The Kentucky Revival,* 17). This paradox is taken up more fully in chapter 5.

4. This divide is not unique or new to the period under study here. Neumann points out this same disconnect with respect to her Puritan subjects: "The narrative of a simple, untroubled exegetical process—whether the translation of scripture into the vernacular or the plain-style explication of the literal sense—is a necessary doctrinal fiction, but the premise of that fiction remains at the core of Puritan literary theory and practice, informing both rhetorical and exegetical preferences" (152).

Chapter 1: Creating the American Bible Reader, 1777–1816

1. In subsequent Carey editions the chart is titled "Analysis of the Bible." This chart or one like it appears in many later American bibles.

2. Writing about "popular" French books of the seventeenth and eighteenth centuries, Roger Chartier focuses on what the producers of books *thought* their potential readers needed, or wanted. "The vast labour of adaptation—shortening texts, simplifying them, cutting them up, providing illustrations—was commanded by how the bookseller-publishers who specialized in that market envisioned their customers' abilities and expectations. Thus the very structure of their books was governed by the way that book publishers thought that their target clientele read." *The Order of Books*, 13. The precise relationship between readers' imagined desires and the preferences and practices of actual readers invites questions more fully discussed in chapter 2.

3. My approach to the imagined reader of American bibles is indebted to Leah Price's discussion in *How to Do Things with Books in Victorian Britain*; see, especially, chapters five and six. See also the essays in Suleiman and Crosman Wimmers, eds., *The Reader in the Text*, especially Wolfgang Iser's "Interaction between Text and Reader." Lastly, Millner, *Fever Reading*, presents an excellent and evocative treatment of these questions (20–4).

4. As Linda Kerber writes of this "Republican Mother": "She was to educate her children and guide them in the paths of morality and virtue. But she was not to tell her male relatives for whom to vote. She was a citizen but not really a constituent" (*Women of the Republic*, 283). See also Robbins, "'The Future Good and Great of Our Land.'"

5. The essays in Saenger and Van Kampen, eds., *The Bible as Book* offer an important material-texts perspective on this history.

6. For an elaboration of this point, see Gilmont, "Protestant Reformations and Reading" in Cavallo, Chartier, and Cochrane, eds., *A History of Reading in the West*.

7. "To the Councilmen of all Cities in Germany that they establish and Maintain Christian Schools" (1524).

8. The Lollards—pre-Reformation proponents of the vernacular—embraced the idea of an English bible out of pedagogical practicality, not from an aspiration to universal access to the Bible itself. "Faced with the necessity of communicating his message to those outside the university, Wyclif moved logically to employing preachers. This move necessitated using the vernacular to convey his message through the use of the pen as well as through preaching." Smeeton, *Lollard Themes in the Reformation Theology of William Tyndale*, 89.

9. See Saenger, "The Impact of the Early Printed Page on the Reading of the Bible."

10. In Wimbush's succinct phrase: "The Protestant mentality is misunderstood if it is assumed to mean that anyone's reading is acceptable." *White Men's Magic*, 255 n. 12. At the same time, the need to annotate scripture did make reformers uncomfortable. See William H. Sherman, "'The Book Thus put in every Vulgar Hand': Impressions of Readers in Early English Printed Bibles" in Saenger and Van Kampen. For observation of this paradox with specific reference to English bibles in America, See Nord, 15; Hall (1990), 27; and Gutjahr.

11. For a bibliography of early English bibles, see A. S. Herbert, *Historical Catalogue of Printed Editions of the English Bible, 1525–1961*.

12. Daniell, *The Bible in English*, 205.

13. *Statutes of the Realm*, 896. As Heidi Brayman Hackel notes, the patriarchal assumptions of bible reading are clear here: it is significant that the act "allows the householder to assign the task of reading to someone—daughter, wife, servant—who could not otherwise lawfully read the Bible aloud." "'Boasting of Silence,'" 103. These assumptions would be carried through the history of family bible reading.

14. *The Bible and Holy Scriptvres conteyned in the Olde and Newe Testament* (Geneva Bible, 1560), "To Our Beloved in the Lord . . . ," unpaged.

15. H. Stout, "Word and Order in Colonial New England," 21.

16. Barlow, *The Summe and Substance of the Conference . . .* , 47.

17. "The Translatours to the Reader," in *The Holy Bible* (1611), unpaged.

18. Norton, *A Textual History of the King James Bible*, 47.

19. Ibid., 291.

20. H. Stout, 29.

21. Norton, 99.

22. Ibid.

23. Quoted in Hitchin, "The Politics of English Bible Translation in Georgian Britain," 68, n. 6.

24. For a consideration of the English bible patent in the context of intellectual property rights in the English book industry at the beginning of the seventeenth century, see St. Clair, *The Reading Nation in the Romantic Period*, 75. For more on this history, see Perry, " 'What the Public Expect' "; Daniell, Hitchin, and Norton.

25. Norton, 101.

26. Herbert, *Historical Catalogue*, 187.

27. See Bentley Jr., "The Holy Pirates" and Carpenter, *Imperial Bibles, Domestic Bodies*, xvi.

28. See Herbert, 1031, 1125, and 1126.

29. St. Clair positions lax enforcement of the bible charter as part of large-scale changes in English intellectual property after a series of legal decisions in 1774 (75–6). See table 3.1 of *The Reading Nation in the Romantic Period* for a summary of St. Clair's timeline of changes in the intellectual property regime from the sixteenth century to the nineteenth.

30. It is worth pausing to note here that at the level of the text the recognition that these words were both constitutive of readers and intended to be appealing to them signals a chicken-or-egg problem endemic to studies of rhetoric and subject-formation: Were these words and the content they promised a response to consumer demand, or did they create, as I am emphasizing here, the consumer who demanded this kind of content? The answer is, well, both. This is a question that this study will continue to grapple with, but in that I am in good company, because the question strikes to the heart of not just the study of popular culture but the study of subjectivity itself. So, Judith Butler: "We cannot presume a subject who performs an internalization if the formation of the subject is in need of explanation. The figure to which we refer has not yet acquired existence and is not part of a verifiable explanation, yet our reference continues to make a certain kind of sense. The paradox of subjection implies a paradox of referentiality: namely, that we must refer to what does not yet exist" (*Psychic Life of Power*, 4). I have found investigations of this question by Thomas Rickert (*Ambient Rhetoric*) and Diane Davis (*Inessential Solidarity*) particularly instructive. For my purposes here, it is important to remember that scripturalization has no "beginning" in the period under consideration. The scripturalized environment of eighteenth-century anglophone culture was an inherited privileged distinctiveness for the Bible, which meant that attaching words such as "Family," "History," and "Complete" to a bible had the rhetorical weight to help constitute particular relationships of subjectivity. At the same time, it meant that such words were part of the ongoing processes of scripturalization—they altered the precise nature of the Bible's privileged status.

31. See Cambers and Wolfe, "Reading, Family Religion, and Evangelical Identity in Late Stuart England"; see also Hill, chapter 13. For a typical contemporary treatment of family bible reading, see Backus, *Family Prayer Not to Be Neglected*.

32. "Paratexts" are, as elucidated by Gerard Gennette, thresholds to texts. This division is never absolute, but it is rhetorically significant enough to be a useful rubric for analysis. Genette, *Paratexts*. See also Gray, *Show Sold Separately*.

33. *The Holy Bible . . . by Samuel Clark*, unpaged.

34. Brown, unpaged.

35. Unpaged.

36. Wesley, *Explanatory Notes upon the New Testament*, iii–iv.

37. Whitefield in *The Holy Bible . . . by Samuel Clark*, unpaged.

38. See Herbert, 1150.

39. See Hills, entry 753. Benedict Anderson holds that "the idea that a particular script-language offered privileged access to ontological truth, precisely because it was an insepa-rable part of that truth" had to "lose its grip on men's minds" before the nation-state could be imagined (*Imagined Communities*, 36). This point, along with the canonization of par-ticular vernacular translations observed by Sheehan, make plain, though, that the identifi-cation of specific languages with ontological truth did not go anywhere. See Sheehan, *The Enlightenment Bible*, 24.

40. "A Catalogue of the Missionaries Library, &c," 44.

In the 1790s, when Thomas Paine sought to mock and undermine biblical authority without recourse to any text other than a bible, he used the chronology that had become so standard as to be inseparable from the biblical text itself. "The chronology that I shall use is the bible chronology, for I mean not to go out of the bible for evidence of any thing, but to make the bible itself prove, historically and chronologically, that Moses is not the author of the books ascribed to him." *Age of Reason Part the Second*, 12.

41. See Sheehan and Brown, *Jonathan Edwards and the Bible*, xxi, 100. In *The Eclipse of Biblical Narrative*, Hans Frei details the intellectual forces that gave rise to this sort of understanding but construes it, as the title suggests, as a fundamentally antinarrative move. Frei found this to be the case because he argued that mapping the events of the Bible onto historical time meant that it could no longer be appreciated in a narrative sense— that bibli-cal stories could not be thought of as both true and temporally locatable relative to the events of profane history. American bible readers, at least, have never made any such dis-tinction. I am arguing here that that is not because they imagined folding their own lives into "sacred time," but because they imagined biblical events as historical. A similar ques-tion is raised here with Anderson's argument that nationalism necessarily drove "a harsh wedge between cosmology and history" (36).

42. Wimbush, *White Men's Magic*, 113–4. See also Carpenter (2003). Though Carpenter does not make this point about the effect of the historicization of English bibles, she care-fully documents the racial themes of this imperial rhetoric, as well as its gendered mean-ings. See also Brown, "Converting the Lost Sons of Adam" and especially Glasson, *Master-ing Christianity*.

43. "The Secret of England's Greatness," National Portrait Gallery. See Howsam, *Cheap Bibles*, 2.

44. See Glasson, 109; see also Monaghan, chapter 5, for an in-depth account of the SPG and literacy.

45. Francis Le Jau to the Secretary, June 13, 1710.

46. "Instructions for Catechists for Instructing Indians," 20.

47. See Monaghan, 149–56. "Slaves were rarely introduced to the Bible through the medium of the printed page," Callahan writes (*Talking Book*, 11).

48. Cooper Harriss has written evocatively about the effect that this enforced illiteracy may have had on African American bible usage in the nineteenth century. Harriss posits "a decided lack of precision in the reception of biblical material received at second- or even third- or fourth-hand" ("On the Eirobiblical," 474). While literate culture, he argues, could produce writers such as Frederick Douglass and Harriet Jacobs who deployed careful, pre-cise biblical references, the ad hoc, overwhelmingly oral experience that the vast majority

of the enslaved had with the Bible enabled a loose sense of the text that gave rise to subversive, ironic forms of citation. While I question the efficacy of the "overwrought determinism" that Harriss argues characterized literate bible usage in the nineteenth century, his insights are important. The current study argues that the processes of scripturalization mean that *all* biblical citation has an effect on the text—adds to it, alters its applications, changes its position relevant to other cultural constellations. I would emphasize that literacy-based biblical pedagogy does not equate with precision in citation, and that irony and all other aspects of "counter" readings depend on a normative sensibility of the text that is itself contingent. Harriss's argument about what he calls "eirobiblical rhetoric," though, gives important clarity to the way that forms of citation exist in greater and lesser degrees of ironic tension with a given discursive community's *expected* forms of biblical usage. Chapter 2 will argue that written biblical paratexts both enabled biblical citation and did so in ways that reinscribed traditional, expected applications of scriptural texts. Harriss's argument suggests that oral forms of citation—lacking direct access to those written aides to the text—were less beholden to those traditional forms.

Harriss's argument is usefully read with Itumeleng J. Mosala's suggestion that even theological traditions that position themselves against presumptively hegemonic readings have tended to reify the notion of "scriptural authority." It would be anachronistic to directly connect Mosala's complaint to Harriss's subjects—the former is making an intervention into a transnational tradition of black theology that developed in the latter part of the twentieth century—but his questions are pertinent to readings of African American biblical citation. Mosala argues that the traditional terms of scriptural authority—acknowledging the Bible as the word of God—necessarily abdicate a critical perspective. "Paradoxically," he argues, "black theology's notion of the Bible as the Word of God carries the implication that there is such a thing as a nonideological appropriation of Scripture" (*Biblical Hermeneutics and Black Theology in South Africa*, 15–16). Biblical citation "colludes with the text," in Mosala's eloquent phrase. In this sense, to aggressively claim the Bible, its meanings, and the right to cite it—typically considered actions toward liberation—is to reinscribe its (always potentially dominating) authority. "Once black theology colludes with the text in obscuring its oppressors and oppression and in presenting the text as divine discourse emanating from among the poor and oppressed, then the way is open for it to defend and claim, as part of the underclass, the program of the dominant classes" (28). Mosala himself pursues a "form of biblical-hermeneutical appropriation" that is "deliberately oblivious to the notion of 'scriptural authority,' which is at the heart of traditional biblical scholarship" (11). Mosala's approach to scripture shares much with Wimbush's notion of scripturalization. See also Johnson, "Scripturalizing Religion and Ethnicity."

49. Warner, *Letters of the Republic*, 12–13.

50. Round, *Removable Type*, 27. See also Fisher, "America's First Bible" and Rivett, "The Algonquian Word and the Spirit of Divine Truth."

51. On the stakes and cultural meanings of literacy for Native Americans in the colonial period, see Wyss, *Writing Indians*, especially chapter 2. Protestant antipathy to African languages would endure. In the mid-nineteenth century, some who questioned missionary organizations would mock efforts to translate the Bible into some African languages as "extreme examples of accommodating the Bible to . . . ignorance and barbarism." Unitarian George Livermore called one such translation—into "the abominable *patois* spoken by the slaves" of Surinam—an "extraordinary volume of gibberish" (Livermore, *Remarks on the Publication and Circulation of the Scriptures*, 12–13).

52. The exception to this would be bibles pirated elsewhere in Europe, which would have counterfeit title pages or no legible publication information at all.

53. Warner, *Letters of the Republic*, 17.

54. Breen 1986, 477. Specifically regarding the colonial trade in imported books, see Raven, "The Export of Books to Colonial North America."

55. *New-York Gazette and Weekly Mercury*, January 17, 1774.

56. Ibid., November 7, 1774.

57. See Howe, *What Hath God Wrought*, and Pred, *Urban Growth and the Circulation of Information*.

58. The authoritative bibliography of American bibles is Hills, *The English Bible in America*. See Gutjahr, *An American Bible*, 182, figure 46; see, especially, Gutjahr's notes about the complexities of edition-counting, discussed further here in chapter 2.

59. For a detailed overview of the development of the American book market in this era with particular attention to bible publishing, see Green, "The Rise of Book Publishing."

60. Weems to Carey, August 22, 1800, in Ford, *His Works and Ways*, 139.

61. The perception that the Bible was scarce in America, at least as compared with England, would persist for decades. In the early nineteenth century, it was sustained by the rhetoric of the American Bible Society's fundraising efforts and self-justifications, and took hold in popular culture. In the 1830s, African American preacher Zilpha Elaw listed the prevalence of bibles in England relative to her homeland among the factors that made her insecure in her ability to preach there: "I often argued the matter before the Lord in prayer, pleading my ignorance, my sex, my colour and my inability to minister the gospel in a country so polished and enlightened, so furnished with Bibles, so blessed with ministers, so studded with temples" (*Memoirs*, 135).

62. Gaines Jr., "The Continental Congress Considers the Publication of a Bible, 1777," 275.

63. Ibid., 276.

64. Ibid.

65. See Hills, *The English Bible in America*, 2. *Pennsylvania Packet*, November 1, 1782.

66. On the promotion of American nationalism in the early national period, particularly through the figure of Washington, see Furstenberg, *In the Name of the Father*.

67. Collins, "Preface" in *The Holy Bible* (1791).

68. Stereotype was a printing technology in which plates were made from blocks of set type, allowing the same text to be printed over and over again while the type was broken down for other uses. See Perry 2014, 138.

69. See the following bible imprints: Albany: E. F. Backus, 1816; Boston: C. Ewer, 1816; Brattleborough, Vermont: J. Holbrook, 1818; Buffalo: Phinney & Co., 1859; Dayton, Ohio: E. A. & T. T. More, 1857; New York: N. and J. White, 1832; Hartford, Connecticut: Sumner and Goodman, 1846; and Philadelphia: W. W. Harding, 1876.

70. *Brown's Self-Interpreting Bible* (1792).

71. A New Testament was printed in Chambersburg, Pennsylvania, in 1813. (Chambersburg is only about 85 miles from Baltimore, but west, nevertheless.) The later 1810s saw several testaments and a full bible printed in Pittsburgh.

72. See Baker, "Jesse Olney's Innovative Geography Text of 1828 for Common Schools."

73. I am indebted to James N. Green for these observations on the Olney bible.

74. Trish Loughran has forcefully questioned the ability of a print culture dominated by Northeastern producers to effectively conjure a "national" public sphere. While this mattered differently for bibles than for other forms of print, it has important implications for understanding the rhetorical worlds created with and for bibles in America. In *The Republic in Print* Loughran argues that until midcentury American print culture was emphatically regional and atomized, and therefore incapable of playing the sort of unifying role in creat-

ing the American nation ascribed to it by Michael Warner and Benedict Anderson. On one hand, the geographic disparity in early national bible production accords with Loughran's findings: "American print-bible culture," where it refers specifically to the production of printed bibles, is not so much "American" as "Northeastern" throughout the period of this study. On the other hand, though, Loughran's caution against accepting, with Anderson, that print could "erase local differences and . . . install, in their place, a formal homogeneity, whether in fact or in feeling" is not really relevant to print bible culture. There were no local differences for very long, and "formal homogeneity"—which, in the context of the bible correlates to textual accuracy—was an established goal. Though particular bibles might have been more commonly owned by readers near their sites of production, there were no "local" bibles. Small local presses turned out newspapers and pamphlets, as Loughran observes, but they had no resources for a printing project as large as a bible or even, with a handful of exceptions, a New Testament. American print bibles themselves, published almost exclusively in a handful of American cities even into the third quarter of the nineteenth century, are textual artifacts of one region's pretense to representing a national consciousness. Unlike the forms of print on which Loughran focuses, though, other regions produced no print bibles with which that pretense could clash. *The Republic in Print*, xix, 3.

75. See Fea, *The Bible Cause*. For an account of the ABS's history with particular attention to its national ambitions and local tensions, see Wosh, *Spreading the Word*; see also Gutjahr, *An American Bible*, chapter 1, and Haselby, *The Origins of American Religious Nationalism*, chapter 6.

76. BFBS 1809 Report, 17–18; see also Nord, 43.

77. *Address of the Bible Society Established at Philadelphia*, 6.

78. Ibid., 7.

79. *Memoir on the Subject of a General Bible Society for the United States of America*, 8.

80. Ibid., 9.

81. Ibid.

82. Wosh, 14.

83. *Memoir on the Subject of a General Bible Society for the United States of America*, 13.

84. Wosh, 13.

85. *The Eighth Report of the Bible Society of Philadelphia*, 19.

86. See *Annual Reports of the American Bible Society with an Account of Its Organization*, 45-8 and Nord, 67–8.

87. *Annual reports of the American bible society*, 420.

88. See Fea, 22.

89. Fea, 26.

90. *Annual Reports of the American Bible Society*, 616–17.

91. Frederick Douglass, "Bibles for the Slaves," *The Liberty Bell*, June 1847, in *Selected Speeches and Writings*, 86–7.

92. For an overview of the "market revolution" and its historiographical treatments with particular attention to the book market, see Gross, "Introduction," 6–8. See also Brekus 1998, 120–2.

93. See Perry, "'What the Public Expect.'"

94. Green, "Rise of Book Publishing," 98.

95. Hartigan-O'Connor, *Ties That Buy*, 131; Kowaleski-Wallace, *Consuming Subjects*, 75. See Breen, "An Empire of Goods"; *The Marketplace of Revolution*; and "'Baubles of Britain'"; Bushman, "Shopping and Advertising in Colonial America." For analysis of the nexus between religion and consumption in the later nineteenth century, with particular attention to gender, see Schmidt, *Consumer Rites*.

96. Hartigan-O'Connor, 131.

97. Braude, 88.

98. Robbins, "The Future Good and Great of Our Land.'"

99. Calculated from Slee, "A Summary of the English editions of illustrated bibles published in America between 1790 and 1825."

100. See Carpenter for more on Judith in English bibles. Gutjahr, *An American Bible* (see 47–59 and 71–4) has also noted the prominence of women in bible illustrations, though with a particular emphasis on what he sees as their potential to distract from the biblical text that relies on a sharp division between reader and text from which I dissent. As I'll argue in the next chapter, paratexts such as illustrations in which readers could see themselves invited readers into the text of the bible, making it more readable, rather than distracting from it.

101. See Kerber and Robbins.

102. Weems to Carey, November 27, 1801, Carey Correspondence, Lea & Febiger Records, Box 35, Historical Society of Pennsylvania. On Weems's aesthetic obsessions, see Garcia, "The 'curiousaffaire' of Mason Locke Weems."

103. Hewitt (James and Caroline Grayson) and Carradine Family Bible, Mississippi Department of Archives and History, Jackson, Mississippi. James Hewitt bought this copy for Caroline, his wife of just less than two years, in late 1806. James was born in Prince George's County, Maryland, and Caroline was from Prince William County, Virginia, "between Dumfries and Colchester." They were married in Washington, DC. This was Weems's home territory—he was on the road constantly, but his family lived in Dumfries during the years he peddled Carey's bibles. It is virtually certain that James Hewitt bought this Carey bible from Weems himself.

104. The family record pages of this bible document the family's (and the bible's) movements. The Hewitt's first four children were born in DC, the fourth in June of 1817. The fifth Hewitt child was born in Washington, Mississippi, though, in April of 1821.

105. See Darnton, "What Is the History of Books?"

Chapter 2: Taking a Text

1. Vision as recounted in *Life Sketches Manuscript*, 137–8. The vision was first printed in 1851 in *A Sketch of the Christian Experience and Views of Ellen G. White*, where the citations appear as an appendix (see pages 35–42).

2. Neuman makes a similar point about the influence of formal theological education on "non-university trained" auditors of Puritan sermons. See *Jeremiah's Scribes*, 15.

3. Monaghan, *Learning to Read and Write in Colonial America*, 12.

4. Ibid., 12–13.

5. For analysis of the "highly self-referential," intensively-read nature of the New England library, see Warner, *Letters of the Republic*, 21. On "reading divinity" see Gilpin, *A Preface to Theology*.

6. Stout, *The New England Soul*, 32.

7. Ibid., 23.

8. Ditmore "A Prophetess in Her Own Country," 360.

9. Hall, ed., *The Antinomian Controversy*, 336–8.

10. Ditmore, "A Prophetess in Her Own Country," 356.

11. See Hall, ed., *Antinomian Controversy*, 311.

12. See Brekus, *Sarah Osborn's World*, especially chapter 9.

13. Other exceptions are found in the case studies of biblical fluency studied by Elrod in *Piety and Dissent*, which bridge the mid-eighteenth and mid-nineteenth centuries.

14. See Monaghan, *Learning to Read and Write in Colonial America*, graphs 1 and 2.

15. Ferdman, "Literacy and Cultural Identity," 187. See also Morton, "South of 'Typographic America.'"

16. Monaghan, "Literacy Instruction and Gender in Colonial New England." See also Hall, *Worlds of Wonder, Days of Judgment*.

17. Tuer, *History of the Horn-book*, 5.

18. Monaghan 2007, 267.

19. This confusion of biblical text and the Book of Common Prayer is still felt today in circumstances of public recitation of the Lord's Prayer, when officiants will often tell an audience whether they will be saying "debt" or "trespass."

20. *The New England Primer*, unpaged; see Gordis, *Opening Scripture*, 33.

21. Murray, *The Duty and Benefit of a Daily Perusal of the Holy Scriptures*, 34.

22. Bickersteth, *A Scripture Help*, 158.

23. James, *The Anxious Inquirer after Salvation Directed and Encouraged*, 15.

24. Pratt's bible is a 1796 Edinburgh edition. The inscription on a back flyleaf—"Phineas Pratt / Saco, Mass."—indicates that it was owned by Pratt prior to 1820, when Maine (where Saco is located) separated from Massachusetts. Mississippi Department of Archives and History.

25. Hosner expressed how often solitary bible reading was her primary religious activity in a poem embedded in her journal:

> Oh how many gloomy Sabbaths
> I have spent here all alone
> No heartcheering Christian friend
> To repel the tedious gloom
> But my bible blessed bible
> Often casts bright rays of light
> When I read the precious promise
> He will give me day for night

Journal of Adeline Cleveland Hosner, Cornell University Special Collections, Sunday, September 22, 1839.

26. This assumes that Hosner's bible did not contain the Apocrypha. Since she was a Baptist, this is a fair assumption: Baptist opposition to these books was the most absolute of all Protestant denominations.

27. Hosner journal.

28. In his study of the American Tract Society, David Paul Nord gets at the difference between reading-guide advice and actual reading practices with a pair of witty chapter titles: "How Readers Should Read," followed by "How Readers Did Read" (*Faith in Reading*).

29. *Confessions* VII.xii (29); see Manguel, *A History of Reading*, 209–11 and Harris, *Ancient Literacy*, 303.

30. Mather, *The Wonders of the Invisible World*, 26. See Cambers, "Demonic Possession, Literacy and 'Superstition' in Early Modern England."

31. Little, "The Mental World of Ralph Merry," 357.

32. See Round 43.

33. Henry, *Letters to an anxious inquirer*, 182–3; 186. See Nord, 123–4.

34. Journal of William Smyth Babcock, American Antiquarian Society, Worcester, Massachusetts, August 2, 1801.

35. Henry, 186.

36. *Eyes and No Eyes and Eyes that See Not, Or How to Read the Bible Aright*, 7–9.

37. Ibid., 11.

38. See Davidson, *Revolution and the Word*, 141, and 408, n. 64.

39. See Darnton, "What Is the History of Books?," 79; Davidson, 141. For thoughts on intensive versus extensive reading with respect to bible reading in America, see also Gutjahr, *An American Bible*, 18, and Jackson, *The Word and its Witness*, 96.

40. Brown, *The Pilgrim and the Bee*, xii.

41. To be sure, a scripturalized text so identified does not have to be a "scripture," as in a religious text, conventionally conceived. Virgil, as noted above, was read for guidance in an indexical mode in antiquity; Roland Barthes famously discussed Proust as, for him, "*the reference work*" (*Pleasure of the Text*, 36). A good argument could be made that the United States Constitution is a scripturalized text, because it is read both ways. The point here is that the same is not true for, say, the United States Code, the notionally discrete set of all federal laws, which is regularly indexed and cited but unlikely to be read through in its entirety, pilgrimage-style. Certainly, though, religious texts are preeminent examples of those likely to be read both ways. Any genre might notionally exist in a scripturalized relationship with some reader or another, but most novels (typically read sequentially) and dictionaries (indexical by definition) do not. In this sense, the discontinuous appeal requisite for potential scriptures is something like the fragmentary nature of cultural artifacts that become "cult" favorites as suggested by Umberto Eco: "I think that in order to transform a work into a cult object one must be able to unhinge it, to break it up or take it apart so that one then may remember only parts of it, regardless of their original relationship to the whole." "'Casablanca,'" 4.

42. Hills lists about 1100 editions during this time span, and about 48% have extensive notes—here I include marginal commentary as well as less-intrusive features such as full cross-references. As Gutjahr (*An American Bible*) notes, however, Hills undercounts the number of editions printed by the ABS, because she did not consistently count each impression from a set of plates as an edition (182). ABS bibles, as discussed here, typically had the least annotation, and so counting up annotated bibles from Hills can give an inaccurate sense of their overall presence in the bible market. The popular circulation of lightly annotated ABS bibles should not be understated. However, as discussed below, ABS bibles were not reliably "without note or comment." Many, if not most, of even the plainest bibles bore guide phrases, chapter summaries, brief charts, and occasional alternative readings in the margins. As Gutjahr argues, "By the 1830s, it had become strikingly clear that a bible was no longer just a bible" (37). My point here is that this variety encouraged indexical reading and, as elaborated more in chapter 5, brought a sense of indeterminacy to readers' perception of the Bible's content and meaning.

43. Nord, 127.

44. *Mary Scott, Eldest Daughter of Rev. T. Scott, the Commentator.*

45. Clifford, *The Good Doctor.*

46. For some thoughts on the effects of "variorum-style annotation" on reading, see Slights, *Managing Readers*, 61–6.

47. *The Family Expositor*, unpaged.

48. For more on Doddridge and the Expositor, see Whitehouse, "The Family Expositor, the Doddridge Circle and the Booksellers."

49. *The Duty and Benefit of a daily Perusal of the Holy Scriptures*, 16.

50. Occom, "To the officers of the English trust for Moor's Indian charity school," 108.

51. Scott, "To the Reader," in *The Holy Bible . . . by Thomas Scott*, unpaged.

52. John Holt Rice to Woodward, February 2, 1805, Woodward letters, Case 8, Box 39, Historical Society of Pennsylvania.

53. *Commercial Advertiser* (New York), January 5, 1811.

54. Gilmore, 64.

55. *Daily Scripture Expositor: Containing a Text of Scripture for Every Day in the Year; with Explanatory Notes and Brief Reflections.*

56. *The New Testament . . . with the learned and excellent Preface of the Rev. Thomas Scott, D. D., Author of the commentary on the Bible, etc.* Hills reports that this is a full bible with the New Testament bound in front. See Hills, 210.

57. *Eastern Argus*, January 9, 1821. The bible was published as *The Columbian Family and Pulpit Bible.*

58. Gordis, 30.

59. Hall Papers, American Philosophical Society, Philadelphia.

60. Bickersteth, *A Scripture Help*, 160–1.

61. Tomes, " 'Scripture Its Own Commentator'."

62. *The English Version of the Polyglott Bible*, iii.

63. *Annual Reports of the American Bible Society*, 617.

64. *The English Version of the Polyglott Bible*, iii.

65. Wilbur 1826, "Key," unpaged.

66. *A Complete Concordance to the Holy Scriptures*, 280–1. The indispensability of concordances may explain the persistence of the Authorized Version's usage in America: the most widely-published concordances in use in nineteenth-century America were all written in the eighteenth century, and all of them were keyed to the King James. New translations would mean new concordances.

67. Shipps and Welch, eds., *The Journals of William E. McLellin, 1831–1836*, 31 and 33.

68. Nathaniel Southard, quoted in *Memoirs of William Miller*, 246.

69. Ibid., 100.

70. Babcock journal, July 3 1802; "Notes on Religion" (octavo 3). Babcock papers, American Antiquarian Society.

71. See "Lectures on Faith," in *Doctrine and Covenants*, 1835. Bowman and Brown, "Reverend Buck's Theological Dictionary."

72. Towle, *Vicissitudes illustrated*, 15; see Brekus 1998, 5.

73. Towle, 15, 25, 35.

74. Ibid., 15.

75. Ibid., 14.

76. *Memoirs of Fanny Newell; written by herself . . .* , 25. The verses are Matthew 9:28, Mark 9:23, Acts 16:31, Luke 8:50, and Mark 9:24.

77. See, for example, page 24, where Elaw cites 1 Thessalonians 4:3, John 17:17, and 1 Peter 1 in a paragraph. Scott connects these passages in his cross-references. Underscoring the contingency of cross-references, Canne, Brown, and the references used by the ABS do not connect these verses.

78. Brekus, 172. Elizabeth Elkin Grammer has called this an attempt to write "over" the Bible as a means of self-definition and a claim to authority, but from a material perspective that claim to authority can be understood as writing *with* the Bible as a demonstration of skill, one enabled by access to indexical materials. See *Some Wild Visions*, 20 and 105.

79. In *The Intelligence of a People*, Daniel Calhoun discusses sermons among a category of creations he calls "professional products": displays of intelligence that validate money or attention paid to an authority. To be successful, Calhoun argues, "most professional products depended to some extent on whether people at large could appreciate them. These products had to be heard or paid for or enforced by people who were not professionally trained" (207).

80. New London County Historical Society, New London, Connecticut.

81. *The Holy Bible . . . Designed for the use of students.*

82. Boudinot bible, Princeton University.

83. Chevalier compiled references for Bagster's Comprehensive Bible, first published in London in 1822; the "polyglotts" that were common in America were drawn from the Bagster's. See Hills, 534 and 753.

84. *The Holy Bible . . . by Thomas Scott*, unpaged.

85. Haynes, *Noah's Curse*, 8.

86. See the pages containing Romans 9 in bibles published by Isaac Collins (Trenton) 1791; Mathew Carey (Philadelphia) 1804; and Langdon Coffin (Boston) 1834.

87. See bibles published by H & E Phinney (Cooperstown, New York) 1828 and Silas Andrus (Hartford, Connecticut) 1828.

88. Hosner journal, July 1847.

89. Babcock journal, June 24, 1802.

90. See Kristeva, "The System and the Speaking Subject" and "Word, Dialogue, and Novel."

91. As will be discussed at length in chapter 4, claims to direct revelation and clerical forms of authority should not be set at sharp odds: they always exist on a spectrum, blended. A distinct form of radical religious authority, though, was defined by a long tradition of would-be prophets and prophetesses who claimed to receive dramatic revelations from the divine affecting belief and behavior.

92. *Review and Herald*, June 17, 1880, 393.

93. Butler, "A Portrait," 8. For comparisons, see, for example, Alley, *Account of a trance or vision of Sarah Alley . . .*; Coy, *A Wonderful account of a little girl of nine years old . . .*; and Thomas, *A vision; tending to edify, astonish, and instruct.*

94. Butler, "A Portrait," 5.

95. For a concise discussion of White's first visionary experiences, see Taves, "Visions"; see also Brekus, 309.

96. James White and Ellen Gould Harmon White, *Life Sketches*, 237.

97. *Spiritual Gifts*, Volume 2, 78.

98. Loughborough, *Rise and Progress of the Seventh-day Adventists*, 134.

99. See *A Word to the Little Flock*, Facsimile Reproduction, 26 and 13; see also Numbers, *Prophetess of Health*, 70.

100. "A Test," *Review and Herald*, October 16, 1855, 61.

101. "Address of the Conference Assembled at Battle Creek," *Review and Herald*, December 4, 1855, 78–9. See also Numbers, *Prophetess of Health*, 74.

102. See Patrick, "Author."

103. Adeline Hosner journal, July 1838.

104. Ibid., May 6, 1839.

105. Ibid., November 3, 1839.

106. Ibid., May 13, 1838.

107. From the beginnings of Sunday school in America the vast majority of teachers were women. Sunday school curricula notionally centered on the Bible, but as with primers and spellers in common schools, students more often read smaller, cheaper books that selected from and summarized the Bible. Anne Boylan discusses the relationship between literacy education and Sunday school at length in her chapter "Sunday School and American Education" (*Sunday School*).

108. Warner, *The Law and the Testimony*, iii.

Part II: Beyond Bibles

1. Wilbur, ed. *The Reference Bible*, unpaged.

2. Barnes, Reminiscences and Diaries, Volume 2, 1; Grant, Journal, 1; Cahoon, Diaries, 11; all Church History Library, Church of Jesus Christ of Latter-day Saints, Salt Lake City.

Chapter 3: Joshua, When the Walls Fell

1. Kennedy and Parker, *Official Report*, 17.

2. On the Vesey conspiracy, see Egerton, "'Why They Did Not Preach up This Thing'" and Johnson, "Denmark Vesey and His Co-Conspirators." Mindful of Johnson's warnings about the admissibility of virtually all sources—primary as well as secondary—relevant to the conspiracy, I am not convinced that the conspiracy was "conjured into being" by the court, abetted by subsequent historians. Johnson's own argument about the fabrication of witness testimony in the Vesey trials takes at face value witness statements touching on the Bible. For a thorough consideration of historiographical arguments surrounding evidence for the conspiracy, see Gross, ed., "Forum: The Making of a Slave Conspiracy, Part II" in *The William and Mary Quarterly*. My use of the *Official Report* here is augmented with recourse to Edward Pearson's transcription of the relevant extant manuscripts, Johnson's many criticisms of that transcription, and a native caution with respect to sources. See Pearson, ed., *Designs against Charleston*.

3. Confession of Rolla, *Official Report*, 68; Pearson, 186.

4. Confession of Jesse, *Official Report*, 82; Pearson, 190.

5. By way of illustrating Vesey's violence, Kennedy and Parker wrote that Zechariah 14:1–3 and Joshua 4:21 were Vesey's "favorite texts when he addressed his own color," but in this context it appears they meant Joshua 6:21.

6. Testimony of Rolla, *Official Report*, 68; Pearson, 186–7.

7. Harriss makes a similar point concerning the violence against children in the *Confession of Nat Turner*: "Nat's claim that 'there was a little infant sleeping in the cradle, that was forgotten, until we had left the house and gone some distance, when Henry and Will returned and killed it' certainly resonates with the Psalm: 'Happy shall he be, that taketh and dasheth thy little ones against the stones' (137:9)" (490 n. 42).

8. "Turn not back till they are consumed," Cotton Mather urged Puritan forces in 1689, rallying them to war with the Indians, "the Amalek that is now annoying this Israel in the Wilderness." Corrigan, "Amalek and the Rhetoric of Extermination," 64.

9. Though his methods and goals are very different from mine, the sense of conjure here is not unlike that elaborated by Theophus Smith. See *Conjuring Culture*, 3.

10. Orson Hyde journal, February–December 1832, Church History Library, Church of Jesus Christ of Latter-day Saints, Salt Lake City..

11. John Fletcher, *Studies on Slavery*; iii, 221. On Abraham as a performative model for slaveholders see Fox-Genovese and Genovese, *Mind of the Master Class*, 506–8, and the supplementary references on Israelite servitude, 755–6.

12. In the tradition of Erving Goffman's dramaturgical analysis of the way meaning is continually created and sustained in the performance of social life, performed biblicism is a means of highlighting the contingency inherent in all authoritative biblical citation. "What is crucial to the dramaturgical vision of social life is that meaning is not a bequest from culture, socialization, or institutional arrangements, nor the realization of either psychological or biological potential. Rather, meaning is a continually problematic accomplishment of human interaction and it is fraught with change, novelty, and ambiguity." Brissett and Edgley, "The Dramaturgical Perspective," 2.

13. Bercovitch's understanding of Mather's typology is strictly ahistorical, an assumption about this type of Bible usage that I will challenge here. He writes, "Winthrop's American aspect, we might say—his association with a particular enterprise—emphasizes his position as governor in order to reveal the individual; his aspect as Nehemiah renders him, as an individual, the exemplum of statesmanship. In this sense, the parallel wrenches him out of time. Insofar as the New Englander is the Hebrew governor, his actions extend beyond any particular situation to demonstrate the principles of just government.

Nehemiah serves here as archetype, an organizing metaphor which allows Mather to vaunt a host of similar parallels that universalize Winthrop's accomplishments. History is invoked to displace historicism." *The Puritan Origins of the American Self*, 35–6.

14. Glaude, *Exodus!*

15. The distinction I am arguing for here is related to that observed by E. Brooks Holifield between types and examples in Puritan thought. Holifield observes that "types were outward signs of future spiritual realities, while examples were not. Types were divinely instituted to represent Christ; examples were not. Types pointed beyond themselves; examples bore their meanings on the surface. The visible types were abolished when they found fulfillment in their Christian antitypes; examples endured as perpetual models for Christian behavior" (*Era of Persuasion*, 46). This distinction separates examples from the dynamic, participatory elements of typology, however. My effort here is to suggest performed biblicism as a way of allowing for both the mimetic prompting of examples with the lived aspect of typology. See also the essays in Earl Miner, ed., *Literary Uses of Typology*; Downing, " 'Streams of Scripture Comfort' "; Henwood, "Mary Rowlandson and the Psalms"; see also Neuman, 21 and 156-67; and Sollors, *Beyond Ethnicity*.

16. Ann Taves has highlighted the identity-making potential of bible-based performance in her thick description of the Methodist shout tradition, emphasizing that dramatic bodily movement in revivalist settings "did not simply involve performance, it also involved narrative, sometimes in the context of performance and sometimes after the fact." She emphasizes the ways in which embodied performances used the "idioms of the biblical narrative" to situate individuals in relation to groups "by placing the individual within the collective narrative of the people of God" (*Fits, Trances, and Visions*, 104). This is an important examination of bible-based performance in the early nineteenth century to which the present study is indebted. As Taves writes, "While the use of typology was not new, scholars have largely missed the way that typological exegesis was employed at the grassroots level, especially in contexts where it was enacted rather than preserved in written commentaries on scripture" (Ibid., 78). I think, though, that Taves's persistent use of a typological model and interest in "experience" renders such performances passive rather than actively creative, eliding the biblical expertise necessary for both their enactment and recognition. Beyond that, here I am concerned with individual rather than ostensibly corporate roles and their consequences for the Bible itself. The notion that the Bible constitutes a singular story of a singular "people of God" is itself a product of scripturalization. The variety of distinct, discontinuous, character-centered narratives that early national Americans performed from the Bible reflects this reality. Performed biblicism as discussed here, further, reveals the necessities imposed upon bible-based performance by the contingencies of everyday life, outside of ritualized settings such as camp meetings.

17. Newell, *Memoirs of Fanny Newell Written by Herself*, 51.

18. McNemar, *The Kentucky Revival*, 22.

19. Ibid., 20.

20. The Kentucky revival, McNemar wrote, "has been one of the greatest wonders that ever the world beheld; and was no doubt included in the visions of that man, who, falling into a trance with his eyes open, cried out—*'How goodly are thy tents, O Jacob! And thy tabernacles, O Israel! as the vallies are they spread forth, as gardens by the rivers side; as the trees of lign-aloes, which the Lord hath planted.*['*]" (Numbers 24: 5-6) Ibid., 31-32. Though primarily interested in typologies promoted through preaching and public speech, Glaude observes something like this in nineteenth-century African-American worship: "The worship ceremonies within most of these institutions—the liturgies, the singing and dancing—invented, maintained, and renewed senses of communal identification that cel-

ebrated, even reveled in the uniqueness of black people and their relation to God" (*Exodus!*, 29).

This is not, to be clear, an assertion of the Bible's monological influence in this period. Extrabiblical precedent clearly played an important part in scripting subsequent activity—every camp meeting had biblical models, but it also had recent, contemporary models. The type of connection made by one Aeneas M'Callister regarding revivals in North Carolina, cited by McNemar, was typical in its use of both biblical and contemporary models: "The like wonders have not been seen, except the Kentucky Revival, last summer, since the apostle's days" (31). Those biblical models, though, are what authorized the contemporary ones: to be acceptable, the rhetorical connection to biblical roles was primary, all others ancillary.

21. A summary of those early martyrologies titled "Account of the Lives, Sufferings, and Martyrdom, of the Apostles and Evangelists" appeared in editions of the *Book of Martyrs* in the eighteenth century and was picked up by John Holbrook for use in his line of bibles published in Brattleboro, Vermont, beginning in the 1810s.

22. Seventeenth-century collections of scripture biography include Clarke, *The Marrow of Ecclesiastical History Divided into Two Parts* and John Merbecke, *The Lives of Holy Saints, Prophets, Patriarchs, Apostles, and Others Contained in Holy Scripture.*

23. Theed, *Sacred Biography*; Enfield, *Biographical Sermons*; Robinson, *Scripture Characters*; Anonymous, *Scripture Characters*. See also Merbecke, *The Lives of Holy Saints, Prophets, Patriarchs, Apostles, and Others Contained in Holy Scripture...*; Stevenson, *The Sacred History*; Goldsmith, *An History of the Lives, Actions, Travels, Sufferings, and Deaths of the Most Eminent Martyrs...*; Priestley, *The New and Complete Evangelical History of the Life of Our Blessed Lord and Saviour Jesus Christ....*

24. "[T]he saints' way cannot really be ours," Berkovitch argued. "Even when we acknowledge their occasionally vivid personal traits, they impress us not as models for emulation but as objects of veneration." *The Puritan Origins of the American Self*, 8.

25. Watkins, *Scripture Biography*, iv.

26. Brewer, "The Afterlife of Character," 2.

27. Ibid., 3

28. Ibid., 10.

29. Though concerned with ostensibly fictional texts rather than scripturalized ones, Brewer's literary-theorist interests align very closely with many questions of scripturalization. "[O]ur investigation of imaginative expansion can substantially complicate and recise three of the most pressing issues in literary and historical study today: namely, the emergence of proprietary authorship, the processes by which canonical texts gain their canonicity, and the related practices through which virtual communities are invented" (10). Brewer's reflections on the study of literary character have been eye-opening to me. Brewer notes a growing literature on the uses of character in the eighteenth century and the way in which this work focusses not on what characters might represent or mean, appearing in the literature of a given time and place, but on what they allowed readers to do. I have found this a fruitful way of thinking about biblical characters. Note that questions about the evolving "importance" of the textual sources of Brewer's characters are very much beside the point to his analysis. Material availability, he argues, created a sense of ubiquity that made literary characters accessible, useful—that is all. I will apply a version of this argument to the presence of the Bible in the late nineteenth century in the conclusion.

30. Macgowan, *The Life of Joseph*, 15.

31. Ibid., vi.

32. Cox, *Female Scripture biography*, iv.

33. On feminist uses of collective biography to recover female roles in the bible in the

later nineteenth century see Rebecca Styler, *Literary Theology by Women Writers of the Nineteenth Century*, chapter 4.

34. Babcock journals, July 27, 1801; August 5, 1801; April 8, 1810, American Antiquarian Society.

35. For a detailed rhetorical analysis of nineteenth-century female preachers' self justifications, see Zimmerelli, "'Heaven-Touched Lips and Pent-Up Voices.'"

36. See Haywood, "Prophesying Daughters."

37. Elaw, *Memoirs*, 75.

38. Ibid., 45.

39. Newell, *Memoirs*, 43, 123

40. Ibid., 80.

41. Wilbur, *Catechism*, 197.

42. Jackson, *Word and its Witness*, 5, 32.

43. Ibid., 21.

44. Elaw, 99.

45. Within the historiography of American religious history, biblically-inspired behavior among Protestants is often discussed under the rubrics of "primitivism" or "restorationism." Although ostensibly descriptive of a set of behaviors based on the depiction of the early church in Acts, historians of American Christianity have complicated the understanding of these behaviors by insisting on a particular view of their subjects' internal experience of them—namely, that those presupposing "to live ancient lives," in Dwight Bozeman's phrase, abandoned any distinction between the biblical era and their own. Bozeman, *To Live Ancient Lives*; see also Hughes and Allen, *Illusions of Innocence*.

Like the "aesthetics of immediacy," this approach relies on a "sense of historylessness" that imagines bible readers imagining themselves living and moving and finding meaning only within textually-based, ritually conjured primordial time, ignoring the multiplicity of real-time factors by which they were constituted. For more on the problems of "historylessness" as applied to early national primitivism, see Perry, "Scripture, Time, and Authority among Early Disciples of Christ." Performed biblicism invites analysis of the full range of social factors within which a text is enacted. It treats the subjects of bible-based performance as relational, not isolated, because the performance of biblical roles depends on the willingness of others to respond to a given performance by engaging in the coordinating roles that it demands. I hope here to draw attention to the problems of analyses relying on "broken time" in the way that Kevin O'Neill has drawn attention to the limitations of "broken space." O'Neill writes that "broken space, methodologically speaking, presumes a world of already existing distinctions. These include distinctions between the sacred and the profane, between the here and the there, between North and South, between the local and the global, and so on. The result is a scholarly imagination interested in meaningful differences rather than hierarchical interconnections" ("Beyond broken," 1094–5).

Thomas M. Allen sees a similar tendency in American studies scholarship's tendency to privilege space over time in the development of American nationalism. "Scholars in the mainstream of American studies scholarship from the mid-twentieth century to the present have largely ignored this tradition of temporal nationalism in order to produce a particular account of the relation of the American nation to its own history. Because the national development of the United States was exclusively spatial, the argument has gone, Americans have lacked a sense of historical change. Mainstream American culture has been immersed in an ideological belief in its own transcendence of history" (*A Republic in Time*, 20).

46. Bercovitch argued that Puritan authors of personal testimonies "fit their most intimate experiences to the contours of christology, subsuming anything unique about them-

selves into a few standard structural and verbal forms" (*The Puritan Origins of the American Self*, 15). By contrast, early national performed biblicism drew on the full set of biblical characters, allowing individuals to represent a much finer degree of personality and eccentricity in biblical forms.

47. Newell, 19.

48. Ibid., 40.

49. The only book-length biography of Dow to date is Sellers, *Lorenzo Dow*; see also Perry, "Cosmopolite's Mount Sinai Domains."

50. *Essex Patriot*, August 12, 1820, 3.

51. As this chapter will be referring frequently to two Dows, I will be using their first names to avoid confusion and tediousness.

52. *Divine Dramatist*, 163.

53. Peggy Dow, *Vicissitudes*, 1814, 7.

54. Peggy Dow 1814, 8; 1833, 150.

55. Hatch, *Democratization*, 36.

56. Peggy Dow 1814, 11.

57. Ibid., 13.

58. Ibid., 77–8.

59. Ibid., 57.

60. Ibid., 14.

61. Wigger, *Taking Heaven by Storm*, 69.

62. Ibid., 71.

63. Peggy Dow 1814, 5.

64. Ibid., 11.

65. Ibid., 61.

66. Ibid., 24.

67. Ibid., 30.

68. Ibid., 31.

69. Ibid., 51, 47.

70. Ibid., 1815, 200.

71. Wigger, 29.

72. Peggy Dow 1815, 200.

73. Ibid., 231.

74. Ibid., 225.

75. Lorenzo Dow, *Travels and Providential Experience*, 87.

76. Quoted in Sparks, *On Jordan's Stormy Banks*.

77. Peggy Dow 1814, 47.

78. Ibid., 1815, 217.

79. Ibid., 259.

80. Ibid., 1818, 105, 136.

81. Ibid., 1833, 149.

82. Ibid., 1814, 105.

83. Ibid., 48.

84. Ibid., 1815, 113–14.

85. *Poulson's American Daily Advertiser*, January 12, 1820.

86. McNemar in fact suggests that the Bible isn't complete until performed. McNemar—who eventually became a Shaker—expressed the importance of bible-based performance in terms of the importance of the Spirit: "It is true, the scriptures contain a copy of the divine will, concerning the redemption of souls: all the promises of God are there re-

corded. But of what use is a bare copy of a will, without witnesses." The scriptures themselves, he wrote, "could effect nothing real; the inheritance itself was not in them" (McNemar, 16–17).

Chapter 4: "Write These Things in a Book"

1. Copy 2, "The Vision of Isaac Childs," 1757 (MC.975.07.019), Quaker & Special Collections, Haverford College, Haverford, PA.

2. In *Teach Me Dreams*, Mechal Sobel argues that "[i]n the period following the Revolution, as reason was more widely seen as replacing emotion and faith and as those in power
sought to limit or control the 'fantasies of freedom' of the downtrodden, there was a widespread reversal in the evaluation of dreams from portentous and likely to be God-sent to
useless or dangerous—something that only blacks and women relied on" (9). This draws too
sharp a line between arguments from reason and from faith in this period. I will argue here
that the ability to compose bible-citing visionary texts was a form of appeal reliant on both
the tools of "emotion and faith" and the print-culture tools of scholarship. Here, I follow
Schmidt's observation in *Hearing Things* that in the nineteenth century rationalism and
eccentric religious practices were imbricated. "So people talked with angels, had tongues of
fire descend upon them, and listened to ancient harmonies, but they did so with distinctly
modern accents" (Schmidt, *Hearing Things*, 11).

3. Susan Juster has written extensively about the proliferation of visionary documents
in the age of revolutions. See *Doomsayers*.

4. For an experience-focused approach to early-national religiosity, see Taves's monumental *Fits, Trances, and Visions*.

5. Juster identified 126 North Americans "who were recognized (by themselves or others) as prophets" between 1750 and 1820 (*Doomsayers*, 64). See also Winiarski, "Souls Filled
with Ravishing Transport," and Bushman, "The Visionary World of Joseph Smith."

6. Lorenzo Dow, *The Life and Travels of Lorenzo Dow*, 214. See Lobody, "Lost in
the Ocean of Love" and Cope, " 'In Some Places a Few Drops and Other Places a Plentiful
Shower'."

7. On the complex relationship between manuscript and print publication, see Hall,
Material Texts; Shields, "The Manuscript in the British American World of Print"; and
Neuman, chapter 1.

8. Bushman, 185.

9. Dow, *The Life and Travels of Lorenzo Dow*, 214.

10. Juster has suggested that one context for understanding anglophone visionaries of
the late eighteenth century is the English Civil War, during which prophets roamed town
and country casting judgment on society and predicting doom. She argues that the difference between seventeenth-century visionaries and their late eighteenth-century successors
is that the latter were less political and, because of the development of the public sphere,
more well known. "For every person who joined a millennial sect or heard an inspired
prophet in the 1640s and 1650s, hundreds of men and women read a millennial tract, followed the careers of itinerant prophets in the daily newspapers, or attended large open-air
assemblies where obscure men and women warned of the dangers to come in the 1780s or
1790s." (*Doomsayers*, 6–7).

11. *The Visions of a Certain Thomas Say*, 1774, 3, 9, 10, 4, 6, 10.
The Bible-echoing visionary texts I am concerned with here are to be sharply distinguished from the kind of texts that Shalev (*American Zion*) discusses under the rubric of
"pseudobiblicism" (see Shalev's chapter 2). Most of those texts are deliberately and manifestly farcical, employing bible-like turns of phrase to satirize, in most cases, political op-

ponents. (For this reason, I think his discussion of the *Book of Mormon* is misplaced, as I will discuss in chapter 5.) The visionary accounts I am interested in here, by contrast, bear not a whiff of irony: they use biblical citation as generic action intended to cue the reader to treat them as scripturalized texts.

12. On the imagery and significance of hell in the early national period, see Lum, *Damned Nation*.

13. *A Vision of Heaven and Hell*, 4.

14. Say, 1792, 5.

15. *A Short Account of the Life and Remarkable Views of Mrs. Chloe Willey of Goshen N.H.*, 9.

16. On the conventions of these narratives, see Hindmarsh, *The Evangelical Conversion Narrative*.

17. *Short Account*, 17.

18. Ibid., 18.

19. "Notes on Religion," Babcock Papers, American Antiquarian Society.

20. Revelation 1:11; Stearns, *The Religious Experience of Norris Stearns*, 3.

21. On the conventions of female authorship in colonial America, see Brekus, "Writing Religious Experience."

22. *The Vision and Wonderful Experience of Jane Cish*, 2.

23. *A Vision of Heaven and Hell*, 1.

24. *The Vision and Wonderful Experience of Jane Cish*, 16.

25. Thomas, *A Vision*; see title page.

26. Alley, *Account of a Trance or Vision of Sarah Alley of Beekman Town Dutchess County State of New York*.

27. Ibid., iv.

28. Ashburn, *Three Remarkable Dreams*, 1.

29. See Ann How sampler, 1794.

30. Ashburn, 2.

31. Ibid., 2–3.

32. Willey, *Short Account*, 19.

33. Ibid., 30.

34. He ends, a bit defensively, by noting that Paul "in his 1st Epistle to the Corinthian Church, 4th chapter, and 5th verse, writes, 'Judge nothing before the time, until the Lord come." Ashburn, 7–8.

35. Willey, 32.

36. Say, 1792, 6.

37. *The Religious Experience of Norris Stearns*, 3.

38. Elaw, *Memoirs*, 114; Ashburn, 7. Pool, *News from Heaven*, title page.

39. McNemar, *The Kentucky Revival*, 68.

40. The titles of the various copies of Childs's vision are inconsistent in giving his name as "Child" or "Childs." I have gone with Childs consistently here because that is how the name is given in the version I believe is the latest one Childs himself edited.

41. Quaker meetings are organized as nesting ecclesiastical units—monthly within quarterly within yearly meetings. See Hamm, *The Transformation of American Quakerism*.

42. See Childs 1766a, 6, 5.

43. Ibid., 5.

44. These sorts of notes, where paratextual explanation is offered by the author, suggest allegorical forebears—texts such as *Pilgrim's Progress* and its lesser-known early American imitator, Joseph Morgan's *The History of the Kingdom of Basaruah* (1715). Neither of those texts position themselves as anything more than literary, however.

45. See Hamm, *The Transformation of American Quakerism*.

46. *Poulson's American Daily Advertiser*, February 8, 1826, 3.

47. See *A Collection of Memorials Concerning Divers Deceased Ministers and others of the People called Quakers*.

48. Childs 1826, 5.

49. Ibid., 5–6.

50. Ibid., 6.

51. Ibid.

52. This is "The Vision of Isaac Child, 1757," MSC 141, Folder 27. Mercer Museum Library, Doylestown, PA.

53. Childs 1826, 6.

54. Ibid., 7.

55. Hamm, *Transformation*, 16.

56. Childs 1826, 8.

57. Ibid., 9.

58. Hamm, 16–17.

59. Childs 1826, 13.

60. See Swarthmore pamphlet collections BX7612 pam.vol.169 and BX7612 pam.vol.43 and Rare Am 1826 Chi(b.w.) 43374.D.1 at the Library Company of Philadelphia.

61. Childs 1826, 9. American Antiquarian Society, Worcester, MA

62. Childs 1840, 9.

63. Ibid., 16.

64. See, for example, the Childs manuscripts in the Henry Warrington and Abraham Warrington piece books in the Friends Historical Library, Swarthmore College, Swarthmore, Pennsylvania.

65. "The Vision of Isaac Childs," 1757 (MC.975.07.019), Copy 2. Quaker & Special Collections, Haverford College, Haverford, PA. Unless otherwise noted, my quotations from Childs manuscripts come from this copy.

66. At the same time, Childs's vision was common enough to inhabit another important aspect of scripturalization: it was taken lightly as well as seriously. The manuscript copy held by the Historical Society of Pennsylvania is, like the Dillwyn copy, neatly written and bound in blue papers, but its copyist, one Margaret Jones of Blockley Township, Philadelphia County, practiced her signature all over it. Her copy of the vision, in fact, might have been little more than an exercise in practicing her handwriting, given that it is unfinished, cutting off mid-line. The Henry Warrington piece book copy at Swarthmore also fits this description.

67. See Marietta, *The Reformation of American Quakerism*.

68. See Bauman, *For the Reputation of Truth*, 118–19. Bauman's brief reference to Childs is the only substantial mention of him I have been able to find in existing scholarship.

69. *Collection of Memorials Concerning Divers Deceased Ministers and others of the People called Quakers*, 273.

70. Marietta, *Reformation of American Quakerism*, Table 1.

71. All of this would later be particularly applicable to Hicksites, making their interest in Childs's vision especially interesting. Hicks himself revered the Bible, but argued that living revelation was much superior to written. "Jesus says I have yet many things to say unto you but ye cannot bear them now Howbeit when he the Spirit of Truth is come he will guide you into all truth. This certainly is better than the journals and epistles of men's writing in a previous age although written by Divine inspiration." Hopper, ed., *Letters of Elias Hicks*, 140. This tension was not new among Quakers in the late eighteenth century, but

was exacerbated by the growth of American print culture and the particular strains of Quaker reform in the eighteenth century and in the 1820s. See Peters, *Print Culture and the Early Quakers*; the essays in Corns and Loewenstein, eds., *The Emergence of Quaker Writing*; and Cadbury, "Early Quakerism and Uncanonical Lore."

72. These two printings share an identical text and both are duodecimos, but one is twelve pages and the other is twenty-four, owing to the much larger type used in one printing.

73. I am indebted to Jim Green for this observation about the capitalization.

74. See Marietta 1984, 87–8.

75. Childs 1766, 20–1.

76. Childs 1791.

77. Willey, 20.

78. Ibid., 25.

79. Ibid., 29.

Chapter 5: The Many Bibles of Joseph Smith

1. Unless otherwise noted, all quotations from the *Book of Mormon* are from Skousen, ed. *The Book of Mormon*. Chapter and verse references are from the contemporary LDS editions.

2. Cowdery to Hyrum Smith, June 14, 1829, in *Early Mormon Documents*, Volume 2, 402–3.

3. Performed biblicism, moreover, means that practical concerns find their way to multiplying the meanings of a text by juxtaposing, for example, apostolic exhortation with the perfectly mundane. Right after the Pauline closing to his letter, Cowdery asks Hyrum to "tell mrs. Rockwell that those shoes fit well and I received them as from the lord."

4. Scholars have long recognized the centrality of the Bible in Smith's career. See Shipps, *Sojourner*, 210–11; Barlow, *Mormons and the Bible*; Jackson, "Joseph Smith and the Bible"; Brown, "Joseph (Smith) in Egypt"; Räisänen, "Joseph Smith as a Creative Interpreter of the Bible."

5. See Perry, "'What the Public Expect.'"

6. Joseph Smith Papers. In quotations from Smith's private papers, I have added punctuation and standardized spelling where appropriate.

7. For a full account of the beginnings of Smith's career, see Shipps, *Mormonism*, chapter 1, and Bushman, *Rough Stone Rolling*.

8. Lucy Smith, *Lucy's Book*, 6.

9. Ibid., 14.

10. Marquardt and Walters 1998, 43, n. 5. William Davis's detailed analysis of Smith's education argues persuasively that it was more extensive than has traditionally been assumed. See "Reassessing Joseph Smith Jr.'s Education."

11. Marquardt and Walters, *Inventing Mormonism*, 43, n. 5; Smith, *Lucy's Book*, 344; see also chapter 2.

12. History, circa Summer 1832, 2. The Joseph Smith Papers, accessed October 23, 2017, http://www.josephsmithpapers.org/paper-summary/history-circa-summer-1832.

13. Shipps, *Mormonism*, 17–21; Vogel, *Joseph Smith*, 128–9; Bushman, *Rough Stone Rolling*, 68–9.

14. All quotations from Smith's revelations are from *The Joseph Smith Papers*, except where noted. Chapter and verse references are from the contemporary LDS editions.

15. For a detailed account of the *Book of Mormon*'s publication history, see Gutjahr, *The Book of Mormon*.

16. Italics were used by the King James translators to mark words they added to the text necessary for English readability but which lacked exact analogues in the original. See Norton, *Textual History of the King James Bible*.

17. I am deeply grateful to Royal Skousen for sharing a prepublication version of his definitive analysis of Isaiah's italicized words as they appear in the *Book of Mormon*; this analysis will be published in Volume 3 of Skousen's *The History of the Text of the Book of Mormon* (Provo, Utah: Foundation for Ancient Research and Mormon Studies). My estimates here are based on Skousen's count of the number of italicized words in the AV Isaiah (438), the number of those italicized words that are altered in the *Book of Mormon* version of the text (171), and the total number of differences between the texts (811). I believe that some of Skousen's methods overrepresent the last number (some edits that could be counted as a single change have been counted as multiple changes); however, his exhaustive and diligent study provides definitive answers to a long-standing point of scholarly controversy. For earlier work on Isaiah's italics and the *Book of Mormon*, see Wright, "Joseph Smith's Interpretation of Isaiah in the Book of Mormon," 182; Tvedtnes, "The Isaiah Variants in the Book of Mormon," 6–19; and Skousen, "Textual Variants in the Isaiah Quotations." For an exploration of similar questions with respect to another part of the *Book of Mormon*, see Larson, "The Historicity of the Matthean Sermon on the Mount in 3 Nephi."

The suggestion that Smith read from a bible for a portion of the dictation process does not accord with first-hand accounts of that process. These accounts differ on a few particulars, but agree that Smith dictated while covering his face with a hat containing, in most reports, his seer stone. The most commonly cited statements, however, date from decades after the fact and come from individuals who witnessed only small portions of the dictation (see Whitmer *An Address to All Believers in Christ*, 12, and Bidamon, "Interview with Joseph Smith III, February 1879," *Early Mormon Documents*, Volume 1, 542). Smith himself and Oliver Cowdery, his most frequent scribe, left no detailed account of the process. Contemporary accounts from Smith's detractors insisted that Smith had copied from a Bible (see, for example, *The Painesville [Ohio] Telegraph*, March 22, 1831); I find these to be no more or less admissible than supporters' accounts insisting that Smith recited the approximately 11,000 words in those fifteen chapters of Isaiah without reference to the text. In any case, it does not seem unreasonable to suggest that Smith and Cowdery referred to a bible for those passages, particularly when the relatively close attention to a printed feature such as italics is considered, nor does it seem necessary to assume that doing so would have undermined Cowdery's confidence in Smith's revelatory powers. For scholarly discussions of the mechanics of the translation process of the *Book of Mormon*, see Lancaster, "The Translation of the Book of Mormon" and Givens, *By the Hand of Mormon*, 30–6.

18. Barlow, *Mormons and the Bible*, 13.

19. Wimbush, *Theorizing Scriptures*, 3.

20. Goodwillie, "Shaker Richard McNemar," 143.

21. Thomas, *A Mosaic for a Religious Counterculture*, 50.

22. See chapter 2.

23. Flake, *Translating Time*, 500.

24. Warner, *Letters of the Republic*, xiii.

25. Ibid., 64–5.

26. Looby, *Voicing America*, 80.

27. Ibid., 80, 44. Loughran, meanwhile, challenges the idea that print was ever separable from other textual forms or ever truly impersonal, owing to the technological realities of print into the mid-nineteenth century (*The Republic in Print* 113–16; see chapter 1).

28. See chapter 2. Amanda Porterfield (*Conceived in Doubt*) has written eloquently

about the early national period as an environment of doubt and the implications of this condition for religious authority.

29. While some paratextual features of the 1611 edition (such as the translators' preface and the dedication to King James) came and went in American editions, this phrase on the title page remained overwhelmingly consistent, even as "newly" became less and less relevant as time passed.

30. Sheehan, *The Enlightenment Bible*, 24. See also Perry, "Scripture, Time, and Authority among Early Disciples of Christ."

31. See Hills, *The English Bible in America*, 860 and 871.

32. "Repeatedly," Holland writes, "another *Bible* became the condemnatory title for threats to the church; these were the terms in which the orthodox had mentally structured their battles" (*Sacred Borders*, 64).

33. *Millennial Harbinger*, February 7, 1831; Holland, *Sacred Borders*, 143.

34. For analysis of the Book of Mormon's narrative structure, see Hardy, *Understanding the Book of Mormon*.

35. Elizabeth Fenton has made the perceptive argument that "through its presentation of variations on biblical texts such as Isaiah, the *Book of Mormon* offers a model of sacred history that centers on iteration and proliferation rather than unity" ("Open Canons," 347). I think that the radical variety of revelation is indeed a key theme of not just the *Book of Mormon* but Smith's entire career, but I would maintain that the book's interest in its material reliability illustrates a continuing concern for a unity of truth—in this view of scripture, there may be multiple iterations of a story, but each must maintain that it is not fundamentally different from another, as they must all accord with a single true account.

36. *Book of Mormon*, 1830, iii–iv. I am indebted to Judith Weisenfeld for this insight on the significance of the Preface's last line.

37. See preface to part I.

38. Genette avers that "truthfulness, or, at the very least sincerity . . . the effort to achieve truthfulness" is in fact the only thing that an author of a text can ascribe to him- or herself in the preface without alienating the reader. The trick of this function of the preface, Genette recognizes, is "to put a high value on the text without antagonizing the reader by too immodestly, or simply too obviously, putting a high value on the text's author." *Paratexts*, 206, 197.

39. Clarke, "Advertisement," unpaged.

40. Huggins, " 'Without a Cause' and 'Ships of Tarshish,' " 163, 165–6, 173.

41. These two bibles are the 1828 Phinney quarto published at Cooperstown, New York, which Smith and Cowdery purchased for the bible-editing project, and the 1831 quarto published by Langdon Coffin of Boston which apparently served as the Smith family bible. See chapter 2.

42. Hyrum Smith Diary and Accounts, 1831–1844, undated entry appears at cell 76 in the microfilm. Church History Library, Church of Jesus Christ of Latter-day Saints, Salt Lake City, Utah.

43. One of Smith's revelations (D&C 91) addresses the value of the Apocrypha. Controversialists have pointed to Smith's use of the Apocrypha as further evidence of his "plagiarizing" of the Bible, which misses the point made in this chapter about biblical facility and scripturalization.

44. Pratt and Goodson, "Preface," v–vi.

45. Marquardt and Walters, *Inventing Mormonism*, 43–4. Hatch has written against any tendency to gentrify Joseph Smith, suggesting that scholars risk turning his "radical, apocalyptic, absolutist, extreme, combustible, and militant" enterprise into "sipping tea in

a drawing room, engag[ing] in polite theological debate with Nathaniel William Taylor and William Ellery Channing" (*Mormon and Methodist*, 73). Letting alone the complicated relationship between formal theology and the rhetoric of radical religious movements, the problem with that warning is that, although he may never have sipped tea in his life, by all appearances Smith wanted to be in that drawing room: he had a respect for learning that belied his more "extreme, combustible, and militant" impulses. Moreover, Smith's choice of close associates throughout his career can be seen as a respect for what he considered learning. The *Book of Mormon* project lay dormant for nearly a year after the loss of the first pages and was revived only when Oliver Cowdery, a schoolteacher, came to meet Smith; Cowdery immediately became Smith's scribe and closest confidant. Cowdery, in turn, was replaced by Sydney Rigdon when Smith met him in late 1830. Rigdon had scarcely more formal education than Smith, but as a Campbellite minister had read much more widely. Another of Smith's associates wrote at the time that "Rigdon was a thorough Bible scholar, a man of fine education, and a powerful orator" who "soon worked himself deep into Brother Joseph's affections, and had more influence over him than any other man living" (Van Wagoner, *Sidney Rigdon*, 73). Rigdon's influence with Smith faded when John C. Bennett joined the Church in 1840: Bennett was a medical doctor and self-styled polymath (Smith, *The Saintly Scoundrel*).

46. See, for example, the following early missionary diaries held by the Church History Library, Church of Jesus Christ of Latter-day Saints, Salt Lake City, Utah: Barnes; Grant; Cahoon; and Hyde.

47. Shipps and Welch, *The Journals of William E. McLellin*, 31, 33.

48. See Bushman, *Rough Stone Rolling*, 131. Fenton makes a similar point, noting that Smith's is the initial voice of narration in the *Book of Mormon* ("Open Canons," 349).

49. As Grant recorded: "[W]e then had a privlige of conversing with elder pursery[?] and of hearing his objections against the *Book of Mormon* one was that he did not believe it another was that Joseph Smith jr got a coppy right I shoed him that that was nothing against the book." Grant, Journal, July 17, 1834, page 3. Church History Library, Church of Jesus Christ of Latter-day Saints, Salt Lake City, Utah.

50. Patten, *Journal*, 2–3.

51. John Taylor, "Discourse, April 13th, 1879," 94.

52. See The Joseph Smith Papers, "Joseph Smith as Revelator and Translator," http://www.josephsmithpapers.org/intro/revelations-and-translations-series-introduction, accessed October 23, 2017.

53. Juster, *Doomsayers*, 166–7.

54. The Joseph Smith Papers, "Revelation Book 1 Historical Introduction," http://www.josephsmithpapers.org/paper-summary/revelation-book-1/201#historical-intro, accessed October 23, 2017.

55. *Book of Commandments* (1833): 3, 6.

56. In addition to their relevance to the intersection of American religious history and print-culture studies and the nature of religious subjectivity in the early national period, the arguments presented here have important consequences for contemporary scholarship on early Mormonism. To argue that Smith is not only an active presence in his early texts, but, further, that his editorial voice was a crucial part of their acceptance as scripture, pushes back against the contemporary bent of early Mormon studies. For more, see Perry, "The Many Bibles of Joseph Smith," 767–9.

57. *Evening and Morning Star*, July 1833.

58. Genesis 1:4 in Smith's text reads: "And I have work for thee, Moses, my son; and thou art in the similitude of mine Only Begotten; and mine Only Begotten is and shall be

the Savior, for he is full of grace and truth; but there is no God beside me; and all things are present with me, for I know them all."

59. "That Rigdon could have been merely 'Sydney the Scribe,' a penman whose sole function was to take down dictation, is implausible," his biographer argues. "A biblical scholar with a reputation for erudition, he was more learned, better read, and more steeped in biblical interpretation that any other early Mormon, despite his common school education." Matthews likewise does not assume that the bible revision was strictly a matter of Smith's dictation, as the production of the *Book of Mormon* had been. Rather, "there must have been frequent periods of discussion about various passages and ideas." Matthews, "*A Plainer Translation*," 39.

60. For example, Acts 17:31: "Because he hath appointed a day, in the which he will judge the world in righteousness by ~~that man~~ **him** whom he hath ordained; ~~whereof~~ **and** he hath given assurance **of this** unto all *men*, in that he hath raised him from the dead."

61. See Doctrine and Covenants of the Church of the Latter Day Saints (1835).

62. Van Wagoner, *Sydney Rigdon*, 73.

63. Campbell, a founder of the movement known today as the Disciples of Christ, was a leader of the early national movement to restore Christianity to what was imagined to be its primitive form, the church as described in the New Testament. Campbell's New Testament, known as the *Living Oracles*, was not a new translation but an edited collection of the work of three British scholars that Campbell found truer to the original languages. It first appeared in 1826 and was probably the most widely read alternative to the King James among Protestants in the early nineteenth century. See Perry, "Scripture, Time, and Authority among Early Disciples of Christ."

64. Huggins, "'Without a Cause' and 'Ships of Tarshish,'" 167; see Perry, "Scripture, Time, and Authority."

65. See, to the point, Thomas Scott's commentary on Isaiah 2:16, which quotes from the eighteenth-century commentaries of Robert Lowth.

66. See Huggins "'Without a Cause,'" 163; Wright, "Joseph Smith's Interpretation of Isaiah in the Book of Mormon."

67. Huggins, 165–6.

68. "Mormonism and the Mormons," *The Methodist Quarterly Review*, January 1843, 113; Huggins, 173.

69. Sheehan, *The Enlightenment Bible*, 12.

70. Orson Hyde journal, 1832 February–December, Church History Library, Church of Jesus Christ of Latter-day Saints, Salt Lake City, Utah. The reference was to 2 Nephi 25:20: "And now, my brethren, I have spoken plainly that ye cannot err."

Conclusion

1. Strickland, *History of the American Bible Society* (1849), 18, 136, 335.

2. See Livermore, *Remarks on the Publication and Circulation of the Scriptures*, 14–15.

3. Fessenden, *Culture and Redemption*, chapter 3, and Gutjahr, *An American Bible*, chapter 4.

4. Strickland 1849, 82.

5. Livermore, 16–17.

6. See Strickland 1856, 18, 132, 124, 76.

7. On these developments see the essays in Casper et.al, eds., *The Industrial Book, 1840–1880*.

8. Strickland 1856, 74; *Sixty-fourth Annual Report of the American Bible Society* (1880), 36; *Eighty-fourth Annual Report of the American Bible Society* (1900), 12.

9. Strickland 1849, 79.

10. John Modern and Sonia Hazard have made a similar point with respect to the reports of the American Tract Society. As Modern suggests, "The presentation of 'data' invited individuals to read the meaning of their own sociality and to organize their lives in accordance with the political imagination being promoted" (*Secularism in Antebellum America*, 102). See also Hazard, "The Touch of the Word," 131–4.

11. *An American Bible*, 173. Robert Alter, meanwhile, places the decline of the Bible a century later, looking back to the mid nineteenth century as the glory days of American letters, owing to the sense of style accompanying widespread biblicism ("American Literary Style and the Presence of the King James Bible").

12. *America's Public Bible* http://americaspublicbible.org, accessed October 23, 2017.

13. "Diversification in American Religious Publishing," in Casper et al, eds., 195.

14. Fessenden, *Culture and Redemption*; Modern, *Secularism in Antebellum America*.

15. Shalev, *American Zion*, 12.

16. Strickland 1856, 20–1.

17. *The Civil War as a Theological Crisis*, 22.

18. Regarding the contest over the Bible and slavery, see also Fox-Genovese and Genovese, *Mind of the Master Class*, chapters 15–17.

19. *A debate on slavery*, 39 and 424, respectively.

20. *Message to the Blackman in America*, 95.

21. *Dispensational Modernism*, 4. See Pietsch, chapter 7, on the Scofield Bible. See also Marsden, "Everyone One's Own Interpreter? The Bible, Science, and Authority in Mid-Nineteenth-Century America."

22. Livermore, 18.

23. "Notices of Recent Publications," *Christian Examiner and Religious Miscellany*, 308.

24. Proust, *Finding Time Again*, 194.

Primary Sources

Address of the Bible Society Established at Philadelphia, An. Philadelphia: Fry & Kammerer, 1809.

Alley, Sarah. *Account of a Trance or Vision of Sarah Alley, of Beekman Town, Dutchess County, and State of New-York* . . . . Philadelphia: Joseph Rakestraw, 1807.

American Bible Society. *Annual Reports of the American Bible Society with an Account of Its Organization*. New York: Daniel Fanshaw for the Society, 1838.

Ashburn, Rebecca. *Three Remarkable Dreams in Succession on Thursday Night April 15th Friday Night April 16th and Saturday Night April 11th 1802*. Philadelphia[?], 1802.

Augustine. Henry Chadwick, trans. *Confessions*. Oxford: Oxford University Press, 1991, 1998.

Babcock, William Smyth. Papers. American Antiquarian Society, Worcester, MA.

Backus, Isaac. *Family Prayer Not to Be Neglected* . . . . Newport, RI: Samuel Hall, 1766.

Barlow, William. *The Summe and Substance of the Conference, which, it pleased his Excellent Maiestie to have with the Lords Bishops . . . in his Maiesties Privie-Chamber, at Hampton Court. Ianuary 14, 1603*. London: V.S. for Mathew Law, 1605.

Barnes, Lorenzo D. Reminiscences and diaries, 1834–1839. Church History Library, Church of Jesus Christ of Latter-day Saints, Salt Lake City, UT.

Bible and Holy Scriptvres conteyned in the Olde and Newe Testament, The. Translated according to the Ebrue and Greke, and conferred with the best translations in diuers langages. . . . Geneva: Printed by Rouland Hall, 1560.

Bible Biography, in the Form of Questions: With References to Scripture for the Answers . . . . Boston: Munroe & Francis, 1830.

Bible Society (Philadelphia, PA). *The Eighth Report of the Bible Society of Philadelphia*. Philadelphia: William Fry, 1816.

Bickersteth, Edward. *A Scripture Help*. Boston: S.H. Parker, 1817.

Bidamon, Emma Smith. "Interview with Joseph Smith III, February 1879," in Dan Vogel, ed., *Early Mormon Documents*, Vol. 1, 534–45. Salt Lake City, UT: Signature Books, 1996.

Book of Commandments for the Government of the Church of Christ: Organized According to Law on the 6th of April, 1830, A. Zion, MO: W. W. Phelps, 1833.

Boudinot, Elias. Bible. Princeton Borough Collection, Princeton University Department of Rare Books and Special Collections, 5179.1791.

Brown, John, ed. *Brown's Self-Interpreting Bible*. New York: Hodge & Campbell, 1792.

Cahoon, Reynolds. Diaries, 1831–1832. Church History Library, Church of Jesus Christ of Latter-day Saints, Salt Lake City, UT.

Carey, Mathew. "Address to the Subscribers for the Doway Translation of the Vulgate Bible." Philadelphia, 1790.

    Correspondence. Lea & Febiger Records, 1785–1982 [Collection 227B]. Historical Society of Pennsylvania, Philadelphia.

    Miscellanies (MS), Library Company of Philadelphia.

Carroll, John. Thomas O'Brien Hanley, S.J., ed. *The John Carroll Papers*, Volume 1. Notre Dame: University of Notre Dame Press, 1976.

"Catalogue of the Missionaries Library, &c, A." in *A Collection of Papers Printed by Order of the Society for the Propagation of the Gospel in Foreign Parts.* London: E. Owen, 1741.

Child(s), Isaac. *The Vision of Isaac Child(s).*

     Philadelphia[?] n.p. 1766 [23pp].

     Philadelphia[?] n.p. 1766a [12pp].

     Das Gesicht des Isaac Childs, welches er gesehen hat, betreffend das Land seiner Geburt. Aus dem Englischen übersetzt. Reading, PA: Barton und Jungmann, 1791.

     Philadelphia: Bickley, 1814.

     Philadelphia: John Simmon, 1826.

     Baltimore: William Wooddy, 1830.

     Sherwoods, NY: David Heston, 1861.

     Emporia, KS: Ezra Lamborn, 1883.

     Glen Rose, PA: Charles Brinton, 1929.

     MS. MSC 141, Folder 27. Mercer Museum Library, Doylestown, PA.

     MS. MSC 163, Folder 95. Mercer Museum Library, Doylestown, PA.

     MS. Department of Rare Books and Special Collections, Princeton University Library, Princeton, NJ.

     MSS. Miscellaneous Manuscripts Collection, Friends Historical Library, Swarthmore College, Swarthmore, PA.

     MS, 1789. Henry Warrington piece book, Friends Historical Library, Swarthmore College, Swarthmore, PA.

     MS, 1812. Abraham Warrington piece book, Friends Historical Library, Swarthmore College, Swarthmore, PA.

     MS, 1780. Historical Society of Pennsylvania, Philadelphia.

     MS, 1780. Ontario County Historical Society, Canandaigua, NY.

     MS, 1778. Oyster Bay Historical Society, Oyster Bay, NY.

     MS. Families of Philadelphia Papers, 1700–1942, Quaker & Special Collections, Haverford College, Haverford, PA.

     MSS. "The Vision of Isaac Childs," 1757 (MC.975.07.019). Quaker & Special Collections, Haverford College, Haverford, PA.

     MS. Vaux Collection of Correspondence, Documents and Graphics, 1659–1978, Quaker & Special Collections, Haverford College, Haverford, PA.

Christian Examiner and Religious Miscellany, Volume 47. Boston: Wm. Crosby & H.P. Nichols, 1849.

Cish, Jane. *The Vision and Wonderful Experience of Jane Cish . . . Being a Copy from Her Own Mouth, and Published at the Request of Several of her Friends.* Philadelphia, 1793.

Clarke, Adam. "Advertisement," in *The Holy Bible.* New York: D. & G. Bruce, 1811[–1825].

Clarke, Samuel. *The Marrow of Ecclesiastical History Divided into Two Parts . . . .* London: William Birch, 1675.

Collection of Memorials Concerning Divers Deceased Ministers and others of the People called Quakers, A. Philadelphia: Crukshank, 1787.

Columbian Family and Pulpit Bible . . . The. Boston: Joseph Teal, 1822.

Commercial Advertiser (New York).

Cowdery, Oliver. "Letter to Hyrum Smith, 14 June 1829," in Dan Vogel, ed., *Early Mormon Documents*, Vol. 2, 402–3. Salt Lake City, UT: Signature Books, 1998.

Cox, F. A. *Female Scripture Biography: Including an Essay on what Christianity has done for Women.* New York: James Eastburn & Co., 1817.

Coy, Hannah. *A Wonderful Account of a Little Girl of Nine Years Old, Who Lives in the Town of Jericho, in the State of Vermont; by the Name of Hannah Coy.* . . . Windsor, VT: A. Spooner for the Purchaser, 1800.

Craig, Frederick. Correspondence. Lea & Febiger Records, 1785–1982 [Collection 227B]. Historical Society of Pennsylvania, Philadelphia.

Cruden, Alexander. *A Complete Concordance to the Holy Scriptures.* Boston: Gould, Kendall, & Lincoln, 1845.

Daily Scripture Expositor: Containing a Text of Scripture for Every Day in the Year; with Explanatory Notes and Brief Reflections. New York: C. Wells, 1835.

Debate on Slavery, Held on the First, Second, Third and Sixth Days of October, 1845, in the City of Cincinnati . . . *A.* Cincinnati: W.H. Moore, 1846.

Doctrine and Covenants of the Church of the Latter Day Saints. Kirtland, OH: F.G. Williams & Co., 1835.

Doddridge, Philip. *The Family Expositor.* Charlestown, MA: S. Etheridge, 1807 [–1808].

Douglass, Frederick, Philip S. Foner, ed. *Frederick Douglass: Selected Speeches and Writings.* Chicago: Chicago Review Press, 2000.

Dow, Lorenzo. *The Life and Travels of Lorenzo Dow.* Hartford, CT: Lincoln & Gleason, 1804.

———. *The Travels and Providential Experience of Lorenzo Dow.* . . . Liverpool: Forshaw, 1807.

Dow, Peggy. *Vicissitudes Exemplified; or, The Journey of Life.* Totten: New York, 1814.

———. *Vicissitudes; or, The Journey of Life.* Philadelphia: Rakestraw, 1815.

———. *Vicissitudes in the Wilderness; or, The Journey of Life; Exemplified in the Journal of Peggy Dow.* Liverpool: W. Forshaw, 1818.

———. *Vicissitudes in the Wilderness; Exemplified in the Journal of Peggy Dow.* Norwich, CT: William Faulkner, 1833.

Eastern Argus (Portland, ME).

Elaw, Zilpha. *Memoirs of the Life, Religious Experience, Ministerial Travels and Labours of Mrs. Zilpha Elaw.* London: Published by the Authoress, 1846.

English Version of the Polyglott Bible, The. Philadelphia: Key & Meilke, 1831.

Enfield, William. *Biographical Sermons, Or, A Series of Discourses on the Principal Characters in Scripture.* Philadelphia: Francis Bailey, 1791.

Essex Patriot (Haverhill, MA).

Evening and Morning Star (Independence, MO).

Eyes and No Eyes and Eyes that See Not, Or How to Read the Bible Aright. Philadelphia: American Sunday School Union, 1827.

Fletcher, John. *Studies on Slavery: In Easy Lessons: Compiled into Eight Studies, and Subdivided into Short Lessons for the Convenience of Readers.* Natchez, MS: 1852.

Ford, Paul Leicester and Emily Ellsworth Ford Skeel, eds. *Mason Locke Weems: His Works and Ways.* Norwood, MA: Plimpton Press, 1929.

Goldsmith, Oliver. *An History of the Lives, Actions, Travels, Sufferings, and Deaths of the Most Eminent Martyrs and Primitive Fathers of the Church in the First Four Centuries.* . . . London: J. Newbery, 1764.

Grant, Jedidiah. Journal. Church History Library, Church of Jesus Christ of Latter-day Saints, Salt Lake City, UT.

Hall, David. Papers. American Philosophical Society, Philadelphia.

Hall, David D., ed. *The Antinomian Controversy, 1636–1638: A Documentary History.* Durham: Duke University Press, 1990.

Henry, Thomas Charleton. *Letters to an anxious inquirer.* Philadelphia: Key & Biddle, 1833.

Hewitt (James and Caroline Grayson) and Carradine Family Bible. Mississippi Department of Archives and History, Jackson.

Hicks, Elias. Isaac T. Hopper, ed. *Letters of Elias Hicks: Including Also a Few Short Essays Written on Several Occasions, Mostly Illustrative of His Doctrinal Views*. New York: Isaac T. Hopper, 1834.

Holy Bible, The. Conteyning the Old Testament and the New: Newly translated out of the originall tongues and with the former translations diligently compared. . . . London: Robert Barker, 1611.

Holy Bible, The. Containing the Old and New Testament: Or, a Family Bible, with Annotations and Parallel Scriptures. . . . by Samuel Clark. London: Sold by J. Fuller, 1760.

Holy Bible, The. Isaac Collins: Trenton, 1791.

  Philadelphia: Mathew Carey, 1802.

  Philadelphia: Mathew Carey, 1804.

  Albany: E. F. Backus, 1816.

  Boston: C. Ewer [1816].

  Brattleborough, VT: J. Holbrook, 1818.

  Cooperstown, NY: H. & E. Phinney, 1828.

  Hartford, CT: Silas Andrus, 1828.

  New York: N. & J. White, 1832.

  Boston: Langdon Coffin, 1834.

  Hartford, CT: Sumner & Goodman, 1846.

  Dayton, OH: E. A. & T. T. More, 1857.

  Buffalo: Phinney & Co., 1859.

  Philadelphia: W. W. Harding, 1876.

Holy Bible, The: Containing the Old Testament; . . . Designed for the use of students. New York: Charles Starr, 1835.

Holy Bible, The: With Original and Practical Observations and Copious Marginal References by Thomas Scott, 5 volumes. Philadelphia: William W. Woodward, 1804–09.

Hosner, Adeline Cleveland. Diary. Cornell University Special Collections, Ithaca, NY.

How, Ann. Sampler. http://www.scarlet-letter.com/samplers/how.php, accessed May 30, 2017.

Hunter, Henry. *Sacred Biography: Or, The History of the Patriarchs: To Which Is Added, the History of Deborah, Ruth, and Hannah*. Boston: Manning & Loring, 1794.

Hurlbut, Lucy. Journal, October 21, 1803, to April 29, 1832. New London County Historical Society, New London, CT.

Hyde, Orson. Journal, February–December, 1832. Church History Library, Church of Jesus Christ of Latter-day Saints, Salt Lake City, UT.

"Instructions for Catechists for Instructing Indians, Negroes, &c.," in *A Collection of Papers Printed by Order of the Society for the Propagation of the Gospel in Foreign Parts*. London: E. Owen, 1741.

James, John Angell. *The Anxious Inquirer after Salvation Directed and Encouraged*. 6th ed. London: Religious Tract Society, 1835.

Le Jau, Francis. Correspondence. British Online Archives, "American Material in the Archives of the USPG, 1635–1812." https://www.britishonlinearchives.co.uk/collection.php?cid=9781851171439&keywords, accessed October 26, 2017.

The Joseph Smith Papers. http://josephsmithpapers.org/.

Kennedy, Lionel H. and Thomas Parker. *An Official Report of the Trials of Sundry Negroes Charged with an Attempt to Raise an Insurrection in the State of South-Carolina. . . .* Charleston, SC: JR Schenck, 1822.

King, Mrs. (Frances Elizabeth). *Female Scripture Characters: Exemplifying Female Virtues*. Boston: Wells & Lilly, 1816.

Livermore, George. *Remarks on the Publication and Circulation of the Scriptures: Suggested by Rev. W. P. Strickland's History of the American Bible Society....* Cambridge, MA: Printed at the University Press, 1849.

Loughborough, John Norton. *Rise and Progress of the Seventh-Day Adventists: With Tokens of God's Hand in the Movement and a Brief Sketch of the Advent Cause from 1831 to 1844.* General Conference Association of the Seventh-day Adventists, 1892.

Luther, Martin. Albert T. W. Steinhaeuser, trans. "To the Councilmen of all Cities in Germany that they establish and Maintain Christian Schools" (1524), in Walther I. Brandt, ed., *Luther's Works vol. 45 The Christian in Society II.* Philadelphia: Muhlenbuerg Press, 1962.

Macgowan, John. *The Life of Joseph, the Son of Israel. In Eight Books: Chiefly Designed to Allure Young Minds to a Love of the Sacred Scriptures.* Sagg-Harbour, NY: David Frothingham, 1792.

Martin, Gregory. *A Discouerie of the Manifold Corruptions of the Holy Scriptures by the Heretikes of our Daies Specially the English Sectaries, and of their Foule Dealing Herein, by Partial & False Translations to the Aduantage of their Heresies, in their English Bibles Used and Authorised Since the Time of Schisme.* Rhemes: John Fogny, 1582.

Mary Scott, Eldest Daughter of Rev. T. Scott, the Commentator. New York: American Tract Society, 1848.

Mather, Cotton. *The Wonders of the Invisible World. Observations as well Historical as Theological, upon the Nature, the Number, and the Operations of the Devils.* Boston: Printed by Benj. Harris for Sam. Phillips, 1693.

McNemar, Richard. *The Kentucky Revival.* Cincinnati: John W. Browne, 1807.

Memoir on the Subject of a General Bible Society for the United States of America. By a Citizen of the state of New York. New Jersey: n.p., 1816.

Merbecke, John. *The Lives of Holy Saints, Prophets, Patriarchs, Apostles, and Others Contained in Holy Scripture....* London: John Williams, 1681.

Methodist Quarterly Review. New York: Lane & Sanford, 1843.

Millennial Harbinger (Bethany, VA).

Miller, William. *Memoirs of William Miller.* Boston: Joshua Himes, 1853.

Muhammad, Elijiah. *Message to the Blackman in America.* Newport News, VA: United Brothers Communications Systems, 1965.

Murray, Lindley. *The Duty and Benefit of a Daily Perusal of the Holy Scriptures.* New York: C. Wiley & Co., 1817.

New England Primer. Germantown, PA: Christopher Sower, 1771.

New Testament, The ... with the learned and excellent Preface of the Rev. Thomas Scott, D.D., Author of the commentary on the Bible, etc. New York: Whiting & Watson, 1812.

New-York Gazette and Weekly Mercury.

Newell, Fanny. *Memoirs of Fanny Newell; written by herself....* 3rd ed. Springfield, MA: O.Scott & E. F. Newell, 1833.

Occom, Samson. Joanna Brooks, ed. *The Collected Writings of Samson Occom, Mohegan: Leadership and Literature in Eighteenth-Century Native America.* New York: Oxford University Press, 2006.

Paine, Thomas. *The Age of Reason Part the Second.* [Paris]: Printed for the Author, 1795.

Patten, David W. Journal, July 1832–November 1834. Church History Library, Church of Jesus Christ of Latter-day Saints, Salt Lake City, UT.

The Painesville [Ohio] Telegraph.

Pearson, Edward A., ed. *Designs Against Charleston: The Trial Record of the Denmark Vesey Slave Conspiracy of 1822.* Chapel Hill: University of North Carolina Press, 1999.

Pennsylvania Packet (Philadelphia).

Phillips, Ann. *A Vision of Heaven and Hell.* Barnard, VT: Joseph Dix, [1812].

Pool, Caleb. *News from Heaven, by Visions / Communicated Miraculously To, and Explained By, Caleb Pool*. Salem, MA: Printed for the Author, 1805.

Poulson's American Daily Advertiser (Philadelphia).

Pratt, Parley P. and John Goodson. "Preface." *The Book of Mormon*. Kirtland, OH: O. Cowdery & Co, 1837.

Pratt, Phineas. Bible. Mississippi Department of Archives and History, Jackson, Mississippi.

Priestley, T. *The New and Complete Evangelical History of the Life of Our Blessed Lord and Saviour Jesus Christ . . . .* London: Alex. Hogg, 1793.

Proust, Marcel. Ian Patterson, trans. *Finding Time Again*. London: Allen Lane, 2002.

Review and Herald (Battle Creek, MI).

Robinson, Thomas. *Scripture Characters: Or, a Practical Improvement of the Principal Histories in the Old and New Testament*. 4th ed. London: J. Mathews, 1800.

Say, Thomas. *The Visions of a Certain Thomas Say, of the City of Philadelphia, which he Saw in a Trance: To which is Added, Another Vision. By the late Reverend Isaac Watts, D.D.* Philadelphia: William Mentz, 1774.

————. *A True and Wonderful Account of Mr. Thomas Say, of Philadelphia, while in a Trance*. [Philadelphia?], 1792.

Scripture Characters; by a Parent for His Children. London: W. Darton, 1811.

"The Secret of England's Greatness," National Portrait Gallery. http://www.npg.org.uk /collections/search/portrait/mw00071/The-Secret-of-Englands-Greatness-Queen -Victoria-presenting-a-Bible-in-the-Audience-Chamber-at-Windsor.

Shipps, Jan and John W. Welch eds., *The Journals of William E. McLellin, 1831–1836*. Urbana, IL: University of Illinois Press, 1994.

Skousen, Royal, ed. *The Book of Mormon: The Earliest Text*. New Haven: Yale University Press, 2009.

Smith, Hyrum. Diary and Accounts, 1831–1844. Church History Library, Church of Jesus Christ of Latter-day Saints, Salt Lake City, UT.

Smith, Lucy. Lavina Fielding Anderson, ed. *Lucy's Book: A Critical Edition of Lucy Mack Smith's Family Memoir*. Salt Lake City, UT: Signature Books, 2001.

Statutes of the Realm. Printed by Command of His Majesty King George the Third. Volume 3. 1817.

Stearns, Norris. *The Religious Experience of Norris Stearns*. Greenfield, MA: Denio & Phelps, 1815.

Stevenson, William. *The Sacred History*. London: James Holland, 1717.

Strickland, W. P. *History of the American Bible Society*. New York: Harper & Brothers, 1849, 1856.

Taylor, John. "Discourse, April 13th, 1879," in *Journal of Discourses*. Volume 21. Liverpool: Albert Carrington, 1881.

Theed, Richard. *Sacred Biography, Or, Scripture-Characters . . . .* London: W. Bowyer, 1712.

Thomas, Eliza. William Billings and Thomas Pitnam, eds. *A Vision; Tending to Edify, Astonish, and Instruct; Experienced by Miss Eliza Thomas . . . .* Stonington, CT: Samuel Trumbull, 1800.

Towle, Nancy. *Vicissitudes Illustrated: in the Experience of Nancy Towle, in Europe and America. . . .* 2nd ed. Portsmouth: John Caldwell, 1833.

[Warner, Susan]. *The Law and the Testimony*. New York: Robert Carter & Brothers, 1853.

Watkins, John. *Scripture Biography . . . .* New York: Simpson & Lindsay, 1810.

Wesley, Jonathan. *Explanatory Notes upon the New Testament*. Philadelphia: Printed by Joseph Crukshank, 1791.

White, Ellen G. *Life Sketches Manuscript*. Ellen G. White Archives and Database Resource.

https://text.egwwritings.org/publicationtoc.php?bookCode=LSMS&lang=en&collection=2&section=253.

———. *A Sketch of the Christian Experience and Views of Ellen G. White*. Saratoga Springs, NY: James White, 1851.

———. *Spiritual Gifts*. Volume 2. Ellen G. White Archives and Database Resource. http://www.gilead.net/egw/books/spiritual-gifts/Spiritual_Gifts._Volume_2/.

———. *A Word to the Little Flock*. Facsimile Reproduction. Washington, DC: Review and Herald Publishing Association, [1847?].

White, James and Ellen Gould Harmon White. *Life Sketches: Ancestry, Early Life, Christian Experience, and Extensive Labors of Elder James White, and His Wife Mrs. Ellen G. White*. Battle Creek, MI: Press of the Seventh-day Adventist Publishing Association, 1880.

Whitmer, David. *An Address to All Believers in Christ, By a Witness to the Divine Authenticity of the Book of Mormon*. Richmond, MO; n.p., 1887.

Wilbur, Hervey, ed. *The Reference Bible . . . .* Boston: Hilliard & Co., 1826.

———. *A Short Biblical Catechism*. Exeter, MA: Norris & Co., 1814.

Willey, Chloe. *A Short Account of the Life and Remarkable Views of Mrs. Chloe Willey of Goshen N.H. Written by Herself*. Amherst, NH: Joseph Cushing, 1807.

Witherspoon, John. "To the Reader," in *The Holy Bible*. Philadelphia: William Young, 1790.

———. Trenton: Isaac Collins, 1793.

Woodward, William. Correspondence. Historical Society of Pennsylvania, Philadelphia.

Young, William. Correspondence, 1792–1827. Historical Society of Pennsylvania, Philadelphia.

Secondary Sources

Allen, Thomas M. *A Republic in Time: Temporality and Social Imagination in Nineteenth-Century America*. Chapel Hill: University of North Carolina Press, 2008.

Alter, Robert. "American Literary Style and the Presence of the King James Bible," *New England Review* 30: 4 (January 1, 2009): 60–75.

Anderson, Benedict. *Imagined Communities: Reflections on the Origin and Spread of Nationalism*. London: Verso, 1991.

Arendt, Hannah. "What is Authority?" in *Between Past and Future*. New York: Penguin, 1954, 1977.

Bakhtin, M. M. *The Dialogic Imagination: Four Essays*, Michael Holquist, ed. Caryl Emerson, trans. Austin: University of Texas Press, 1982.

———. *Art and Answerability: Early Philosophical Essays*. Michael Holquist and Vadim Liapunov, eds. Liapunov, trans. Austin: University of Texas Press, 1990.

Baker, Simon. "Jesse Olney's Innovative Geography Text of 1828 for Common Schools," *Journal of Geography* 95, no. 1 (January–February 1996): 32-8.

Barlow, Philip L. *Mormons and the Bible*. Oxford: Oxford University Press, 1991, 2013.

Barthes, Roland. Richard Miller, trans. *The Pleasure of the Text*. New York: Hill & Wang, 1975.

Bauman, Richard. *For the Reputation of Truth: Politics, Religion, and Conflict among the Pennsylvania Quakers, 1750–1800*. Baltimore: Johns Hopkins Press, 1971.

Beeman, Richard R. *The Varieties of Political Experience in Eighteenth-Century America*. Philadelphia: University of Pennsylvania Press, 2004.

Bell, Catherine M. *Ritual Theory, Ritual Practice*. Oxford: Oxford University Press, 2009.

Bentley, G. E., Jr. "The Holy Pirates: Legal Enforcement in England of the Patent in the Authorized Version of the Bible ca. 1800," *Studies in Bibliography* 50 (1997).

Berkovitch, Sacvan. *The Puritan Origins of the American Self.* New Haven: Yale University Press, 1975.

Bielo, James, ed. *The Social Life of Scriptures: Cross-Cultural Perspectives on Biblicism.* New Brunswick, NJ: Rutgers University Press, 2009.

Bowman, Matthew and Samuel Brown, "Reverend Buck's Theological Dictionary and the Struggle to Define American Evangelicalism, 1802–1851," *Journal of the Early Republic* 29, no. 3 (2009): 441–73.

Bourdieu, Pierre. Gino Raymond and Matthew Adamson, trans. *Language and Symbolic Power.* Cambridge: Harvard University Press, 1991.

Boylan, Anne M. *Sunday School: The Formation of an American Institution, 1790–1880.* New Haven: Yale University Press, 1988.

Bozeman, Theodore Dwight. *To Live Ancient Lives: The Primitivist Dimension in Puritanism.* Chapel Hill: University of North Carolina Press, 1988.

Braude, Ann. "Women's History *Is* American Religious History," in Thomas A. Tweed, ed., *Retelling U.S. Religious History.* Berkeley: University of California Press, 1997.

Breen, T. H. "An Empire of Goods: The Anglicization of Colonial America, 1690–1776," *Journal of British Studies* 25, no. 4 (October 1, 1986): 467–99.

———. *The Marketplace of Revolution: How Consumer Politics Shaped American Independence.* New York: Oxford University Press, 2004.

———. "'Baubles of Britain': The American and Consumer Revolutions of the Eighteenth Century," *Past & Present* 119 (May 1, 1988): 73–104.

Brekus, Catherine A. *Strangers and Pilgrims: Female Preaching in America, 1740–1845.* Chapel Hill: University of North Carolina Press, 1998.

———. *Sarah Osborn's World: The Rise of Evangelical Christianity in Early America.* New Haven, CT: Yale University Press, 2013.

———. "Writing Religious Experience: Women's Authorship in Early America," *The Journal of Religion* 92, no. 4 (October 1, 2012): 482–97.

Brewer, David A. *The Afterlife of Character, 1726–1825.* Philadelphia: University of Pennsylvania Press, 2005.

Brissett, Dennis and Charles Edgley. "The Dramaturgical Perspective," in Brissett and Edgley, eds., *Life as Theater: A Dramaturgical Sourcebook,* 2nd ed. New York: Aldine de Gruyter, 1990.

Brown, Matthew. *The Pilgrim and the Bee: Reading Rituals and Book Culture in Early New England.* Philadelphia: University of Pennsylvania Press, 2007.

Brown, Robert. *Jonathan Edwards and the Bible.* Bloomington: Indiana University Press, 2002.

Brown, Samuel M. "Joseph (Smith) in Egypt: Babel, Hieroglyphs, and the Pure Language of Eden," *Church History* 78, no. 1 (2009): 26–65.

Brown, Sylvia. "Converting the Lost Sons of Adam: National Identities and the First Publication of the 'Society for the Propagation of the Gospel in New England,'" *Reformation* 4, no. 1 (January 1, 1999): 169–96.

Bushman, Richard. "Shopping and Advertising in Colonial America," in Cary Carson et al., *Of Consuming Interests: The Style of Life in the Eighteenth Century.* Charlottesville: University Press of Virginia, 1994.

———. "The Visionary World of Joseph Smith," *BYU Studies* 37, no. 1 (1997–98): 183–204.

———. *Rough Stone Rolling.* New York: Knopf, 2005.

Butler, Jon. *Awash in a Sea of Faith.* Cambridge: Harvard University Press, 1990.

Butler, Jonathan M. "A Portrait," in Terrie Dopp Aamodt, et al. eds., *Ellen Harmon White: American Prophet.* Oxford: Oxford University Press, 2014, 1–29.

Butler, Judith. *The Psychic Life of Power.* Stanford: Stanford University Press, 1997.

Byrd, James P. *Sacred Scripture, Sacred War: The Bible and the American Revolution.* Oxford: Oxford University Press, 2013.

Cadbury, Henry J. "Early Quakerism and Uncanonical Lore," *The Harvard Theological Review* 40, no. 3 (1947): 177–205.

Calhoun, Daniel. *The Intelligence of a People.* Princeton: Princeton University Press, 1973.

Callahan, Allen Dwight. *The Talking Book: African Americans and the Bible.* New Haven: Yale University Press, 2006.

Cambers, Andrew and Michelle Wolfe, "Reading, Family Religion, and Evangelical Identity in Late Stuart England," *The Historical Journal* 47, no. 4 (December 2004): 875–96.

Cambers, Andrew. "Demonic Possession, Literacy and 'Superstition' in Early Modern England," *Past and Present* 202, no. 1 (2009): 3–35.

Carpenter, Mary Wilson. *Imperial Bibles, Domestic Bodies Women, Sexuality, and Religion in the Victorian Market.* Athens, OH: Ohio University Press, 2003.

Casper, Scott E., et. al. eds. *The Industrial Book, 1840-1880: A History of the Book in America.* Volume 3. Chapel Hill: University of North Carolina Press, 2007.

Cayton, Mary Kupiec. "The Expanding World of Jacob Norton: Reading, Revivalism, and the Construction of a 'Second Great Awakening' in New England, 1787-1804," *Journal of the Early Republic* 26 (Summer 2006): 221–48.

Chartier, Roger. Lydia G. Cochrane, trans. *The Order of Books: Readers, Authors and Libraries in Europe between the Fourteenth and Eighteenth Centuries.* Stanford: Stanford University Press, 1992, 1994.

Clifford, Alan C. *The Good Doctor: Philip Doddridge of Northampton—A Tercentenary Tribute.* Norwich: Charenton Reformed Publishing, 2002.

Cope, Rachel. "'In Some Places a Few Drops and Other Places a Plentiful Shower': The Religious Impact of Revivalism on Early Nineteenth-Century New York Women." PhD. diss., Syracuse University, 2009.

Corns, Thomas N. and David Loewenstein, eds. *The Emergence of Quaker Writing: Dissenting Literature in Seventeenth-Century England.* Portland, OR: Frank Cass, 1995.

Corrigan, John. "Amalek and the Rhetoric of Extermination," in Chris Beneke and Christopher S. Grenda, eds., *The First Prejudice: Religious Tolerance and Intolerance in Early America.* Philadelphia: University of Pennsylvania Press, 2011.

Daniell, David. *The Bible in English: Its History and Influence.* New Haven: Yale University Press, 2003.

Darnton, Robert. "What Is the History of Books?" *Daedalus* 111, no. 3 (Summer 1982): 65–83.

Davidson, Cathy N. *Revolution and the Word: The Rise of the Novel in America.* New York: Oxford University Press, 1986, 2004.

Davis, Diane. *Inessential Solidarity: Rhetoric and Foreigner Relations.* Pittsburgh, PA: University of Pittsburgh Press, 2014.

Davis, William. "Reassessing Joseph Smith Jr.'s Formal Education," *Dialogue* (Winter 2016): 1–58.

Ditmore, Michael G. "A Prophetess in Her Own Country: An Exegesis of Anne Hutchinson's 'Immediate Revelation,'" *William and Mary Quarterly* 57, no. 2 (April 2000): 349–92.

Downing, David. "'Streams of Scripture Comfort': Mary Rowlandson's Typological Use of the Bible," *Early American Literature* 15, no. 3 (1980): 252–9.

Eco, Umberto. "'Casablanca': Cult Movies and Intertextual Collage," *SubStance* 14, no. 2 (1985): 3–12.

Egerton, Douglas R. "'Why They Did Not Preach up This Thing': Denmark Vesey and Revolutionary Theology," *The South Carolina Historical Magazine* 100, no. 4 (October 1, 1999): 298–318.

Elrod, Eileen Razzari. *Piety and Dissent: Race, Gender, and Biblical Rhetoric in Early American Autobiography.* Amherst, MA: University of Massachusetts Press, 2008.

Engelke, Matthew. "Angels in Swindon: Public Religion and Ambient Faith in England," *American Ethnologist* 39, no. 1 (February 1, 2012).

Fea, John. *The Bible Cause: A History of the American Bible Society.* New York: Oxford University Press, 2016.

Fenton, Elizabeth. "Open Canons: Sacred History and American History in the Book of Mormon," *J19* (2013): 339–61.

Ferdman, Bernardo M. "Literacy and Cultural Identity," *Harvard Educational Review* 60, no. 2 (May 1990).

Fessenden, Tracy. *Culture and Redemption: Religion, the Secular, and American Literature.* Princeton: Princeton University Press, 2007.

Fisher, Linford D. "America's First Bible: Native Uses, Abuses, and Reuses of the Indian Bible of 1663," in Philip Goff, Arthur E. Farnsley II, and Peter J. Thuesen, eds., *The Bible in American Life.* New York: Oxford University Press, 2017, 35–47.

Flake, Kathleen. "Translating Time: The Nature and Function of Joseph Smith's Narrative Canon," *Journal of Religion* 87, no. 4 (2007): 497–527.

Fox-Genovese, Elizabeth and Eugene D. Genovese. *Mind of the Master Class: History and Faith in the Southern Slaveholders' Worldview.* Cambridge, UK: Cambridge University Press, 2005.

Franchot, Jenny. *Roads to Rome: The Antebellum Protestant Encounter with Catholicism.* Berkeley: University of California Press, 1994.

Freadman, Anne. "Anyone for Tennis," in Ian Reid, ed., *The Place of Genre in Learning: Current Debates.* Waurn Ponds, Australia: Typereader Publications, 1987, 91–124.

———. "Uptake," in Richard Coe, Lorelei Lingard, and Tatiana Teslenko, eds., *The Rhetoric and Ideology of Genre: Strategies for Stability and Change.* Cresskill, NJ: Hampton Press, 2002, 39–53.

———. "The Traps and Trappings of Genre Theory," *Applied Linguistics* 33, no. 5 (2012): 544–63.

Frei, Hans. *The Eclipse of Biblical Narrative.* New Haven, CT: Yale University Press, 1974.

Frerichs, Ernest S., ed. *The Bible and Bibles in America.* Atlanta, GA: Scholars Press, 1988.

Furey, Constance M. "Body, Society, and Subjectivity in Religious Studies," *Journal of the American Academy of Religion* 80, no. 1 (2012): 7–33.

Furstenberg, Francois. *In the Name of the Father: Washington's Legacy, Slavery, and the Making of a Nation.* New York: Penguin, 2007.

Gaines, William H., Jr. "The Continental Congress Considers the Publication of a Bible, 1777," *Studies in Bibliography* 3 (1950–51).

Garcia, John J. "The 'curiousaffaire' of Mason Locke Weems: Nationalism, the Book Trade, and Printed Lives in the Early United States," *The Papers of the Bibliographical Society of America* 108, no. 4 (December 1, 2014): 453–75.

Gebarowski-Shafer, Ellie. "Catholics and the King James Bible: Stories from England, Ireland and America," *Scottish Journal of Theology* 66, no. 3 (August 2013): 253–60.

Genette, Gérard. Jane E. Lewin, trans. *Paratexts: Thresholds of Interpretation.* Cambridge, UK: Cambridge University Press, 1997.

Gilmont, Jean-François. "Protestant Reformations and Reading," in Guglielmo Cavallo, Roger Chartier, and Lydia G. Cochrane, eds., *A History of Reading in the West.* Amherst, MA: University of Massachusetts Press, 1999.

Gilmore, William J. *Reading Becomes a Necessity of Life: Material and Cultural Life in Rural New England, 1780–1835.* Knoxville: University of Tennessee Press, 1989.

Gilpin, W. Clark. *A Preface to Theology.* Chicago: University of Chicago Press, 1996.

Givens, Terryl. *By the Hand of Mormon: The American Scripture That Launched a New World Religion.* Oxford: Oxford University Press, 2002.

Glasson, Travis. *Mastering Christianity: Missionary Anglicanism and Slavery in the Atlantic World.* New York: Oxford University Press, 2011.

Glaude, Eddie S. *Exodus!: Religion, Race, and Nation in Early Nineteenth-Century Black America.* Chicago: University of Chicago Press, 2000.

Goodwillie, Christian. "Shaker Richard McNemar: The Earliest Book of Mormon Reviewer." *Journal of Mormon History* 37 (2011): 138–45.

Gordis, Lisa M. *Opening Scripture: Bible Reading and Interpretive Authority in Puritan New England.* Chicago: University of Chicago Press, 2002.

Grammer, Elizabeth. *Some Wild Visions: Autobiographies by Female Itinerant Evangelists in Nineteenth-Century America.* New York: Oxford University Press, 2002.

Gray, Jonathan. *Show Sold Separately: Promos, Spoilers, and Other Media Paratexts.* New York: New York University Press, 2010.

Green, James N. "The Rise of Book Publishing," in Robert A. Gross and Mary Kelley, eds., *A History of the Book in America.* Volume 2. Chapel Hill: University of North Carolina Press, 2010, 75–127.

Greenblatt, Stephen. *Renaissance Self-Fashioning: From More to Shakespeare.* Chicago: University of Chicago Press, 1980, 2005.

Gross, Robert A. "Introduction: An Extensive Republic," in Gross and Mary Kelley, eds., *A History of the Book in America.* Volume 2. Chapel Hill: University of North Carolina Press, 2010.

———. "Forum: The Making of a Slave Conspiracy, Part II," *The William and Mary Quarterly* 59, no. 1 (January 2002).

Guillory, John. *Cultural Capital: The Problem of Literary Canon Formation.* Chicago: University of Chicago Press, 1993.

Gutjahr, Paul C. *An American Bible: A History of the Good Book in the United States, 1777–1880.* Stanford: Stanford University Press, 1999.

———. *The Book of Mormon: A Biography.* Princeton: Princeton University Press, 2012.

Hackel, Heidi Brayman. "'Boasting of Silence': Women Readers in a Patriarchal State," in Kevin Sharpe and Steven N. Zwicker, eds., *Reading, Society and Politics in Early Modern England.* New York: Cambridge University Press, 2003.

Hall, David D. *Material Texts: Ways of Writing: The Practice and Politics of Text-Making in Seventeenth-Century New England.* Philadelphia: University of Pennsylvania Press, 2011.

———. *Worlds of Wonder, Days of Judgment: Popular Religious Belief in Early New England.* New York: Knopf, 1990.

Hamm, Thomas D. *The Transformation of American Quakerism: Orthodox Friends, 1800–1907.* Bloomington: Indiana University Press, 1988.

Hardy, Grant. *Understanding the Book of Mormon: A Reader's Guide.* New York: Oxford University Press, 2010.

Harris, R. Blaine, ed. *Authority: A Philosophical Analysis.* Tuscaloosa: University of Alabama Press, 1976.

Harris, William V. *Ancient Literacy.* Cambridge, MA: Harvard University Press, 1991.

Harriss, M. Cooper. "On the Eirobiblical: Critical Mimesis and Ironic Resistance in *The Confessions of Nat Turner*," *Biblical Interpretation* 21, nos. 4–5 (2013): 469–93.

Hartigan-O'Connor, Ellen. *Ties That Buy: Women and Commerce in Revolutionary America*. Philadelphia: University of Pennsylvania Press, 2011.

Haselby, Sam. *The Origins of American Religious Nationalism*. New York: Oxford University Press, 2015.

Hatch, Nathan O. *The Democratization of American Christianity*. New Haven, CT: Yale University Press, 1989.

——. "Mormon and Methodist," in Dean L. May, et al, eds., *The Mormon History Association's Tanner Lectures*. Urbana, IL: University of Illinois Press, 2006, 65–80.

Hatch, Nathan O. and Mark Noll, eds., *The Bible in America: Essays in Cultural History*. New York: Oxford University Press, 1982.

Haynes, Stephen R. *Noah's Curse: The Biblical Justification of American Slavery*. New York: Oxford University Press, 2002.

Haywood, Chanta M. "Prophesying Daughters: Nineteenth-Century Black Religious Women, the Bible, and Black Literary History," in Vincent L. Wimbush and Rosamond C. Rodman, eds., *African Americans and the Bible: Sacred Texts and Social Textures*. New York: Continuum, 2000.

Hazard, Sonia. "The Touch of the Word: Evangelical Cultures of Print in Antebellum America." PhD diss., Duke University, 2017.

Henwood, Dawn. "Mary Rowlandson and the Psalms: The Textuality of Survival," *Early American Literature* 32, no. 2 (1997): 169–86.

Herbert, A. S. *Historical Catalogue of Printed Editions of the English Bible 1525–1961; Revised and Expanded from the Edition of T. H. Darlow and H. F. Moule, 1903*. London: The British and Foreign Bible Society, 1968.

Hill, Christopher. *Society and Puritanism in Pre-Revolutionary England*. 2nd ed. London: Schocken Books, 1967.

Hills, Margaret T. *The English Bible in America: A Bibliography of the Bible and the New Testament Published in America, 1777–1957*. New York: American Bible Society, 1961.

Hindmarsh, D. Bruce. *The Evangelical Conversion Narrative: Spiritual Autobiography in Early Modern England*. New York: Oxford University Press, 2005.

Hitchin, Neil W. "The Politics of English Bible Translation in Georgian Britain," *Transactions of the Royal Historical Society* 9 (1999): 67–92.

Holifield, E. Brooks. *Era of Persuasion: American Thought and Culture, 1521–1680*. Boston: Twayne Publishers, 1989.

Holland, David. *Sacred Borders: Continuing Revelation and Canonical Restraint in Early America*. New York: Oxford University Press, 2011.

Hollywood, Amy. "Performativity, Citationality, Ritualization," *History of Religions* 42, no. 2 (2002): 93–115.

Holquist, Michael. *Dialogism: Bakhtin and His World*. 2nd ed. New York: Routledge, 2002.

Howe, Daniel Walker. *What Hath God Wrought: The Transformation of America, 1815–1848*. New York: Oxford University Press, 2007.

Howsam, Leslie. *Cheap Bibles: Nineteenth-Century Publishing and the British and Foreign Bible Society*. Cambridge, UK, and New York: Cambridge University Press, 1991.

Hughes, Richard T. and Leonard Allen. *Illusions of Innocence: Protestant Primitivism in America, 1630–1875*. Chicago: University of Chicago Press, 1988.

Huggins, Ronald V. "'Without a Cause' and 'Ships of Tarshish': A Possible Contemporary Source for Two Unexplained Readings from Joseph Smith," *Dialogue* 36, no. 1 (2003): 157–79.

Jackson, Greg. *The Word and its Witness: The Spiritualization of American Realism*. Chicago: University of Chicago Press, 2009.

Jackson, Kent P. "Joseph Smith and the Bible," *Scottish Journal of Theology* 63, no. 1 (2010): 24–40.

Johnson, Curtis D. *Islands of Holiness: Rural Religion in Upstate New York, 1790–1860*. Ithaca, NY: Cornell University Press, 1989.

Johnson, Michael P. "Denmark Vesey and His Co-Conspirators," *The William and Mary Quarterly* 58, no. 4 (2001): 915–76.

Johnson, Paul E. *A Shopkeeper's Millennium: Society and Revivals in Rochester, New York, 1815–1837*. New York: Hill & Wang, 1978.

Johnson, Sylvester A. "Scripturalizing Religion and Ethnicity: The Circle Seven Koran," in Philip Goff, Arthur E. Farnsley II, and Peter J. Thuesen, eds., *The Bible in American Life*. New York: Oxford University Press, 2017, 35–47.

Juster, Susan. *Doomsayers: Anglo-American Prophecy in the Age of Revolution*. Philadelphia: University of Pennsylvania Press, 2003.

Kerber, Linda K. *Women of the Republic: Intellect and Ideology in Revolutionary America*. New York: Norton, 1986.

Kling, David. "A Contested Legacy: Interpreting, Debating, and Translating the Bible in America," in Catherine A. Brekus and W. Clark Gilpin, eds., *American Christianities*. Chapel Hill: University of North Carolina Press, 2011.

Kowaleski-Wallace, Elizabeth. *Consuming Subjects: Women, Shopping, and Business in the Eighteenth Century*. New York: Columbia University Press, 1996.

Kristeva, Julia. "The System and the Speaking Subject" and "Word, Dialogue, and Novel," in Toril Moi, ed., *The Kristeva Reader*. New York: Columbia University Press, 1986.

Lancaster, James E. "The Translation of the Book of Mormon," in Dan Vogel, ed., *The Word of God: Essays on Mormon Scripture*. Salt Lake City, UT: Signature Books, 1990, 97–112.

Larson, Stan. "The Historicity of the Matthean Sermon on the Mount in 3 Nephi," in Brent Lee Metcalfe, ed., *New Approaches to the Book of Mormon*. Salt Lake City, UT: Signature Books, 1993, 115–63.

Lincoln, Bruce. *Authority: Construction and Corrosion*. Chicago: University of Chicago Press, 1994.

Little, J. I. "The Mental World of Ralph Merry: A Case Study of Popular Religion in the Lower Canadian-New England Borderland, 1798–1863," *Canadian Historical Review* 82, no. 3 (September 2002).

Lobody, Diane Helen. "Lost in the Ocean of Love: The Mystical Writings of Catherine Livingston Garrettson." PhD diss., Drew University, 1990.

Looby, Christopher. *Voicing America: Language, Literary Form, and the Origins of the United States*. Chicago: University of Chicago Press, 1996.

Loughran, Trish. *The Republic in Print: Print Culture in the Age of U.S. Nation Building, 1770–1870*. New York: Columbia University Press, 1999.

Lum, Kathryn Gin. *Damned Nation: Hell in America from the Revolution to Reconstruction*. New York: Oxford University Press, 2014.

Manguel, Alberto. *A History of Reading*. New York: Penguin, 1997.

Marietta, Jack D. *The Reformation of American Quakerism, 1748–1783*. Philadelphia: University of Pennsylvania Press, 1984.

Marquardt, H. Michael and Wesley P. Walters. *Inventing Mormonism: Tradition and the Historical Record*. Salt Lake City, UT: Signature Books, 1998.

Marsden, George. "Everyone One's Own Interpreter? The Bible, Science, and Authority in Mid-Nineteenth-Century America," in Hatch and Noll, eds., *The Bible in America: Essays in Cultural History*. Oxford: Oxford University Press, 1982.

Matthews, Robert J. "A Plainer Translation": Joseph Smith's Translation of the Bible—A History and Commentary. Provo, UT: Brigham Young University Press, 1975, 1980.

Mercado, Monica L. "'Have You Ever Read?': Imagining Women, Bibles, and Religious Print in Nineteenth-Century America," U.S. Catholic Historian 31, no. 3 (2013): 1–21.

Miller, Carolyn. "Genre as Social Action," The Quarterly Journal of Speech 70, no. 2 (1984): 151–67, 151–2.

Millner, Michael. Fever Reading: Affect and Reading Badly in the Early American Public Sphere. Durham, NH: University of New Hampshire Press, 2012.

Miner, Earl, ed. Literary Uses of Typology: From the Late Middle Ages to the Present. Princeton: Princeton University Press, 1977.

Modern, John Lardas. Secularism in Antebellum America. . . . Chicago: University of Chicago Press, 2011.

Monaghan, Learning to Read and Write in Colonial America. Amherst, MA: University of Massachusetts Press, 2007.

———. "Literacy Instruction and Gender in Colonial New England," in Cathy N. Davidson, ed., Reading in America: Literature and Social History. Baltimore: Johns Hopkins University Press, 1989.

Morton, Clay. "South of 'Typographic America': Orality, Literacy, and Nineteenth-Century Rhetorical Education," South Atlantic Review 71, no. 4 (Fall 2006), 45–61.

Mosala, Itumeleng J. Biblical Hermeneutics and Black Theology in South Africa. Grand Rapids, MI: W. B. Eerdmans Pub. Co., 1989.

Mullen, Lincoln. America's Public Bible: Biblical Quotations in U.S. Newspapers. Website, code, and datasets, 2016. http://americaspublicbible.org.

Neuman, Meredith Marie. Jeremiah's Scribes: Creating Sermon Literature in Puritan New England. Philadelphia: University of Pennsylvania Press, 2013.

Noll, Mark America's God: From Jonathan Edwards to Abraham Lincoln. Oxford: Oxford University Press, 2002.

———. In the Beginning Was the Word: The Bible in American Public Life, 1492–1783. Oxford: Oxford University Press, 2015.

———. The Civil War as a Theological Crisis. Chapel Hill: University of North Carolina Press, 2006.

Nord, David Paul. Faith in Reading: Religious Publishing and the Birth of Mass Media in America. Oxford: Oxford University Press, 2004.

Norton, David. A Textual History of the King James Bible. Cambridge, UK: Cambridge University Press, 2005.

Numbers, Ronald L. Prophetess of Health: Ellen G. White and the Origins of Seventh-day Adventist Health Reform. Grand Rapids, MI: W. B. Eerdmans Pub. Co., 1975, 2008.

O'Neill, Kevin. "Beyond broken: Affective spaces and the study of American religion," Journal of the American Academy of Religion 81, no. 4 (December 2013): 1093–1116.

Pasley, Jeffrey L., Andrew W. Robertson, and David Walstreicher, eds. Beyond the Founders: New Approaches to the Political History of the Early American Republic. Chapel Hill: University of North Carolina Press, 2004.

Patrick, Arthur. "Author," in Terrie Dopp Aamodt, et al. eds., Ellen Harmon White: American Prophet. Oxford: Oxford University Press, 2014, 91–109.

Perry, Seth. "'What the Public Expect': Consumer Authority and the Marketing of Bibles, 1770–1850," American Periodicals 24, no. 2 (2014): 128–44.

———. "Cosmopolite's Mount Sinai Domains: Lorenzo Dow Dreams of Empire in the Era of Good Feelings," Common-place 15, no. 3 (April 2015).

———. "The Many Bibles of Joseph Smith: Textual, Prophetic, and Scholarly Authority in

Early-National Bible Culture," *Journal of the American Academy of Religion* 84, no. 3 (September 2016), 750–75.

———. "Scripture, Time, and Authority among Early Disciples of Christ," *Church History* (December 2016).

Peters, Kate. *Print Culture and the Early Quakers.* New York: Cambridge University Press, 2005.

Pietsch, B. M. *Dispensational Modernism.* New York: Oxford University Press, 2015.

Porterfield, Amanda. *Conceived in Doubt: Religion and Politics in the New American Nation.* Chicago: University of Chicago Press, 2012.

Pred, Allan R. *Urban Growth and the Circulation of Information: The United States System of Cities, 1790–1840.* Cambridge, MA: Harvard University Press, 1973.

Price, Leah. *How to Do Things with Books in Victorian Britain.* Princeton: Princeton University Press, 2012.

Räisänen, Heikki. "Joseph Smith as a Creative Interpreter of the Bible," *International Journal of Mormon Studies* 2 (2009): 1–22.

Raven, James. "The Export of Books to Colonial North America," *Publishing History* 42 (January 1, 1997): 21–49.

Rickert, Thomas. *Ambient Rhetoric: The Attunements of Rhetorical Being.* Pittsburgh: University of Pittsburgh Press, 2013.

Rivett, Sarah. "The Algonquian Word and the Spirit of Divine Truth John Eliot's Indian Library and the Atlantic Quest for a Universal Language," in Matt Cohen, Jeffrey Glover, Paul Chaat Smith, eds. *Colonial Mediascapes: Sensory Worlds of the Early Americas.* Lincoln: University of Nebraska Press, 2014.

Robbins, Sarah. *Managing Literacy, Mothering America: Women's Narratives on Reading and Writing in the Nineteenth Century.* Pittsburgh, PA: University of Pittsburgh Press, 2006.

———. "'The Future Good and Great of Our Land': Republican Mothers, Female Authors, and Domesticated Literacy in Antebellum New England," *The New England Quarterly* 75, no. 4 (December 1, 2002): 562–91.

Roth, Randolph A. *The Democratic Dilemma: Religion, Reform, and the Social Order in the Connecticut River Valley of Vermont, 1791–1850.* New York: Cambridge University Press, 1987.

Round, Phillip. *Removable Type: Histories of the Book in Indian Country, 1663–1880.* Chapel Hill: University of North Carolina Press, 2010.

Saenger, Paul Henry and Kimberly Van Kampen, eds. *The Bible as Book: The First Printed Editions.* London: British Library, 1999.

St. Clair, William. *The Reading Nation in the Romantic Period.* New York: Cambridge University Press, 2004.

Satlow, Michael L. *How the Bible Became Holy.* New Haven, CT: Yale University Press, 2014.

Schmidt, Leigh, *Consumer Rites: The Buying & Selling of American Holidays.* Princeton: Princeton University Press, 1995.

———. *Hearing Things: Religion, Illusion, and the American Enlightenment.* London: Harvard University Press, 2000.

Sellers, Charles Coleman. *Lorenzo Dow: The Bearer of the Word.* New York: Minton, Balch & Company, 1928.

Sennett, Richard. *Authority.* New York: Knopf, 1980.

Shalev, Eran. *American Zion: The Old Testament as a Political Text from the Revolution to the Civil War.* London: Yale University Press, 2013.

Sheehan, Jonathan. *The Enlightenment Bible: Translation, Scholarship, Culture.* Princeton: Princeton University Press, 2005.

Shields, David S. "The Manuscript in the British American World of Print," *Proceedings of the American Antiquarian Society* 102 (January 1, 1993): 403–16.

Shipps, Jan. *Mormonism: The Story of a New Religious Tradition*. Urbana, IL: University of Illinois Press, 1985.

———. *Sojourner in the Promised Land: Forty Years among the Mormons*. Urbana, IL: University of Illinois Press, 2000.

Skousen, Royal. "Textual Variants in the Isaiah Quotations," in Donald W. Parry and John W. Welch, eds., *Isaiah in the Book of Mormon*. Provo, UT: Foundation for Ancient Research and Mormon Studies [FARMS], 1998, 369–90.

Slee, Jaquelynn B. "A Summary of the English Editions of Illustrated Bibles Published in America between 1790 and 1825, with Indices of Subjects Illustrated and Engravers." MA thesis, University of Michigan, 1973.

Slights, William W. E. *Managing Readers: Printed Marginalia in English Renaissance Books*. Ann Arbor: University of Michigan Press, 2001.

Smeeton, Donald. *Lollard Themes in the Reformation Theology of William Tyndale*. Kirksville, MO: Sixteenth Century Journal Publishers, 1986.

Smith, Andrew F. *The Saintly Scoundrel: The Life and Times of Dr. John Cook Bennett*. Chicago: University of Illinois Press, 1997.

Smith, Theophus. *Conjuring Culture*. New York: Oxford University Press, 1994.

Smith, Wilfred Cantwell. *What is Scripture?: A Comparative Approach*. Minneapolis: Fortress Press, 1993.

Sobel, Mechal. *Teach Me Dreams: The Search for Self in the Revolutionary Era*. Princeton: Princeton University Press, 2000.

Sollors, Werner. *Beyond Ethnicity: Consent and Descent in American Culture*. New York: Oxford University Press, 1986.

Spangler, Jewel. *Virginians Reborn: Anglican Monopoly, Evangelical Dissent, and the Rise of the Baptists in the Late Eighteenth Century*. Charlottesville: University Press of Virginia, 2008.

Sparks, Randy J. *On Jordan's Stormy Banks: Evangelicalism in Mississippi, 1773–1876*. Athens, GA: University of Georgia Press, 1994.

Stanwood, Owen. "Catholics, Protestants, and the Clash of Civilizations in Early America," in Chris Beneke and Christopher S. Grenda, eds., *The First Prejudice: Religious Tolerance and Intolerance in Early America*. Philadelphia: University of Pennsylvania Press, 2011, 218–40.

Stout, Harry S. *The New England Soul: Preaching and Religious Culture in Colonial New England*. Oxford: Oxford University Press, 1986.

———. *The Divine Dramatist : George Whitefield and the Rise of Modern Evangelism*. Grand Rapids, MI: W. B. Eerdmans Pub. Co., 1991.

———. "Word and Order in Colonial New England," in Mark Noll and Nathan Hatch, eds., *The Bible in America: Essays in Cultural History*. Oxford: Oxford University Press, 1982.

Stout, Jeffrey. *Blessed Are the Organized: Grassroots Democracy in America*. Princeton: Princeton University Press, 2010.

Styler, Rebecca. *Literary Theology by Women Writers of the Nineteenth Century*. Farnham, Surrey, UK: Ashgate, 2010.

Suleiman, Susan and Inge Crosman Wimmers, eds. *The Reader in the Text: Essays on Audience and Interpretation*. Princeton: Princeton University Press, 1980.

Taves, Ann. "Visions," in Terrie Dopp Aamodt, et al. eds., *Ellen Harmon White: American Prophet*. Oxford: Oxford University Press, 2014, 30–51.

——. *Fits, Trances, and Visions: Experiencing Religion and Explaining Experience from Wesley to James*. Princeton: Princeton University Press, 1999.

Thomas, Mark D. "A Mosaic for a Religious Counterculture: The Bible in the Book of Mormon," *Dialogue: A Journal of Mormon Thought* 29, no. 4 (1996): 47–68.

Thuesen, Peter J. *In Discordance with the Scriptures: American Protestant Battles over Translating the Bible*. New York: Oxford University Press, 1999.

Tomes, Roger. " 'Scripture Its Own Commentator': A History of English Cross-Reference Bibles," *The Expository Times* 119, no. 10 (July 1, 2008): 487–94.

Tuer, Andrew W. *History of the Horn-book*. London: Leadenhall Press; New York: C. Scribner's Sons, 1896.

Tvedtnes, John A. *The Isaiah Variants in the Book of Mormon*. Provo, UT: FARMS, 1981.

Van Wagoner, Richard S. *Sidney Rigdon: A Portrait of Religious Excess*. Salt Lake City, UT: Signature Books, 1994.

Vogel, Dan. *Joseph Smith: The Making of a Prophet*. Salt Lake City, UT: Signature Books, 2004.

Waldstreicher, David. *In the Midst of Perpetual Fetes: The Making of American Nationalism, 1776–1820*. Chapel Hill: University of North Carolina Press, 1997.

Warner, Michael. *The Letters of the Republic: Publication and the Public Sphere in Eighteenth-Century America*. Cambridge, MA: Harvard University Press, 1990.

Whitehouse, Tessa. "The Family Expositor, the Doddridge Circle and the Booksellers," *The Library: The Transactions of the Bibliographical Society* 11, no. 3 (2010): 321–44.

Wigger, John H. *Taking Heaven by Storm: Methodism and the Rise of Popular Christianity in America*. New York: Oxford University Press, 1998.

Wimbush, Vincent. ed. *African Americans and the Bible*. New York: Continuum, 2000.

——. *Theorizing Scriptures: New Critical Orientations to a Cultural Phenomenon*. New Brunswick, NJ: Rutgers University Press, 2008.

——. *White Men's Magic: Scripturalization as Slavery*. Oxford: Oxford University Press, 2012.

Winiarski, Douglas L. "Souls Filled with Ravishing Transport: Heavenly Visions and the Radical Awakening in New England," *The William and Mary Quarterly* 61, no. 1 (2004): 3–46.

Wosh, Peter J. *Spreading the Word: The Bible Business in Nineteenth-Century America*. Ithaca, NY: Cornell University Press, 1994.

Wright, David P. "Joseph Smith's Interpretation of Isaiah in the Book of Mormon," *Dialogue: A Journal of Mormon Thought* 31, no. 4 (1998): 181–206.

Wyss, Hilary E. *Writing Indians: Literacy, Christianity, and Native Community in Early America*. Amherst, MA: University of Massachusetts, 2000.

Zimmerelli, Lisa. " 'Heaven-Touched Lips and Pent-Up Voices': The Rhetoric of American Female Preaching Apologia, 1820–1930," in Michael-John DePalma and Jeffrey M. Ringer, eds., *Mapping Christian Rhetorics*. New York: Routledge, 2015, 180–202.

A NOTE ON THE TYPE

THIS BOOK has been composed in Miller, a Scotch Roman typeface designed by Matthew Carter and first released by Font Bureau in 1997. It resembles Monticello, the typeface developed for The Papers of Thomas Jefferson in the 1940s by C. H. Griffith and P. J. Conkwright and reinterpreted in digital form by Carter in 2003.

Pleasant Jefferson ("P. J.") Conkwright (1905–1986) was Typographer at Princeton University Press from 1939 to 1970. He was an acclaimed book designer and AIGA Medalist.

The ornament used throughout this book was designed by Pierre Simon Fournier (1712–1768) and was a favorite of Conkwright's, used in his design of the *Princeton University Library Chronicle*.